The Theory and Interpretation of Narrative Series

Politics, Persuasion, and Pragmatism:

A Rhetoric of Feminist Utopian Fiction

Ellen Peel

The Ohio State University Press
Columbus

Library of Congress Cataloging-in-Publication Data

Peel, Ellen Susan.
Politics, persuasion, and pragmatism : a rhetoric of feminist utopian
fiction / Ellen Peel.
p. cm. -- (The theory and interpretation of narrative series)
Includes bibliographical references and index.
ISBN 0-8142-0910-6 (hard : alk. paper)
1. Utopias in literature. 2. Fiction--20th century--History and
criticism. 3. Feminism and literature. I. Title. II. Series.
PN3448.U7 P44 2002
809.3'9372--dc21
2002010389
Cover design by Dan O'Dair
Printed by Thomson-Shore Inc.

The paper used in this publication meets the minimum requirements of the
American National Standard for Information Sciences—Permanence of Paper
for Printed Library Materials. ANSI Z39.48-1992.

9   8   7   6   5   4   3   2   1

For my parents,
Evelyn Osovitz Peel and Fred Welch Peel,
with love and gratitude.

[T]he future depends on the nobility of our imaginings.
—Barbara Grizzuti Harrison (174)

Contents

Acknowledgments

Writing is a curious mix of individual and collective effort. One of the pleasures of writing this book has come from experiencing the generosity of the many people who have helped me over the course of a long process. I want to offer my warmest thanks for their aid, including the good-humored patience of my friends.

For research time and travel funds, I am grateful to my former institution, the University of Cincinnati, and my current one, San Francisco State University. In its earliest form, this project received the sympathetic guidance of Peter Brooks, Peter Demetz, and Margaret Homans. My gratitude also goes to the Bain Research Group of the University of California at Berkeley, where I was an Affiliated Scholar in 1995, as well as to the Institute for Research on Women and Gender at Stanford University, where I was a Visiting Scholar in 1995 and 2001; the support and stimulating environment were invaluable. Thanks go to my cheerful, highly competent research assistants, especially John Buckley, Cathy Flynn, Megan Pruiett, Catherine Thompson, and Eric Thompson.

A number of people have made helpful comments on this project, in some cases reading the entire manuscript: Shuli Barzilai, William Bush, Linda Dowling, William Dowling, Gillian Gill, Helen Heise, renée hoogland, Evelyn Peel, Frank Palmeri, Jenefer Robinson, Anita Silvers, Loretta Stec, Mihoko Suzuki, and the Theory Reading Group. This book could not have been written without the advice and encouragement of Miriam Solomon and my writing group: Judith Breen, Yvonne Daley, Elise Earthman, jo keroes, and Elizabeth Sommers. In working with Ohio State University Press, I have benefited greatly from the suggestions of reader Raffaella Baccolini; my acquisitions editor, Heather Lee Miller; and the editors of the Theory and Interpretation of Narrative Series, James Phelan and Peter J. Rabinowitz. My deepest gratitude goes to my parents and William Bush for their indispensable help.

I thank the University of Tennessee Press for permission to use material developed from an essay of mine: "Utopian Feminism, Skeptical Feminism, and Narrative Energy" (which appeared in *Feminism, Utopia, and Narrative,* ed. Libby Falk Jones and Sarah Webster Goodwin, *Tennessee Studies in Literature* 32 [Knoxville: University of Tennesee Press, 1990], 34–49).

Introduction

> When you are a fiction writer, you're confronted every day with the question . . . : what kind of world shall you describe for your readers? The one you can see around you, or the better one you can imagine? If only the latter, you'll be unrealistic; if only the former, despairing. But it is by the better world we can imagine that we judge the world we have. If we cease to judge this world, we may find ourselves, very quickly, in one which is infinitely worse.
>
> —Margaret Atwood ("Witches," 6)

I am obsessed with reading. As a toddler, I talked constantly, and ever since learning to read, I have read constantly. Nowadays a novel can still stun me, holding me paralyzed in my chair as I read for hours. The effects of reading fascinate me: those that occur during the well-defined time when our gaze is crossing the page and those that take place later, as the words sink fitfully, unpredictably, deeper into our minds. So in one sense this study was prompted by a question that animates my writing and my teaching: "What effects does reading have on us—especially on our beliefs—and how does it create those effects?" This book was also prompted by my intense interest in feminism, fantasy, and science fiction, a passion fueled by my parents' interests and by my experiences in academia as well as by my coming of age in the 1960s.

All these influences inspired the central question of this study: "How does persuasion work in feminist utopias?" (In the pages that follow the meanings of both "feminist" and "utopia" are honed, but for now we can simply take "feminist utopia" to mean a narrative about a society that is free from the patriarchal subordination of women.[1]) Such texts call for reflection, because, perhaps surprisingly, feminists have devoted less attention to how feminist texts convey their beliefs than to how patriarchal texts convey theirs. I have chosen to focus on three provocative examples: *The Marriages Between Zones Three, Four, and Five* (1980), by British author Doris Lessing; *The Left Hand of Darkness* (1969), by American author Ursula K. Le Guin; and *Les Guérillères* (*The Women Warriors*, 1969), by French author Monique Wittig.

Thus *Politics, Persuasion, and Pragmatism* is a book about how people come to believe what they do—how their beliefs are instilled or reinforced. In particular, it is about how people are influenced by reading feminist utopian novels. My chief argument is that the devices I identify are important in subtle literary persuasion, as exemplified in three feminist utopian narratives that go beyond stasis to pragmatism. After developing its theories of utopia, persuasion, and feminism, this book integrates them through an examination of how persuasion functions in these three narratives. Although this study is devoted largely to such novels, the theoretical framework I construct is not limited to them but also articulates broader issues in contemporary literary and cultural theory.

Literature matters—in part because it can persuade people, for good or ill. Amidst current debates about the value of the humanities, *Politics, Persuasion, and Pragmatism* is meant to help us understand this rhetorical and ethical power. It begins with the premise that all literature exerts such power, attempting not necessarily to shape readers' actions but to shape their beliefs—beliefs that concern the world inside the text and, to varying degrees and through a complex sort of translation, the world outside as well. This literary persuasion, conventionally dismissed as propaganda or simple parables, in fact can affect lives without being crudely didactic. While of course only one of the roles played by literature, persuasion is nevertheless a major role.

This book's focus on literary persuasion is unusual. Although, as Robert Scholes reminds us, people have been thinking about persuasion and literature from at least Aristotle's day onward,[2] few scholars in recent years have been thinking about the two together. To contemplate the overlap is to take up an unfashionable task but a necessary one, for we still have a long way to go before truly comprehending how literary persuasion moves us. By considering how literature persuades—specifically, how narrative form affects feminist belief—I hope to show that a formal approach can meld with a political one.[3] Some political and formal theorists may write as if each approach precluded the other, but in fact the two can be combined, as in the increasingly appreciated writings of Mikhail Bakhtin. The formal helps explain *how* the political functions; the political helps explain *why* the formal matters. Adding form to politics means that, to use Susan Sniader Lanser's terms, while initially drawn to the novels I discuss by their "explicit ideology," I primarily trace their more intriguing "embedded ideology" (*The Narrative Act,* 216). What interests me are the delicate devices, such as those I call "belief-bridging" and "protean metaphor," that nudge readers toward feminism, perhaps without their conscious awareness. And so I employ reader response theory to forge a link between form and belief.

The insufficiently studied point where form, belief, and reader response come together is *persuasion,* which we can consider for the moment to mean *changing someone's beliefs, if only slightly, if only making a new belief more palatable.* This study traces how narrative *form* can shape *belief* by having a persuasive effect, in this case a feminist effect, on *readers' responses.* I posit that the key to persuasion lies in a complex phenomenon that I call *matching:* the more closely real readers resemble implied readers, the more likely it is that the text will succeed at persuading the real readers. The major formal devices I identify are aimed at implied readers; the more matching that occurs, the more the devices persuade real readers. After sketching out how matching leads to persuasion in general and, more particularly, in novels, I take up the question of matching and persuasion in specifically political novels, feminist utopias.

To examine literary persuasion, why—aside from personal interest—choose feminist utopias? First of all, the most interesting place to study literary persuasion is a text that is political in the broad sense, literature by authors who emphasize power relations; James Baldwin, Charles Dickens, and many others come to mind. Because political literature gives a good deal of attention to the world outside the text as well as to the one inside, it can offer intriguing examples of persuasion, powerful without necessarily being propagandistic. Meanwhile, since political authors often write against the cultural grain, seeking sympathy for unpopular ideas and characters, it is especially pressing, in reading their texts, to have a precise notion of how literary persuasion works.

Among political beliefs toward which novels have urged readers, feminism is a uniquely significant, complex, and contested site, a fitting example for the analysis of persuasion. This belief has its roots in ethics, and so I intend this book as a contribution to the broader recent effort to study ethics in literature.[4] Feminism stands out as one of the most truly radical

beliefs of the last two centuries, questioning the very roots of societies all
over the globe. Nor is the process over: the questions continue, many of
them posed by feminists to each other. This study presents a new definition of feminism in order to comprehend what belief it is that feminist
novels are inviting readers to adopt. The definition is meant to answer the
need for inclusiveness and nuance at a moment when people are complaining that the academy has drifted away from many women's concerns.

Within the category of political novels, feminist and otherwise, one of
the most rewarding places to seek literary persuasion is the utopia, partly
because of its "explicit ideology." In utopias, ideology (what I will be calling "belief") is brought to the fore in a way that permits us to reflect fruit-
fully on how the ideology creates its effects. Something else intriguing
about utopias is how they manage to persuade, given the tension between
their extreme fictitiousness (utopias being by definition unreal) and their
sturdy ties to the extrafictional world (for example, feminism's potential
for sparking profound transformations in millions of people). Some people feel that the two forces cancel each other out; that, for instance, the
very physiology that makes possible the aliens' feminism in *The Left Hand
of Darkness* dooms the book to irrelevance for those of us with human
bodies who are engaged in feminist struggles. I strongly disagree. Instead,
I belong to the group that claims utopias need not supply a blueprint for
change; they can speak to us emotionally or metaphorically, inspiring us,
even if we need to find our own means to reach the ends they portray.[5]
Furthermore, because these novels encourage change, at least of belief, in
the extrafictional world, they avoid the standard charges of being mere
opiates or safety valves for discontent.

This volume is intended to cast light not only on feminist utopian narrative in general but on specific examples. Among feminist utopias, why
choose these particular ones by Lessing, Le Guin, and Wittig? Certain
commonalities make them comparable: all are engaging on many levels, for
instance. Thus, while it is rewarding to read them as feminist and utopian,
by doing so I do not intend to imply that they offer nothing more; rather,
I hope my interpretations will prompt people who have not yet read the
novels to discover for themselves what all three have to say about language
and nationhood, love and war, betrayal and bliss. The texts are also linked
by their authors: white Western female writers—prominent and influential, though not conventionally canonical—who are working in overlapping intellectual communities.[6] The novels, published between 1969 and
1980, all grew out of Second-Wave feminism, an era close enough to be

remembered in detail, yet distant enough for scholars to have achieved some perspective on it. More complex than some other feminist novels, these three present multiple sorts of feminism, each with its advantages, thus engaging readers in making judgments instead of accepting some monolithic belief.

Furthermore, these texts—in no way preachy or message-ridden—exercise utopian techniques with rare skill. Setting always matters in utopias since they are rooted in *topos,* but these examples go on to employ it as a central metaphor. Their geography is gendered: each of the three narratives introduces one land representing women and another representing men, then complicates the relation between the two places, figuratively complicating our understanding of the relation between women and men. The fact that the gender/geography metaphor systematically changes makes it not just a metaphor but what I call a protean one.

Marriages, Left Hand, and *Les Guérillères* also solve a problem that plagues many utopias: utopian visions of perfection can effectively critique the present and inspire hope for the future, but when perfection is static, they also run the risk of rigidity and tedium. Certain novels, such as those I consider, confront the dilemma not by retreating back to patriarchy but by including a static utopian moment and then going past it to something more possible and more vital: an ongoing, intricate, vibrant process of rethinking what feminism might entail, a process akin to philosophical pragmatism. The stretching beyond has literary as well as political consequences, for it creates the narrative energy that is often lacking in static utopian literature. These rich and strange tales thus follow a surprisingly common pattern: unlike some other feminist utopias, such as Charlotte Perkins Gilman's *Herland,* these "ambiguous utopias" endorse feminism not only by constructing utopian societies but also, more interestingly, by questioning them.[7] In fact, one source of the complexity in my argument is the idiosyncratic if not problematic role played by feminism in each author's beliefs. So the three texts deserve attention both because at one moment they exemplify the rigid, perfectionist mode within the feminist utopian genre and because later they critique that mode.

In spite of all these similarities, the novels were also chosen because they differ in significant ways. To approach feminist utopias with at least some thoroughness, from more than one angle, and to show how broadly my theories apply, I have used a comparative method: for example, selecting texts that present a range of sexual orientations—basically lesbian in *Les Guérillères,* basically heterosexual in *Marriages,* almost unimaginable in *Left Hand.* In a similarly comparative way, the books represent the different novelistic genres normally used in utopian writing—*Marriages* combines fantasy with allegory, *Left Hand* is science fiction, and *Les Guérillères* employs an experimental form, the *nouveau roman.* Moreover, the three come from a range of national traditions and construct implied readers with a range of political beliefs. Coverage of all possibilities would be an unattainable goal, however, and so I hope the theories may apply to other orientations, genres, traditions, and readers as well.[8]

This book is plural in theoretical orientation. While purists in particular camps might decry my effrontery, as a *bricoleuse* I believe that we can pick and choose among the tenets of various theories—indeed, that making such choices is the only responsible method. I first tried to apply existing theory to the three novels to determine how these feminist utopias create their effects. Finding no theories truly suitable to my task, I realized I needed to invent my own and decided to emulate Gérard Genette's approach to *Remembrance of Things Past,* drawing not only on facets of extant theories but also on the novels themselves (22–23).

To grasp why literature matters, theorists must connect it with persuasion; yet most scholars of persuasion, such as rhetoricians, neglect literature, while most literary scholars, even reader-response theorists, neglect persuasion. Whereas reader-response theorists tend to inquire *how readers interpret a text's meaning,* I shift attention from interpretation of meaning to persuasion of belief, inquiring *how readers shape their beliefs in response to the form of a text.* Literary scholars' lack of concern with persuasion has meant that few have devoted themselves to the issue on which *Politics, Persuasion, and Pragmatism* concentrates: the point—or rather the vast, poorly mapped region—where form, belief, and reader response meet.

These three are often studied individually, sometimes studied in pairs, rarely studied all together, and even more rarely studied all together in the way that I shall be doing it. Many critics see form and belief as incompatible or see only one as worthy of inquiry. Admittedly, some critics have combined the two in their thinking about the author, investigating how an *author's* beliefs affect form.[9] Few critics, however, have added reader response to form and belief, investigating how a *reader's* beliefs are affected by form, which is the tack I am taking—using reader response as the link between form and belief. The lack of inquiry into the three together stems partly from the delay of twentieth-century scholars, with rare exceptions such as I. A. Richards and Louise Rosenblatt, in considering readers from any angle. Until the last quarter of the twentieth century, only in an anecdotal, piecemeal way did people refer to the link between reader response and political belief—for instance, in observing that *The Golden Notebook,* by Doris Lessing, inspired many feminists. Now that reader-response criticism has developed, theorists tend to pair it with one but not both of the other subjects that interest me. It is sometimes linked with belief, including feminism, but such dual studies rarely delve into particular formal techniques.[10] In contrast, most reader-response theorists pay less attention to belief and more to form, particularly to how it causes readers to interpret meaning.[11] My addition of belief to form and reader response makes possible the shift just mentioned, from examining interpretation toward asking how readers shape their beliefs in response to the form of a text—an understudied part of the reading process. One consequence of this shift is that, instead of assuming readers remain fixed entities, I ask how a text might change them.[12]

The point where reader response, belief, and form come together to create persuasion has also begun to be emphasized by some thinkers with strong ethical or political concerns. My approach shares the concentration on specific forms that characterizes the work of a few such theorists—in fact, I focus on two techniques—but I differ from them in that I discuss texts I admire.[13] Some scholars have connected reader response and form with beliefs they to some degree admire but without primarily emphasizing feminist beliefs.[14] There is, however, a small but growing number of feminist narratologists who bring together form and belief; some, such as Susan Sniader Lanser and Robyn Warhol, include reader response as well.[15] In sum, I count myself among those feminist narratologists who analyze *reader response* and narrative *form* in conjunction with *beliefs,* specifically feminist ones, that the narratologists hold.

In relation to scholarship on feminist belief in particular, my work is unusual in several respects, starting with the new definition of feminism referred to above. More importantly, I am studying *persuasive aspects of feminist texts,* whereas other feminist critics—from Simone de Beauvoir on—have tended to criticize persuasive aspects of nonfeminist texts or to study nonpersuasive aspects of feminist texts. I also aim to synthesize the traditionally French emphasis on otherness and difference—exemplified in the writings of Julia Kristeva—with the traditionally American emphasis on social critique—exemplified in the prose of Adrienne Rich. Most

significantly, while a number of feminists have written about utopias, I am
introducing the distinction between the static and pragmatic modes.

Having located myself in terms of feminism, an approach emphasizing
belief, I now turn to two approaches emphasizing form: structuralism and
deconstruction, which strongly color this book. My choice of structuralism might seem old-fashioned, but this vein has yet to be fully mined, for
the structuralist method still has a good deal to offer, particularly in the
scrutiny of narrative. I turn to deconstruction as well, especially for its
unsettling of binary oppositions, chiefly the one constructed between
women and men. As I employ the two approaches, they do not conflict: I
use structuralism to explore the core and deconstruction to explore the
margins. Much of the force of the three novels comes from the way they
prompt readers to make, unmake, and remake a series of structures; structuralism helps me construct a model, deconstruction helps me criticize it,
and pragmatism (in the philosophical sense) helps me repeat the process
on a higher level.

Another point needs to be made about my employment of structuralism and deconstruction, for each is transformed into something new by
my commitment to feminist political values. Structuralists generally have
not studied values, but they can, and therefore in studying feminist ones
I call myself a "neo-structuralist." Feminism also takes me beyond deconstruction, largely because I see deconstruction as primarily critical, a dou-
ble-edged sword that can hurt you as well as your opponents, and
that—to mix metaphors—therefore provides shaky foundations for political commitment. For instance, if "women" and "subordination" are
drained of meaning, it is hard to fight the subordination of women.[16] I
like the notion "'good enough' foundations" introduced by Marilyn
Edelstein "to suggest that there may be foundational claims . . . that are
always subject to scrutiny and even revision, but can still serve as grounds
for action" (47). For example, while I think we need to challenge the binary opposition between women and men, I also think we have a good
enough foundation to believe that women and men exist, as do various
relations between them, some of which are oppressive. Thus I can be considered a "post–poststructuralist," someone who, aware of the theory,
retains some of its strands and replaces others.[17]

A word about what might be called style: much theory is written in an
opaque style, and a disturbing conflict still smolders between readers who
claim the topic requires it and readers who, after a taste of such a style,
refuse to swallow any more, claiming it is nothing but jargon. I attempt

in this volume to present a third alternative: a style intended to protect complexity but to do so in an accessible way, by breaking formidable concepts down into smaller parts and then slowly savoring each in turn. Having adapted something from each of the other groups of readers, I beg the indulgence of both, hoping they will take the time to find not only the complexity but also the accessibility I am aiming for. A related conflict arises between those who favor generalization and those who are suspicious of it. Again, I follow a third course: I contend that certain generalizations are possible—indeed, imperative (such as generalizing enough here to define feminism), but I strive for adequate texture, for sufficient care and granularity (in this case creating a definition that includes four separate elements).

I would like to say a few words about what this book is not. To begin with, while I hope it will resonate with my readers, of course it is not written from any standpoint other than my own, that of a person of privileged circumstances who is very American in her multiple forms of hybridity. Although my work is of course constrained by historical circumstances—those of the authors, those represented in the novels, and my own as a contemporary Westerner—this book is not itself about historical development. I am not claiming the techniques identified have universal applicability, but I am not tracing their evolution either. A survey of their development over time would be interesting; it would not, however, be this book.

Nor is this a book that tries to be comprehensive by foregrounding categories other than its chief ones: sex and gender, with some consideration of sexual orientation. The treatment of ethnicity, race, and nationality mostly confines itself to the key question of how they serve as metaphors for sex, gender, and sexual orientation. For instance, although the authors are based in three different nations, my argument does not rely on national difference; and, although all the authors apparently are white, the argument does not rely on racial similarity. Concerning such categories, I share the hope expressed by renée c. hoogland that "explicit contextualization may offer a possibility to sidestep the pitfalls of the demand for an exhaustive 'political correctness' which . . . would make it almost impossible to assume a speaking stance at all" (16). I would, of course, be gratified if subsequent studies would apply my ideas more widely, inflecting them with categories beyond the ones I employ.

* * *

How does this study relate theories to examples? *Politics, Persuasion, and Pragmatism* consists of two parts, the first laying out the theories, the second illustrating them by applying them to the three novels. Part I creates a number of discrete concepts, theories that are not necessarily related to each other, but this study is about narratives in which they are all in effect, as will become clear when part II applies the theories, laying one atop another. While utopias, say, are not always feminist, and feminism takes forms other than utopias, these novels combine the two. Applications of all the theories overlap in the three narratives analyzed in part II, and in others like them, but the theories also extend beyond such texts and may, I hope, also prove helpful in other instances—as, for instance, in the study of nonfeminist utopian narratives.

The figures illustrate the relations among the theories. "Societal Theories" shows how this study concentrates on feminist utopias, both static and pragmatic. "Textual Theories" shows the concentration on persuasive texts (all of which employ belief-bridging), specifically on narratives, and—still more specifically—on narratives employing protean metaphor. Although it cannot be shown in only two dimensions, the most accurate figure would combine the societal with the textual, for the three novels actually lie at the intersection of the two figures: feminist utopias that include protean metaphor.

Within part I, chapter 1 addresses the problem of the unsatisfying flatness of some utopias, including some feminist ones, by distinguishing between the *static* and *pragmatic* modes. Looking at the three novels through the lens of philosophical pragmatism makes it possible to respect their dynamic stages, to acknowledge the specificity of their varied moments, instead of imposing some grand grid on them.

Chapter 2 presents my theory of the persuasive process, explaining that, for persuasion to succeed, real readers and implied ones must *match* on a variety of levels, ranging from linguistic skill through openness to change. The idea of matching removes the need to assume that either the text or the reader must dominate; the concept thus resolves a dilemma that has bedeviled many reader-response theorists. This chapter also explains why I highlight implied rather than real authors and readers.

People often have an intuitive sense of what makes a heroine heroic or how a narrative changes readers' minds, but chapter 3 embraces such questions more fully in order to identify and define the two chief persuasive devices in these novels. So as to put forward a new belief, such as admiration of feminism, *belief-bridging* connects it with an old belief

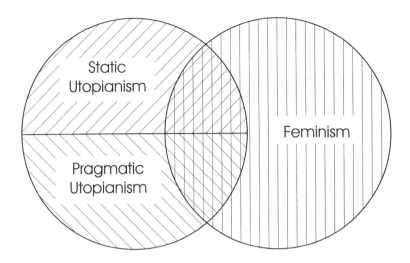

Figure 1: Societal Theories

already held by implied readers, such as respect for intelligence. This widely used device becomes especially interesting and effective when it involves beliefs about narrative itself. *Protean metaphor* is the other major persuasive device in the three novels, in each of which one nation acts as a metaphor for women and another represents men. Each initial pair of metaphors shapes readers' beliefs about the sexes; then, as the novels progress, they move readers through stages of an argument by changing the relations between countries and thus, metaphorically, between the sexes. Each novel thus sets up a geographical and sexual structure that it gradually deconstructs.

Chapter 4 gives a multifaceted definition of feminism, rooted in its rejection of patriarchy. Having observed in that chapter what bonds feminists together, I turn in chapter 5 to what separates them from each other. There I present a range of feminisms, each type dialectically addressing troublesome points in the others. I sketch out the feminist patterns of power (inequality, equality, and difference) and of focus (singularity, centrality, duality, and multiplicity).

Part II braids together my theories of utopia, persuasive techniques, and feminism. Here in three chapters are presented readings of feminist utopias that typify those whose narrative energy takes them beyond stasis to pragmatism. Lessing's novel, developing in clear stages, brings implied

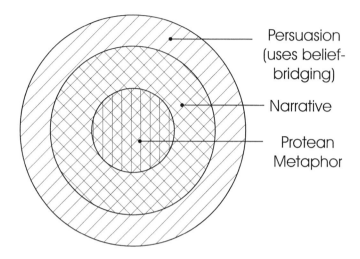

Figure 2: Textual Theories

readers to a place of extreme otherness. Le Guin complicates the sexes, as well as the protean metaphor representing them, in order to address a very specific—and recalcitrant—group of implied readers. Wittig's challenging *nouveau roman* risks alienating many readers but eventually draws on belief-bridging and protean metaphor to win them over. A brief conclusion situates the three narratives in relation to each other and suggests further ways in which the theories might be applied.

Utopias deserve attention because, contrary to appearances, utopian longing permeates our culture.[18] I would suggest, for example, that the current political malaise in the United States—often interpreted as a rejection of earlier ideals—derives instead from discouragement about attaining them. I have found that idealism still burns, or at least flickers, among many of my students, and I have witnessed how readily, whenever we do feel a twinge of hope, we again make our stumbling, poignant efforts to define "values." *Politics, Persuasion, and Pragmatism* responds to our utopian longing.

PART I

Persuasion in Feminist
Utopian Narratives

CHAPTER 1

Static and Pragmatic
Utopian Feminism

If at first you don't succeed, try another method.
—Sally Foldenauer[1]

Feminists have been galvanized, especially in the last thirty years, by utopian narratives, and yet discourse about utopias has a long history of neglecting women and their concerns. To begin with, quite a few utopian proposals claim to value sexual equality but in fact assign women an inferior status.[2] And feminist utopias tend to get neglected by nonfeminist commentators: for instance, Frank E. Manuel and Fritzie P. Manuel wrote in their magisterial *Utopian Thought in the Western World* that at the time of their publishing the book (1979) "in the midst of societies seething with utopian experiments, there is unfortunately no significant utopian thought" (813). Even as they made that statement, however, the Second Wave of feminism was well underway, along with its outpouring of feminist utopian writing.[3] A body of feminist commentary on utopian texts has also developed.[4] Building on such commentary as well as on the nonfeminist sort, this chapter distinguishes between two levels of utopia—societal and textual—and then, on each level, between two modes—static and pragmatic. I conclude by describing the pragmatism in my own method, in its striving for ongoing evolution rather than definitive answers.

We can most simply define the utopia corresponding to a particular political belief as an ideal society that would put into practice the goals of those holding that belief.[5] Thus, given the definition of feminism that will be presented in a later chapter, a feminist utopian society would reject patriarchy. Under that umbrella concept, however, different subgroups of feminists would envision different utopias: for example, not every feminist's ideal society would grant equal power to the two sexes. And of course different cultures, at different historical moments, would have different ideals as well. The term utopia also works on another level, for it can refer to a literary genre, texts that describe an ideal society.[6]

I would like to start my discussion by telling part of a story:

OSEA BALKIS SARA NICEA
IOLA CORA SABINA DANIELA
GALSWINTHA EDNA JOSEPHA

You are probably wondering why I called this a story. It is certainly not "boy meets girl," not even "girl meets girl." It is just a list of women's names—nouns with no verbs. Yet it is part of a narrative, Monique Wittig's *Les Guérillères* (13).

Politics, Persuasion, and Pragmatism explores novels like this one, mysterious because of their ability to remain compelling stories even though they contain potentially dull elements, such as long lists of women's names, that threaten to alienate readers. The problem addressed in this study is that, to be blunt, an ideal society, while resolving the problem of patriarchy, risks introducing a new problem: the utopia might bore its inhabitants, and a book about such a society might bore its readers. Each of the three novels discussed is in some sense about a feminist utopia—an ideal feminist society—and it is that presentation of the ideal that runs the risk of hobbling the action and movement that normally characterize narratives. While presenting perfection, though, these subtle novels somehow generate narrative energy as well, the energy to keep readers excited, to keep them reading. How is this accomplished? Feminism, like most other political beliefs, is manifested in two basic utopian modes: *the static mode emphasizes fixed ideals, while the pragmatic mode entails provisional models and ceaseless, striving questioning.* The static ideal resembles a noun, a state of affairs; the pragmatic ideal resembles a series of verbs, a process. This chapter explains how novels employ the pragmatic mode of utopian feminism in various ways to avoid the threat of stasis.

Although touching on other theories, my concept of the two modes has more specific literary and philosophical ramifications than others usually do. The distinction I draw between static and pragmatic modes recalls differentiations made by other theorists; mine, however, is developed in greater detail than most.[7] Some theorists see little alternative to stasis but negativity,[8] whereas I agree with Daphne Patai that "the protest against injustice implies a vision of justice" (150). Pragmatism envisions the possibility of provisional models—positive though not unchanging.[9] Some theories resemble mine to a degree but do not look into the literary problem of narrative energy.[10] A few writers do consider the problem of bore-dom;[11] others are concerned more specifically about the lack of narrative energy but still don't consider the value of a pragmatic component.[12] And so the theory outlined here differs from others because it links dynamic utopias to both narrative energy and philosophical pragmatism.

Static Utopian Belief

The Societal Level

Utopias have frailties. To say so may sound like a contradiction in terms, but it must be admitted that a certain grit disturbs the glossiness. To begin with, it is very difficult, perhaps impossible, to bring into being a society that is a "good place" but "no place." Indeed, all my references to utopia include the implication that it is a society we may be able to work toward but have not, or not yet, reached. In addition, other shortcomings would arise even if it were easy to reach utopia, to translate a perfect society from plan to reality. We do not actually know, for instance, what perfection would be—at least we do not yet know. The present inevitably shackles our imaginings of the future; as Christina Thürmer-Rohr says, because they "are based on this-worldly experiences, paradises are never really in the beyond, but rather always extrapolations from the here and now" (22).[13] Moreover, it is hard to enumerate ideals with any specificity; for instance, feminists may agree to reject dominant male power, but should they do so by pursuing equal power, different power, or dominant female power?

And, once we have honed specific ideals, we may find that ideals in dif-ferent realms clash with each other. Ursula K. Le Guin paints the prob-lem starkly in "The Ones Who Walk Away from Omelas," which tells of a society that is ideal in almost every conceivable way but owes its exis-tence to the complete misery of one child. Because achieving one ideal can interfere with achieving another, it is difficult to imagine a society that could simultaneously achieve all possible perfections or even all of what one person would consider ideal.

So far I have been writing as if we had a picture in our minds of an ideal society and as if the picture were marred only by blurriness or clashing colors. But utopias, if static, are also hampered by another problem, the one I wish to emphasize: even if the picture could be clear and harmo-niously colored, a certain tedium would make the society's inhabitants feel they were living in a still life. Le Guin's novel *Always Coming Home* criticizes "smartass utopians. Always so much healthier and saner and sounder and kinder and tougher and wiser and righter than me and my family and friends. People who have the answers are boring. . . . Boring, boring, boring" (316). Thürmer-Rohr makes a similar remark about "utopian constructions": "This is stasis, stagnation, an unendurable, constricted non-happiness. Here there is no connection with real people, with their craziness, their real and dramatic dreams, with their unpredictability, their outbursts, their occasional laughter" (21–22). Even as we yearn to live in a perfect society, we may feel, with a twinge of guilt, that such a life would bring enervating immobility. Anyone who has felt the exhilaration of fighting for good can imagine the deflation of living in a world where good would not require any effort, where few profound struggles would challenge us. I by no means intend to suggest that wrongs should exist simply for the stimulation they provide; I do, however, intend to suggest that living in utter perfection would exact a price: dullness.

The Textual Level

More problems arise on the other level, where the term "utopia" refers to a text that describes an ideal society. When we move to this level, the main failing we find in a static utopia is that of unsatisfying thinness—potential boredom this time not only of the society's inhabitants but also of the text's readers. Among the examples that come to mind are classic utopian books such as Thomas More's *Utopia* and Charlotte Perkins Gilman's *Herland*.[14] They lack what, inspired by Peter Brooks, I call *narrative energy:* what keeps a story moving, what compels us to keep turning pages instead of turning off the light and going to sleep (Brooks, xiii–xiv). It is no wonder that many novels—Alice Walker's *The Color Purple* among them—save their utopianism for their final pages, when it is appropriate for narrative energy to decline.

More than most other fiction, that which presents a static utopia runs a special risk of insipidity. Admittedly, the choice of presenting the utopia in a narrative probably makes the account more absorbing (as well as more persuasive) than it would be in an essay, for the ideal society is rendered palpable in concrete details. But figuratively speaking, that description consists of adjectives and nouns, not verbs. Moreover, the description of a perfect society especially causes plot to droop, for plot usually feeds on imperfection.[15] Utopian texts sometimes contain conflict, especially in a romantic subplot, but the static utopian plot, at its dreariest, just presents a guided tour for a character visiting from another land, with dialogue that amounts to: "On your left is the Temple of Hygiene."

One could argue that tedium on the textual level does not pose a seri-ous threat: perhaps readers who get bored are the type who demand sen-sationalism, readers to whom the text should not cater in the first place. But even readers who do not demand a car chase in every chapter never-theless tend to desire some plot. And since utopian texts—more often than average texts—attempt to inspire people, they would do well to hold their readers' interest. Something about the bland serenity of a static utopian society is fatal to narrative; a pure, perfect utopia can never be narrated. Because a story needs conflict, desire, or unhappiness to gener-ate the energy required to launch it, contentment will never propel it off the ground. In short, good news is no news.

The Societal and Textual Levels

Because of the peculiar nature of utopia, the societal and textual levels also interpenetrate: although no completely ideal society has ever exist-ed, many such societies *have* had inhabitants in the form of people who, while reading a textual utopia, imagine themselves living there. Therefore a static utopian text might bore readers because its narrative lacks con-flict, desire, and unhappiness, and it might also cause readers to fear that, if they lived in the society represented in the text, the same lacks would bore them. A dull goal will hardly incite readers to long for it. The two levels connect through the reader, who experiences the textual and imag-ines experiencing the societal. Such a utopia would be a nice place to visit, but I wouldn't want to live there, nor do I particularly enjoy read-ing about it.

Pragmatic Utopian Belief

The Societal Level

Anti-utopians, those who criticize utopianism, usually fall into two groups. Some people have utopian dreams but resign themselves to the status quo, renouncing their dreams, because they despair of ever attain-ing a better world. Other people imply that utopia is immoral, foolish, or dangerous and that we should leave well enough alone. This notion of utopia's undesirability is part of the broader tradition that has long con-demned overreaching in general, as in folktales such as the Grimm Brothers' "The Fisherman and His Wife" and classics such as Christopher Marlowe's *Doctor Faustus*. Even on a small, nonutopian scale, the tradition attacks overreaching by associating it with consequences almost anyone

would consider dangerous: Jane Austen mocks Emma Woodhouse's meddling, Nathaniel Hawthorne reproaches Aylmer for removing his wife's
birthmark, and Jonathan Swift ridicules the mad scientists in book 3 of
Gulliver's Travels.

Although I, too, am criticizing a type of utopianism, I want to stress that
I am doing so from a different standpoint, for, unlike the anti-utopians just
mentioned, I believe major changes are both possible and desirable—I just
want them to take a form other than paralyzed perfection. In spite of the
inadequacies of static utopian belief—both societal and textual—those
who dream of change need not give up on progress and resign themselves
to the status quo. Instead, they can still envision change but through *pragmatism,* with its provisional models, continual questioning, and distrust of
premature closure. Thus, most political beliefs, including feminism, need
not halt at utopian stasis but can go beyond it, in a pragmatic mode.[16]

The term pragmatism is used here not exactly in its everyday sense but
with reference to the tradition in American philosophy that includes such
thinkers as Charles Sanders Peirce, William James, John Dewey, and
Richard Rorty.[17] This philosophy is appealing in its experimental spirit
and its willingness to admit fallibility. Faced with an existing structure—even one of their own creation—pragmatists neither leave it intact
nor destroy it in a spirit of knee-jerk subversion. Rather, they tear down
part of it in order to remodel: they critique something, modify their
model a bit, critique something else, amend another part of the model,
and so on. Through *bricolage,* in short, pragmatists create models provisionally, in stages, and criticize them in order to improve them.

Dewey, according to John P. Murphy, wanted such an experimental
method for values as well as for ideas: "It is because culture is ever-changing that the work of the philosopher, like that of the housekeeper, is never
finished" (77). Rorty says, "For the pragmatists, the pattern of all
inquiry—scientific as well as moral—is deliberation concerning the relative attractions of various concrete alternatives" ("Pragmatism, Relativism,
and Irrationalism," 164). This seemingly modest project has a value of its
own, for, he notes, "James, in arguing against realists and idealists that
'the trail of the human serpent is over all,' was reminding us that our glory
is in our participation in fallible and transitory human projects, not in our
obedience to permanent nonhuman constraints" (ibid., 166). Henry
Steele Commager has summed up the "philosophical preconceptions" that
characterized James, one of the most influential pragmatists: "a suspicion
of all absolutes, all rigidities, and all systems; an inclination to leave all

questions open to reconsideration; an indulgence of eccentricity and non-conformity; a preference for what was artistically and emotionally as well as intellectually appealing; a compelling consciousness of moral obligation" (91).

Pragmatists are not nihilists or utter skeptics. While leery of essences, grand claims, and simplistic teleology, pragmatists base their critiques on working principles that help them define progress. Pragmatists reserve final judgment, for they regard absolutes with suspicion, but they should not be confused with relativists, who reserve all judgment (see Rorty, "Pragmatism, Relativism, and Irrationalism"). For pragmatists the bad news is that certainty is elusive; the good news is that certainty may not matter too much (Rorty, "Introduction," xv–xvii). Pragmatists' optimism stems from their conviction that we do not always need certainty, for what matters about a belief is not whether we are certain it is true but whether it works well (with "working" to be broadly construed), helps us cope with the world, and stands the test of experience, of practice. My theory is neutral on whether we can ever reach certainty (in this case a notion of perfect feminism); what matters is to acknowledge that we are still far from it and so must continue the process of experimenting.[18]

Philosophical pragmatism can sharpen our sensitivity to types of political belief, by enabling us to make a distinction between a pragmatic mode and a static one. Static utopians think there is only one ideal society (or at least a small, well-defined group of ideal societies) for which we should strive; they also think they know what that ideal is. Pragmatic utopians, in contrast, often like bits of the static utopians' ideal but find flaws in other parts. Some pragmatists even think there never can be a single ideal society (or even a small, well-defined group of ideal societies). Other pragmatists think such an ideal is conceivable, though remote. If we construct a model, then go beyond it to another, and then go beyond the second to a third—and go through these stages in a responsible, considered way, pragmatists agree that such movement should be labeled not "failure," as a static utopian would have it, but "progress."

Pragmatism can help answer various objections to utopianism. Many people in the United States today are haunted by yearnings for utopia but feel despair about its possibility or cynicism about its desirability. The pragmatic type of utopianism may, however, offer a way out: its emphasis on change can make it possible, and its on-going self-criticism can aid in guarding against undesirable, dangerous consequences. Another kind of objection to utopias comes from those who are suspicious of positive political programs as necessarily implying stasis and complacency. Pragmatism, however, makes positive goals possible without imprisonment in any particular one. And criticizing one goal need not mean abandoning all of them.[19]

In setting forth my conceptions of static and pragmatic belief throughout this book, I give examples from feminism, but the two modes make sense for other political beliefs as well. For instance, despite Karl Marx's well-known distaste for utopianism, some of his thought could itself be considered unattainable and rigid—particularly as interpreted by his more reductive disciples. The move away from such inflexibility by the Frankfurt School and postmodern thinkers can be read as a move from the static to the pragmatic mode of Marxism. While the distinction between the static and the pragmatic probably could not stretch to fit every belief (a pragmatic fascism sounds improbable, for example), the distinction might well prove fruitful for a range of beliefs.

Although many feminists think in a static mode, since at least the 1970s some have been working in a pragmatic mode, though they have not characterized it as such or fully discussed its ramifications. Now feminism and pragmatism are beginning to be linked explicitly, in particular by Charlene Haddock Seigfried in her groundbreaking book *Pragmatism and Feminism: Reweaving the Social Fabric* and by her and others in the special issue of *Hypatia* that she has edited. For several reasons, the pragmatic mode is even more appropriate for feminism than for Marxism or psychoanalysis. Unlike these latter belief systems, feminism has no single founder, much less a Founding Father. No monolithic body of writings inspires devoted adherents to vie with each other to be the most faithful, for from the beginning—the location of the beginning being itself debatable—feminism has followed multiple paths, complexly intertwining. Moreover, if feminism is the rejection of patriarchy, then in a sense every feminist's critique of patriarchy is by definition touched with pragmatism—a questioning, doubting, inquiring attitude, a tendency to be suspicious of settled convictions. The thoroughly pragmatic feminist meanwhile directs suspicion not only toward patriarchy but also toward the pat answers of static feminism. Pragmatism is manifested clearly in no single variety of feminism but in the thought process that investigates and compares all the varieties.[20]

Feminism particularly needs pragmatism at the current time. Despite dazzling progress, a daunting amount of work remains to be done, and yet some of the initial flames have died out instead of settling into the steady glow that is needed over the long term. Pragmatism could supply the necessary energy. Feminism also needs pragmatism at the moment because feminism has burgeoned only in comparatively recent times: even if *future* feminists will be able to come up with goals both precise and compatible, *at this point* a tidy program could only prove simplistic. At present we need pragmatism in order to remain critical of old schemes and flexible enough to try new ones. I would like to stress, however, that in suggesting that a complete utopian feminist scheme is unlikely or undesirable in our own time, I do not mean to endorse aimless drifting or some banal dilution of pluralism. Nor, of course, do I mean to endorse falling backward into acceptance of patriarchy. On the contrary, I believe that these weaknesses of current utopian feminism mean that we need to move beyond stasis by means of pragmatism.

Pragmatic feminism offers an especially revealing lens for looking at the three authors discussed in this volume, because of the problematic—in some cases even troubled—relation they have with feminism. Doris Lessing has frequently condemned the whole movement, Ursula K. Le Guin developed her feminism largely *after* writing *The Left Hand of Darkness,* and Monique Wittig has excoriated other prominent French feminists. This book argues that feminism pervades each of the three novels but takes an exploratory form—as one might expect from authors with such complex beliefs—and so requires an analytical model, such as pragmatism, that is adequate to its nuances.

Now suppose that future feminists do manage to imagine an ideal society, to paint a picture free of blurriness, clashing colors, and untidiness. It will nevertheless remain a still life, for inhabitants of the utopia will find its chilly perfection tedious. They, too, will need pragmatism—to help them keep re-inventing their society, to stimulate them to make it alive and dynamic. Thus, pragmatism functions on the societal level in two ways: it fosters critical, flexible thought both by people who envision a better society and by those who might inhabit such a society. In other words, people trying to sketch out a better future can benefit by imagining multiple possibilities, and even people living in a better society than ours can benefit by remaining open to further possibilities.

The Textual Level

The pragmatic mode responds to the weaknesses of the static mode not only on the societal level but also on the textual level, by generating narrative energy.[21] Reading a static feminist novel, I often feel I should enjoy it, but I rarely do, whereas the dynamism of a pragmatic feminist novel enables it to be enjoyable as well as feminist—I can have my cake and eat it too. In the three novels discussed in this book, a static tendency threatens to reduce the narrative energy, but the texts guard against that loss by moving onward to an intricate, vibrant pragmatism.

Pragmatic feminism characterizes a number of other narratives as well. In some of these texts, the heroine goes through stages, rejecting one or more ostensibly ideal relationships with men and choosing to move beyond them, alone. One thinks of *The Princess of Cleves,* by Madame de Lafayette; *The Awakening,* by Kate Chopin; and *Their Eyes Were Watching God,* by Zora Neale Hurston (see Nancy K. Miller, "Emphasis Added: Plots and Plausibilities in Women's Fiction"). Because science fiction lends itself to the presentation of alternative societies, the genre abounds with pragmatic texts, such as Samuel R. Delany's *Triton* ("an ambiguous heterotopia"), in which characters can fulfill their every wish except, as it ironically turns out, the masochistic wish to be a woman subordinated to a man. *The Silent City,* by Elisabeth Vonarburg, and the Riding Women series, by Suzy McKee Charnas, each follow a heroine as she rebels against a post-apocalyptic patriarchal society, then goes through stages in which she creates or encounters a series of feminist utopian places, each of which is appealing yet ultimately proves imperfect.[22] Most notably, both *The Silent City* and *The Furies* (the last novel in Charnas's series) even present all-female societies aiming to conquer and enslave all-male ones; both texts then pose questions about whether feminists would really desire such utopias of unequal power. Various societies, each with its own types of power and focus, are also described in *The Female Man,* by Joanna Russ, and *Daughter of Elysium,* by Joan Slonczewski. Although the plots shift around among the different societies instead of setting each forth in turn, both books are pragmatic in guiding implied readers through stages of questions about whether alternatives such as violence or an all-female society may be necessary in striving for feminist ideals.

Textual pragmatism has an impact on form. Its energy lends itself particularly well to the narrative genre—as opposed, for instance, to lyric. Because pragmatism demands change and stages, it requires a text that is protean on the formal level, be it through what I have called protean metaphor or through the plot development inherent in narrative. Pragmatism and protean metaphor can exist independently of each other, but, as we shall discover in later chapters, together they can also function in a powerful symbiosis.

In each of the three novels examined here, the interaction within and between various societies challenges the unitary concept of static perfection. Sometimes the novels produce narrative energy by representing societies that change pragmatically, while at other times the energy is created when the societies themselves remain static but are compared with each other pragmatically by readers (in some cases emulating characters, especially those who travel to a new place).[23] Both devices appear, for instance, in *The Marriages Between Zones Three, Four, and Five*. At first, when the zones are mired in complacency, pragmatism can be found only in readers' and individual characters' comparisons of the various places; later, however, the zones themselves recognize and act on the need for transformation. While the three novels in this study differ in technique, all of them represent a process of lively pragmatism that energizes the narrative.

Textual pragmatism can strengthen a narrative in other ways as well. For instance, it can help a novel avoid splitting everything simplistically into the heroic and the villainous. Since a stage giving an evaluation tends to be followed by a stage modifying that evaluation, a feminist novel can praise a society without idealizing it and can critique one without dismissing it as irredeemably patriarchal; pragmatism thus offers one path toward subtlety. Whether the stages are fuzzy or clear-cut, recognizing the text's pragmatic movement enriches reading in several ways, such as helping resolve seeming contradictions. For example, recognizing textual pragmatism aids understanding of how a book such as *Marriages,* which finds fault with a utopian feminist society, can still be regarded as feminist. And, when pragmatic stages structure a text, acknowledging them makes possible a reading more sensitive to complexities, for one need no longer dismiss most of them in favor of one neat reading. Nor need one follow the New Critical practice of doing only a retrospective reading that would consider all the stages simultaneously, squeezing them into an organic unity that would discount the development of one stage into another. Alertness to textual pragmatism can, in short, enable readers to honor rather than repress the itch in the back of their minds, the recognition that a particular book is not seamless.

The Societal and Textual Levels

For pragmatic utopian belief, as for the static sort, the two levels also interpenetrate—again, through the readers' imagination. As we have found, when readers of a static text imagine themselves living in the society it represents, they might well fear it would bore them. In contrast, a pragmatic text makes living in the imagined society seem interesting to implied readers. The pragmatic narrative avoids monotony by means of the two devices it employs to generate narrative energy. By representing more than one desirable society—even if each is static—the text encourages readers to imagine that, if they lived in one of those places, it would be thought-provoking to compare alternatives. Secondly, when a narrative represents a society that itself changes pragmatically, the text urges readers to imagine how engrossing the process of transformation would be.

Most strikingly, instead of simply being persuaded toward a course of action to follow *later,* implied readers of each novel I discuss are drawn into a process of pragmatic feminism that proceeds *simultaneously* with their experience of the narrative, for they are to engage in the process about which they are reading. Instead of merely presenting an ideal for readers to pursue in the future, these books present a model, then modify it, then replace it with another, which in turn is modified, and so on; in order to follow the narrative, readers need to employ the very agility and openness that the book is advocating. Because novels based on pragmatic feminism urge readers to participate more actively than usual in the reading process, these narratives combat passivity and gain persuasive force.

The Cook and the Carpenter, by June Arnold, provides a memorable example of this process. Most of the novel employs invented, genderless pronouns, and so readers do not receive definite information on the sex of each character until near the end. Since the cook has female-associated traits and the carpenter has male-associated ones, implied readers are tempted to imagine the sexes of the two lovers accordingly. Because the two live countercultural lives on a commune, however, some readers may start to wonder if the text is trying to subvert convention by means of a male cook and a female carpenter. In the next stage, the previously binary plot is thickened—and deconstructed—by the intrusion of another character, appropriately named Three, who stretches the relationship into a triangle. Finally, the revelation of the characters' sexes tosses a paradigm shift at any readers who have been mumbling to themselves: "If this one is female, then that one must be male." In this way *The Cook and the Carpenter* urges readers to give thought to gender and sex not only in the future; every page, by depriving readers of accustomed pronouns, demands that such issues be rethought continually, during the reading process.

But, as this example suggests, such involvement may discomfit readers. In novels of pragmatic feminism, just when readers have had a chance to integrate one point comfortably, another comes along to challenge it; welcoming the difference of the second point requires a disconcerting questioning of the first. Since the implied authors tend to take a position provisionally, only to slide away from it later, the feminist argument in these novels may prove frustrating to some readers.

In sum, given the alternatives of patriarchy, which is oppressive, and static utopian feminism, which is rigid and possibly tedious, pragmatic utopian feminism offers a third choice—a necessary, flexible process. No matter how much a static utopia appeals to those feminists whose ideals it brings to life, its very fixity calls for the doubts of feminist pragmatists. There may come a society to which we will say, "Abide, you are so fair," but at the moment most of us have been molded by patriarchal thought too much to imagine a society that would truly deserve that response from feminists (Goethe, line 1700). The novels discussed here suggest that feminism can mean a revolution in thought that is much more thoroughgoing—and more intimidating—than the achievement of such admittedly worthy goals as equal pay for equal work. Some feminists would condemn the pragmatic approach for being a means without a definite end. Others would accept the paradox that the end is the means, the answer is the question.

Pragmatism also informs my own practice in this book, especially as I describe one pattern of feminism in dialectic with another. My positions are provisional and utilitarian, since I am hopeful that I am making progress but not declaring that I have found the ultimate answer. Like a parent who nurtures a child so that daughter can outdistance mother, this study will, I hope, enable others to outdistance it in the future.

CHAPTER 2

The Process of Feminist Narrative Persuasion

> In reading a novel, any novel, we have to know perfectly well that the whole thing is nonsense, and then, while reading, believe every word of it. Finally, when we're done with it, we may find—if it's a good novel—that we're a bit different from what we were before we read it, that we have been changed a little, as if by having met a new face, crossed a street we never crossed before. But it's very hard to *say* just what we learned, how we were changed.
> —Ursula K. Le Guin (Introduction, *The Left Hand of Darkness*, n.p.)

Feminist Literary Persuasion

Groundbreaking feminist literary critics, such as Simone de Beauvoir and Kate Millett, chose to challenge patriarchal literature. Such attacks were indeed necessary since that literature not only expressed patriarchal beliefs but also helped promote them; yet the question remained—what kind of literature would be preferable? If that kind were feminist, what might feminist literature consist of?

I define *feminist literature as literature that encourages feminism in its readers, literature whose implicit or explicit goals include feminist persuasion.* If the readers are not feminists, then such literature urges them to change, and successful persuasion means the change occurs. If the readers are already feminists, then such literature urges them to retain their beliefs—at times deepening or elaborating them—and successful persuasion means the retention occurs. So my earlier definition of persuasion can be expanded to *changing someone's beliefs—if only slightly, if only making a new belief more palatable—or actively causing someone to retain beliefs.*[1] *Politics, Persuasion, and Pragmatism* explores these processes.

I belong to the motley group, ranging from theorists of ethics such as Wayne Booth to Marxist theorists such as Terry Eagleton, which holds that literature can be persuasive even if it is not obviously didactic, even if it presents no clear-cut religious or political doctrine but only a personal, shifting, internally contradictory vision. Of course, literature offers a whole gamut of pleasures and cannot be reduced to persuasive devices. And persuasion indeed functions in a more intricate way in literature than in a political speech, a sermon, or any other nonfictional text. Nonetheless, all literature has an "implied author"—a figure this chapter will describe in more detail—and to a greater or lesser degree every implied author is attempting to affect readers' beliefs, not only in the fictional world but also, in an indirect and complex way, in the readers' world.

Oddly enough, a sort of taboo keeps most feminist critics from examining persuasion in feminist literature.[2] In addition to criticizing persuasion in patriarchal texts, they often analyze nonpersuasive aspects of female or feminist texts, inquiring, for instance, about the significance of a female or feminist *author or character*. Except in work on feminist utopias, however, critics rarely devote their attention to feminist persuasion, to how literature fosters feminism in its *readers*. Why has feminist persuasion been so rarely acknowledged, much less analyzed or celebrated? Because I myself felt ambivalent at first about broaching the subject, I have contemplated my own hesitation in order to understand the topic's relative neglect by other critics.

I felt squeamish about looking closely at feminist persuasion because I thought I might find something wrong with it. It was easy to condemn patriarchal persuasion, as when seconding Kate Millett's scathing denunciation of Norman Mailer in *Sexual Politics*—the Mailer examples were both misogynistic and heavy-handed. But if we imagine a text that eschews both those traits, we confront the tougher issue of whether the very use of persuasion deserves distrust—a problem that plagued Saint Augustine (book 4) and has not gotten easier since his day. Should we be suspicious of persuasion in a text that is both feminist and subtle—the type of novel I discuss in this book?

Some feminists mistrust persuasion of any sort, perhaps because it smacks of coercion (within which I include unethical methods such as lying). One such feminist is Sally Miller Gearhart, who condemns persuasion for its very "*intention* to change another" (196). Yet even Gearhart, it turns out, thinks "principled advocacy" is possible.[3] Among the most impressive of her suggestions for such advocacy is the idea that each participant be "willing on the deepest level to yield her/his position entirely to the other(s)" (199).[4] Such proposals have renewed my faith in the potential of (what I call) persuasion. *Politics, Persuasion, and Pragmatism* thus grows from the premise *that persuasion need not be coercive in its methods and that noncoercive persuasion is necessary and desirable when directed toward a good purpose, toward conveying worthy beliefs, which for me include feminism.*[5]

Even if some feminist scholars are untroubled by feminist persuasion, they may neglect it for another reason: some of its techniques are not unique to feminism. The desire for a female or feminist aesthetic can make it hard to settle for study of persuasive methods that are not necessarily restricted to women or feminism. But, once admitted, the broader relevance of such techniques can prove intriguing in its own right.

In short, feminist scholars have given too little attention so far to the persuasive aspect of feminist literature—apparently because some are reluctant to confront persuasion in subtle literature whose values they share; because, having confronted it, they are concerned that it may be coercive; or because they may prefer to pursue topics that are uniquely female or feminist. This book, however, is grounded in the principles that all types of persuasion deserve study, that persuasion can be noncoercive and desirable, and that feminists can benefit from grappling with certain issues that extend beyond women and feminism. I also realize that, despite the laudatory tone in which this book refers to feminist persuasion, my very decision to reveal its workings might strike some feminists as a dismaying betrayal and might strike some antifeminists as a welcome exposé. But the attempt to understand is essential, and the understanding can help in reading—or writing—other feminist novels.

Rhetoric, Belief, and Literary Persuasion

Terry Eagleton has called for a return to rhetoric, saying, "Rhetoric, which was the received form of critical analysis all the way from ancient society to the eighteenth century, examined the way *discourses* are constructed in order to achieve certain *effects*" (205, emphasis added). An important way discourses are constructed is through *formal* techniques, and an important category of their effects is the realm of the *political;* so my combination of the formal with the political is rhetorical in the sense that it asks about the *effects* of fictional narrative *discourse* on beliefs about feminism. While nonliterary persuasion has been studied at least since antiquity, the literary sort remains less explored and more intriguing. A "rhetoric of fiction," to which my subtitle alludes, was proposed back in 1961 by Wayne Booth, who examined the "technique of non-didactic fiction, viewed as the art of communicating with readers—the rhetorical resources available to the writer of epic, novel, or short story as he tries, consciously or unconsciously, to impose his fictional world upon the reader" (*The Rhetoric of Fiction,* iii). Scholars have pursued his narratological questions more than his political ones; my study is meant to address both, linking the formal and the political, taking on part of the question of why literature matters.

A word of explanation is needed about the nature of belief in the literary domain.[6] Tricky though it may be at times to determine an actual person's beliefs, the issue of beliefs in literature requires still more care. To begin with, we can speak of literary characters as holding feminist beliefs, but not in the same sense as actual people, since characters appear in a highly mediated form. Nevertheless, insofar as characters are "people," they do hold "beliefs." Furthermore, this book goes beyond asking whether an individual character holds feminist beliefs, for its inquiry includes studying choices about narrative elements such as metaphor, plot, causality, and the selection of details.[7] All these elements together constitute the text's beliefs or—since it is hard to imagine texts possessing beliefs—the beliefs of its implied author. The implied author is not an actual person and sometimes differs startlingly from the real author, but, as the projection of a person, the implied author does have "beliefs" that it is valid and rewarding—in fact, crucial—to analyze. The analysis becomes most interesting when, as in the novels investigated in part II, those beliefs resist fitting neatly into any single category—feminist or otherwise.

In this book the notion of "belief," whether or not in reference to literature, is a comprehensive one.[8] It includes matters of the heart as well as the head, and everything ranging from a delicately entertained possibility, through a way of conceiving of a situation, to a building block in a systematic worldview. Beliefs may be large-scale ("Women in general are oppressed") or small-scale ("This boss is discriminating against this woman").[9] Beliefs may be conscious or unconscious, certain or tentative, consistent or inconsistent. They may be true, false, or a bit of each. A belief may be superstition, prejudice, knowledge, or some hodgepodge of all three. In this volume "belief" extends to what others might call a "state of mind" or even a certain kind of "emotional response": when a Christian gives in to temptation and commits adultery, for instance, one would say that belief in the attractions of adultery has at least temporarily outweighed an aspect of that person's religious belief.

M. H. Abrams makes an observation about readers' beliefs that I would apply to beliefs in general: "These subsist less in propositional form than in the form of unverbalized attitudes, propensities, sentiments, and dispositions; but they stand ready to precipitate into assertions the moment they are radically challenged . . . " ("Belief," 16). While aware that literary beliefs take the low-key form Abrams describes, I must, for lack of any other accepted vocabulary, talk about them in terms more often applied to beliefs "in propositional form"—blaring terms like "argument" and "convince." In employing such words, I do not mean to suggest that literature functions like an infomercial; instead, I aim only to bring into relief what might otherwise lie submerged and undetectable.

Ever since Plato claimed that poetical art seemed "to be a corruption of the mind of all listeners who do not possess as an antidote a knowledge of its real nature," the relation of belief to literature in particular has been a fascinating riddle (419; 595a). This is not the place to plunge deeply into the many debates about pseudo-statements and possible worlds; the two issues that concern us here are how literature *expresses* belief and how literature *instills* belief.

A novel may not express beliefs obviously, but it does express them: in novels the "question, what is the man saying, occurs so universally that . . . to ignore it is both foolhardy and critically irresponsible" (Sacks, 27). John Hospers, especially interested in literary statements that are implied rather than explicit, offers an account of them that gives a taste of what I would call how literature most commonly *expresses* belief:

> We are probably convinced that the novels of Balzac give us a reasonably accurate picture of certain aspects of life in Paris in the early nineteenth century, . . . whether or not they were so intended. . . . Nor do the novels of Thomas Hardy contain sentences telling us what Hardy's view of life and human destiny was; yet, from the way the novels are plotted, and the chance character of the events upon which the major developments turn, even the least perceptive reader, before he finishes even one of the novels, has a pretty good idea of what that view was. (39)

Hospers goes on to explain how we can find clues to Theodore Dreiser's beliefs: "[b]y observing carefully which passages contain the greatest passion and intensity, which themes are most often reiterated, how the plot is made to evolve, which characters are treated with the greatest sympathy, and so on" (41). A major goal of this book is to provide a theoretical framework for observations such as those of Hospers.

Given that literature expresses beliefs, critics have written an enormous amount on how readers are to deal with those beliefs. Most of the criticism has dealt with interpreting a text's meaning or assessing a text's value[10]—asking, for instance: Need a reader share a text's beliefs in order to understand its meaning or appreciate its value? If a text expresses false beliefs, does that lower its value? Such questions assume that a reader's beliefs remain basically unchanged—even the suspension of disbelief during the reading process is often conceived of as only temporary. In contrast, this book asks what happens when readers' beliefs change, when literature *instills* beliefs, when it persuades (if only by altering readers' thinking so that a certain belief starts to seem like an attractive, plausible, or reasonable possibility). It begins with the assumption that literature often influences beliefs and goes on to ask how that occurs.

The most obvious examples of inculcating beliefs come from biblical parables or popular media—the soap opera fan who sends a baby gift when a character gives birth, or the *X-Files* viewer who started to believe, maybe not in an alien that Agent Mulder saw, but in the more general possibility of aliens, or at least of government conspiracies. Whether or not such people are considered competent interpreters, their reactions need to be accounted for. On a different plane, think of the theater-goer who weeps, not only during the last scene of *Romeo and Juliet,* but also in brooding on it later, after suspension of disbelief has supposedly ceased. I know a Californian who built most of his early beliefs about the South on Faulkner's novels, and fiction has created much of my own understanding of England. For some cultures, such as that of the Heian period in Japan, the bulk of our beliefs are grounded in fiction, since that is the chief source available. Some of these beliefs are more sophisticated and well-founded than others; my overall point is that literature can instill beliefs in readers, and we need to think about how that happens.

In pondering literary persuasion, we can draw on a helpful distinction that Peter Rabinowitz makes between the "authorial audience" ("a *hypothetical* audience" for whom the author designs the text) and the "narrative audience" ("the imaginary narrative audience for which the narrator is writing"), which in turn "is quite different from the narratee, the person to whom the narrator is addressing himself or herself" (*Before Reading,* 21, 95).[11] Rabinowitz explains:

> The narrator of *War and Peace* . . . is writing for an audience that not only knows (as does the authorial audience) that Moscow was burned in 1812,

but that also believes that Natasha, Pierre, and Andrei "really" existed. . . . In order to read *War and Peace*, we must therefore do more than join Tolstoy's authorial audience; we must at the same time pretend to be a member of the imaginary narrative audience for which the narrator is writing. . . . [T]he narrative audience of *Cinderella* accepts the existence of fairy godmothers (although the authorial audience does not share this belief). (95–96)[12]

Rabinowitz says, "The pretense involved in joining the narrative audience . . . is [close] to Coleridge's 'willing suspension of disbelief,' except that I would argue . . . that disbelief . . . is both suspended and not suspended at the same time" (95).

Rabinowitz complicates his model in several ways. He points out, for instance, that the distance between the narrative and authorial audiences varies in different texts (with the interesting result that one can define realism as having relatively little distance between the two audiences).[13] He also points out that the role of the narrative audience can be ambiguous.[14] For a given narrative audience, however, Rabinowitz seems confident about identifying its relationship to the authorial audience, both when he explains how they are similar (in that some of their beliefs overlap) and when he explains how they differ ("The characteristics of the narrative audience . . . must be marked in some systematic way that is understood [usually intuitively] by author and reader alike") ("Assertion and Assumption," 412–13). I suspect, however, that in some texts the relationship of the two audiences may not be very clear, and so I would like to add an additional ambiguity, further complicating his model.

In particular, beliefs supposedly limited to that credulous narrative audience may affect the authorial audience more than one might think. Take the example of how Honoré de Balzac's *Le Père Goriot* molds people's beliefs about nineteenth-century Paris. Presumably only the narrative audience acquires the narrow belief that a person named Père Goriot ever lived, but the authorial audience might or might not be meant to believe in something more general: the notion that someone very like him, or a group of people somewhat like him (if he is a Balzacian "type"), once lived, and one could say the same of a tremendous number of other elements in the novel.[15] Rabinowitz might assert that I am confusing the authorial audience (of Balzac or another author) with what he calls the "actual audience"—that is, real readers (*Before Reading*, 20–21)—that I am blaming the author for how people actually react, but my point is that one reason the actual audience's responses are so unpredictable is that the text itself does not always make clear who is to believe what.[16]

Thus, *those beliefs that are to be instilled* in the actual audience as it identifies with the authorial one may be infiltrated more than is commonly thought by *those beliefs that are to be adopted only temporarily* as the actual audience identifies with the narrative one. (This very ambiguity makes me avoid reading historical fiction. I fear I will mistake the fictional for the historical.) It is possible, though, to determine what beliefs are expressed in a text, regardless of which audience is to adopt them; indeed, determining those beliefs is a major concern of this book. While novels cannot—and do not claim to—provide a nonfictional representation of reality, a surprising number of ideas about the world inside a text do leak out to tinge our ideas about the world outside the text. My consideration of belief therefore includes notions about extratextual beliefs (directed toward the authorial and actual audiences) as well as intratextual ones (directed toward the narrative audience).

Description and Evaluation in the Persuasive Process

The persuasive process, in literature and elsewhere, has two strands: convincing people to believe a certain *description* of what is going on in the world and convincing them to accept a certain *evaluation* of that state of affairs.[17] Within feminist literature, for example, a text can affect readers' beliefs about facts by pointing out that patriarchy exists and can affect their beliefs about value by pointing out that patriarchy is objectionable.

It is the first strand, the descriptive one, that usually establishes that some of the narrative audience's beliefs are relevant to the authorial audience—a relatively easy task when the setting is nineteenth-century Paris, a tougher one when the story involves talking horses. Yet Jonathan Swift manages to suggest that Houyhnhnms are relevant to humans. Even science fiction can succeed at such a task, for it need not depend on point-by-point imitation of our reality but can exploit metaphor, allegory, and a host of other techniques. For example, *Frankenstein* needs to convince only the narrative audience—not the authorial one—that scientists can create people from body parts, but in order to affect the authorial readers' notions about their world, the novel does need to convince them that Victor and his creature correspond to them in certain ways, such as in the capacity for love, betrayal, and revenge. This correspondence helps the authorial audience consider that Victor's overreaching might have some relevance to real people. Note that I am not claiming the descriptive strand in any single novel is so powerful that it will immediately transform everyone's beliefs; I am simply claiming it can put out a feeler of relevance to tickle them.

In a book whose descriptive strand establishes the text's relevance to issues involving women and gender, the nature of that strand determines whether or not readers will be nudged in a feminist direction. The direction will be nonfeminist if a novel describes women's sufferings as inevitable or as nonexistent, whereas a feminist novel encourages readers to believe that feminist change is both possible and not yet completed. The texts examined here offer such descriptions. The second strand of the persuasive process suggests how readers should evaluate the state of affairs represented in the first one. If the first presents women's condition under patriarchy, and the second evaluates that condition as oppressive, then the way is smoothed for feminist persuasion. If, however, a novel presents women's condition under patriarchy but evaluates it as acceptable, the text will have a feminist effect only on real readers who believe the descriptive strand but doubt the complacent judgment made in the second strand and who, on their own, evaluate women's condition as unsatisfactory.

The second, evaluative strand takes on special importance for feminist persuasion: because women, unlike most other subordinated groups, are present throughout Western society, readers already have some idea of women's situation. For instance, many people know that in the United States white women generally earn less than white men doing comparable work; if a novel merely presents this state of affairs without evaluating it negatively, readers who regard it as acceptable will probably continue to do so. To cause readers to change their values to feminist ones, a text must be feminist in the evaluative as well as in the descriptive strand.

Therefore we must consider more than the first strand in describing a text—for instance, we must not label a book sexist solely because it has sexist characters. Such a book can still have a feminist effect if those characters are evaluated negatively, like Mr. _____ in Alice Walker's *The Color Purple.* Nor does the mere presence of feminist characters necessarily imply feminist persuasion, for those characters can be evaluated as unappealing, like Henrietta Stackpole in *The Portrait of a Lady,* by Henry James. Distinguishing between the two strands helps reveal that, in analyzing literary persuasion, it is vital to study not only *what* a text represents, but especially *how* it does so.

Why We Should Study the Implied Author's Intention to Persuade Implied Readers

I care about authors and readers because they give a text its significance as political persuasion; feminist utopias gain much of their fascination not as self-contained artifacts but as entities that are written and read, that persuade. Because a number of hues fill the spectrum that runs from the author who composes the manuscript, through the text, to the reader who buys the book, I must identify the points on the spectrum on which this book concentrates: *how the implied author intends to persuade the implied readers*.[18]

Even an anonymous text sketches an image of its author, an image theoretically distinct from the narrator and from the real author who actually produced the text.[19] The counterpart of this implied author is the implied reader, the "audience presupposed by a text," who is to be distinguished from the narratee and the real reader (Prince, 43).[20] Access to the implied author and readers is available in the text, but access to the real ones poses severe problems.[21]

The reasons for giving up the goal of discerning the real author's intention are familiar by now,[22] and feminist intentions are particularly hard to state reliably, partly because the variegated nature of feminist belief means that many people have trouble deciding whether they themselves, much less other people, are feminists. Even if the real author's intention can be known, problems remain. Meanwhile, the real reader gives rise not only to problems similar to those posed by the real author, but also to additional obstacles. For instance, a text is usually read by more than one person, each reacting at least a bit differently to it; until the work of recent feminist scholars, women formed one of the largest groups whose difference as readers had been ignored. Moreover, readers can be differently situated in myriad other ways, including sexual orientation, race, class, nationality, and historical moment.

My emphasis on belief rather than meaning gives rise to additional reasons for doubt about studying real authors and readers; for instance, accurate determination of a text's impact on political beliefs can be extremely elusive. Rarely does a woman read a feminist novel, see the light, then dash out immediately to join NOW. More likely, she will read a range of novels—including some feminist ones—get into a debate with her brother, talk to a couple of friends, be harassed once too often on the street, see a thought-provoking television show, and only then, moved in an immeasurably complicated way by all these forces, start thinking about feminism. Because the kind of effect that interests me is often unconscious, minute, or both, readers may not be aware of it until (or unless) an external event brings the effect to consciousness, or they feel the cumulative effect of exposure to other low-key persuasive influences. This vagueness does not mean literature lacks all political effect; it just means that, because the effect can be unconscious and delicate rather than flashy, asking real readers about it may not be enough.[23]

The mists that veil the real author and readers do not, however, obscure the implied ones, because those exist in the text, a relatively more dependable and precise source. It is through our understanding of linguistic and cultural conventions that, regardless of the real author's (possibly unfulfilled) intentions, we can identify the implied author's intentions, and, regardless of real readers' (possibly poorly motivated) reactions, we can read how implied readers are intended to react.[24]

This book concentrates on how implied authors *intend* to persuade the implied audience rather than on whether they actually *succeed in completing the act* of persuading, because texts rarely give direct evidence of their success or failure at persuading implied readers. Indirect evidence often exists, though, if only because one page must persuade implied readers of one belief in order for the next page to convince them of a belief built on the first one. And, though the book concentrates on implied authors, it does not suggest that real authors and readers should be ignored; information about them, while not definitive, can help generate effective questions to ask about their implied counterparts. For instance, before taking up each novel I shall review the real author's statements about feminism because they supply one sort of evidence among others that it is wise to look for feminism in the text. (In fact, as we shall observe, the type of feminism in the novel can differ considerably from the beliefs espoused by the writer.) Real authors and real readers provide, not the last word about what is going on in the text, but a jumping-off point.

Having considered why information about implied authors and readers is more available and reliable, we can now approach the more significant question of why it is indispensable, especially in understanding feminist utopias. Even if some magical window could accurately show us "the real thing," the implied "thing" would still reward study by the politically concerned critic, for the textually implied figures mediate between the real ones, serving as the means by which the real author actually evokes those real responses. Thus my study emphasizes the textually inscribed figures not only because they are more accessible than the real ones but also—and more importantly—because they play an essential role in the process of literary persuasion. (Despite the distinctions just drawn in this section, in what follows I shall occasionally need to talk about real and implied figures together; in those cases I will simply refer to "authors" and "readers.")

The Matching of Implied and Real Readers

Persuasion relies on the relationship between real and implied readers, for through implied readers the implied author invites real readers to be persuaded. One of my fundamental premises is that *the more closely a real reader fits the profile of a text's implied reader, the more likely it is that the real reader will be persuaded as the implied author intends.* If the real reader does not fit such a profile, then she or he may be unmoved or may be moved in a way not intended by the implied author.

Successful persuasion relies, then, on what I call *matching—pairing the implied reader with a real reader who has relevant corresponding traits*—in terms of reading ability, prior knowledge, openness to change, beliefs about states of affairs and their value (such as beliefs about feminism), and so on.[25] Sometimes the relevant characteristics include class, sex, sexual orientation, ethnicity, and the like. For example, among real readers of Samuel Richardson's *Pamela,* someone who disapproves of certain upper-class privileges will resemble the implied reader and will therefore tend to sympathize, as intended by the implied author, with the servant heroine in her struggle against Mr. B., the well-born man who is trying to seduce her.[26]

Most real authors hope their texts will find as close a matching relationship as possible with as many real readers as possible; the real author draws on knowledge of societal and literary conventions to create an implied reader resembling the real ones who are to be convinced. Note that matching does not mean a resemblance between *author and readers* but between the *implied reader and real readers;* for example, a feminist implied author may, in an effort to persuade, address a nonfeminist implied reader who in turn is meant to match a nonfeminist real reader.[27] The notion of matching helps us understand not only intended readings but also unintended readings, for we can describe many of the unintended ones as cases in

which few real people match the implied reader. Books written ahead of
their time, such as Gustave Flaubert's *Madame Bovary* (1856) and Kate
Chopin's *The Awakening* (1899), did not, at the time of publication, find
a large group of real readers to match their implied ones, whereas recent
audiences have responded more as intended. On the other hand, books
precisely tuned to the time in which they were written may have trouble
later in finding many well-matched real readers. Mixed cases may exist as
well: I suspect that, in the decades since *Marriages, Left Hand,* and *Les
Guérillères* were published, the proportion of real readers who understand
them has gone up, while the proportion who are persuaded by them has
gone down.

Central to the concept of matching is that it resolves the dilemma that
has haunted many reader-response theorists: the question of whether it is
the text (via the implied author and implied reader) or the real reader that
ultimately dominates, that ultimately determines reading.[28] Briefly put,
people who think the text dominates cannot adequately explain why different readers disagree about a given text, while people who think the
reader dominates cannot adequately explain why different readers agree
about a given text or why one reader finds differences between various
texts. To phrase that more specifically in terms of persuasion: the text-ori-
ented group cannot explain why a given text fails to persuade some people, while the reader-oriented group cannot explain why a given text succeeds in persuading anybody or why a reader is persuaded by one text and
not another. Each group assumes that either the text or the reader must
exercise a sort of macho dominance. Some other theorists have attempted
to resolve the dilemma by positing that both text and reader exercise
power, interacting with each other, an appealing concept that nevertheless
begs the question of exactly how the two relate.[29] The three
notions—omnipotence of the text, omnipotence of the reader, and interaction between the text and the reader—suffer from the same problem: all
assume determination as an accurate model for the reading process.

In contrast, the model employed here is one of pattern matching, akin
to tuning a radio; when listeners tune to a frequency on which a station is
broadcasting, they hear the program. Just as broadcasts and listeners exist
independently of each other, so do implied and real readers: a program is
broadcast, whether or not anybody happens to be listening at the
moment, and listeners may tune to a given frequency, whether or not a
program is being broadcast. Normally, though, broadcasters and listeners
hope to be on the same wavelength.

It would be politically and psychologically naive to believe that every real reader acts solely as an atomistic individual; instead we need to think about real readers as members of a cluster of people who share one or more relevant traits and so are likely to be persuaded in the same direction by the same methods. An implied reader intended to appeal to the type of person who is a woman, a feminist, and a city dweller will be constructed to appeal to the smaller cluster that consists of the intersection of those three larger clusters. Since it is hard to be sure of influencing many people at once, various texts attempt to influence different numbers of readers with different gradations of likelihood: a text can have a strong chance of influencing a small cluster of people with many traits in common or a weak chance of influencing a large cluster of people with few traits in common.

Although critics tend to neglect the possibility of *multiple* implied readers, in fact it is one way a text can influence a larger number of people, since a real person who does not match one implied reader may instead match another. The premise mentioned earlier about matching can now be stated more precisely: the more closely a real reader fits the profile of a text's implied reader, *or fits the profile of one of a text's various implied readers,* the more likely it is that the real reader will be persuaded as the implied author intends. The large number of implied viewers and readers in Shakespeare's oeuvre may well have contributed to its longevity and so to its canonicity. No text can be all things to all the readers it implies, much less to all readers in general, but, as we find in Shakespeare's plays, a single text can indeed be inhabited by different but compatible implied readers. As we approach the novels to be studied here, the concept of multiple implied readers will prove helpful in understanding how feminist persuasion reaches out to a variety of readerships.

Matching in Degree of Persuasion

The examples given so far have dealt only with the *kind* of persuasion—whether it is intended for someone who is an admirer of the upper classes, a feminist, someone with a large vocabulary, and so forth.[30] For a match to take place, persuasion of the implied reader must suit the real reader in *degree* as well as kind. In other words, the real reader must find congenial not only the nature but also the strength—the loudness—of the persuasion directed at the implied reader.[31]

The persuasive process demands a degree of energy appropriate to each particular rhetorical situation. In the context of interpretation, Christine Brooke-Rose has introduced terms that will prove helpful here: she remarks that "overdetermination" must be balanced by "underdetermination"; a text must be clear without insulting the reader's intelligence (131). Her ideas can be adapted from interpretation to persuasion: persuasion will fail if it is too vehement (overdetermination) or if it goes over the reader's head (underdetermination).[32] Authors face a tricky task, since some readers require a fervent book that sweeps them along while others find subtlety more convincing. Some narratives delicately avoid the two extremes, often by presenting what Sheldon Sacks calls a "fallible paragon," who embodies many of the implied author's values and who nevertheless possesses enough flaws to avoid being an irritating prig (110–11).[33] Think of Christa Wolf's tentative, adulterous, yet courageous Christa T.; the meddling, clumsy, but wise Kwan in Amy Tan's *The Hundred Secret Senses;* or the passively resistant Offred in Margaret Atwood's *The Handmaid's Tale.* The problem of degree worsens over time, for a book such as Marge Piercy's *Woman on the Edge of Time,* which seemed bold to an appropriate degree when it came out, may today seem overdetermined to real readers who take for granted the feminist values that were fresh in 1976. Conversely, a book like Murasaki Shikibu's *The Tale of Genji,* which seemed nuanced to a suitable degree when it was written, may seem underdetermined today, almost a thousand years later, when read in a vastly dissimilar culture.

Thus, to be urged toward feminism, nonfeminist real readers must match implied readers in both the kind and the degree of persuasion they find appealing. We also need to consider what happens when there occurs a *mismatch in kind,* as when an admirer of George Eliot's ethic of sympathy confronts the righteous violence of a Joanna Russ novel. When such a mismatch in kind is aggravated by a *mismatch in degree,* persuasion is of course doomed (as when the Eliot devotee encounters Kathy Acker's gonzo sensibility). Interestingly, when combined with a *mismatch in kind,* even a *match in degree* can backfire: a text's degree of persuasion may suit a particular reader—may succeed in avoiding both obscurity and crassness—but that very success might cause a mismatch in kind to affect the reader strongly, driving that person away from the feminist stance intended by the implied author. For instance, a reader who finds Norman Mailer's vehemence invigorating might find Acker's over-the-top degree of persuasion equally appealing but then might feel all the more betrayed by her values.

Mismatches: Arbitrary and Negatively Implied Readers

This book will center on successful matching, but for now we must examine unsuccessful cases in some detail, so that the contrast will provide a deeper understanding of how matching works.[34] A classic example of mismatching in kind is *The Jungle,* by Upton Sinclair. The implied author intends that the implied reader will react to the horrifying account of the Chicago meatpacking industry by taking socialist action to improve the workers' lives. In other words, the implied reader of *The Jungle* already cares about workers in general, and the implied author intends that, building on that old value, the reader will primarily be motivated to adopt a new value—socialist commitment to helping Chicago meat workers. But, because most actual American readers lacked sufficient concern for workers, a mismatch occurred, and they failed to react as intended; *The Jungle* ended up moving them only to agitate for improved sanitation in meatpacking.

Every mismatch, whether in degree or kind, between a real and an implied reader is one of two types: an *arbitrary* relationship or a *negatively implied* one. When a real reader's reaction to a text bears no discernible connection to it (other than the mere fact of having read it), then the relationship between the real and implied reader is *arbitrary:* the reaction cannot be accounted for by the text. Someone who found the inspiration to wage war in every word of George Sand's *Lélia,* for instance, would have an arbitrary relationship with its implied reader. If such arbitrary responses can be predicted at all, it is in cases where some *idée fixe* causes the real reader to respond in a similar way to every text, regardless of what it says; a particularly sensational example is Charles Manson's response to the Beatles' song "Helter Skelter," which his fantasy of impending racial war caused him to interpret as inspiration to commit the Tate-LaBianca murders (see Bugliosi).

The *negatively implied* relationship, on the other hand, holds more interest for the student of persuasion. Since in a matching relationship a real reader corresponds to an implied one, we could say that in a mismatched relationship of the negatively implied sort the real reader corresponds to a *negatively implied reader, a sort of un-implied reader who lacks one or more of the implied reader's traits.* For example, because the implied reader of a *nouveau roman,* such as Nathalie Sarraute's *The Planetarium,* is someone who can decipher elliptical books, then a reader who requires clearer explanations is not implied. If a real reader corresponds to the un-implied one who needs clearer explanations, the matching process has failed in a particular way, and so the real reader's response diverges in that way from the persuasion intended by the implied author.

Although at first glance it may seem surprising, a negatively implied relationship *can* be accounted for by the text, even though the relationship does not fulfill the implied author's intentions: a negatively implied relationship does complement a matching one in a systematic way and so, if we know what a text's implied reader is like, we can also predict its negatively implied ones, and vice versa. An implied reader who can cope with Sarraute's obscurity enables us to predict a negatively implied reader who cannot. This book highlights implied readers and the matching process, only rarely mentioning negatively implied readers, but they can be deduced throughout, as complements.

Just as every conventional photograph must also have a negative, so every match entails the possibility of a mismatch. Trade-offs result: if certain real readers match an implied one, other real readers must match the negatively implied one, so no text can influence all the people all the time.[35] Therefore, a mismatch does not necessarily mean a failure on the part of the author or readers, implied or real; in fact, when an implied author intends to attract certain readers, that automatically entails resignation to losing other types of readers or even a Joycean glee in repelling them.

To sum up, the following table displays what happens to a real reader, depending on how well the person's traits match those of an implied reader. This particular example illustrates what happens when, as in the novels to be analyzed in part II, the implied author intends for the implied reader to be a feminist by the end of the persuasive process. As the table shows, only a match in both degree and kind is likely to make nonfeminists change their views and to reinforce the views of those real readers who are already feminists.

The use of a table entails certain simplifications. Relationships between real and implied readers comprise a spectrum rather than the set of discrete positions shown on the table. And for brevity the table refers to sudden changes, such as the conversion of a nonfeminist to a feminist, whereas in reality change occurs more slowly.

For the purposes of explanation, I have been presenting matching, arbitrary, and negatively implied relationships as if a real reader could participate in only one at a time. Usually, though, given a particular real reader and a particular implied one, they might match in terms of reading ability, taste in persuasive fervor, and most—but not all—prior knowledge;

Table 2.1

Possibilities for Feminist Persuasion of Real Readers Who Match or Do Not Match Implied Readers (Whether in Kind or Degree)

Relationship of real and implied readers	Result
Match	
Real and implied readers have matching relationship in kind and degree.	*Real reader ends as feminist, whether started as one or not.*
Mismatches	
Real and implied readers have arbitrary relationship.	Real reader's reaction cannot be predicted from text.
Real and implied readers have negatively implied relationship; real reader matches negatively implied reader and is unmoved. There is a mismatch in kind, in degree (via over or underdetermination), or in both.	Real reader stays as is (feminist or not).
Real and implied readers have negatively implied relationship; real reader matches negatively implied reader and is annoyed. There is a mismatch in kind, in degree (via overdetermination), or in both.	Real reader ends as nonfeminist (whether started as one or not).

maybe they share a good number of beliefs, but the real reader is indifferent to some other beliefs and opposed to still others. And within the areas of overlapping belief, they may differ in how strongly they hold them. Perhaps the real reader even responds arbitrarily to certain beliefs. The relationship between the implied and real reader thus comprises a mosaic, a composite of factors.

This chapter, having investigated the nature of feminist literary persuasion concerning beliefs about states of affairs and their value, and having considered the flow from real to implied authors and from them through implied to real readers, has now developed a theory of the matching that makes successful persuasion possible. "Matching" and related terms will rarely be mentioned explicitly in my treatment of specific novels, for that analysis centers on how the implied authors intend to persuade the implied readers, not on how the implied readers relate to real readers. But the idea of matching is indispensable for that analysis, since it is the relationship with real readers that gives the implied authors and implied readers their weight in the world.

CHAPTER 3

Two Major Techniques of Narrative Persuasion: Belief-Bridging and Protean Metaphor

[T]he great writer does not merely play upon the beliefs and propensities we bring to literature from life, but sensitizes, enlarges, and even transforms them. But in order to get sufficient purchase on our moral sensibility to accommodate it to the matters he presents, any writer must first take that sensibility as he finds it.

—M. H. Abrams ("Belief," 30)

Many of us feel that a particularly compelling novel has transformed us in some way—has persuaded us to change our minds about what is going on in the world or about how to evaluate that state of affairs. We often feel our readings have exerted subtler influences as well. Yet all these processes are elusive, if only because they involve the vexed relationship between fiction and life outside it. We need more satisfying explanations of how specific textual devices persuade us to adopt a new belief: what makes it appealing?

In any particular case the answers may seem self-evident—we recognize, for instance, that representing the heroine of a novel as a feminist can make feminism seem attractive. Such intuitions are not wrong, but I would like to press further, reopening ostensibly simple questions. What, for example, tells readers that a given character is heroic in the first place? And what are the exact steps by which a narrative persuades us? Rarely do we step back and theorize the process as a whole. In seeking to understand how feminist persuasion runs so powerfully through *Marriages, Left Hand, Les Guérillères,* and other texts, I have found that it goes deeper than the feminist actions performed by various characters, and it goes deeper than the feminist statements—no matter how convincing—made by a narrator or characters. How, for example, does feminist persuasion manage to succeed in *Left Hand,* a novel in which women are almost invisible? To go further than feminist actions and statements, I found I needed to identify the texts' subtler persuasive techniques by taking analysis down to the level of form; there I discovered devices that in fact contribute to persuasion not only in feminist texts but elsewhere as well.

On this deeper level, the two strongest techniques proved to be *belief-bridging* and *protean metaphor*. Belief-bridging repeatedly engages implied readers with the text by linking the implied author's beliefs to their pre-existing beliefs, especially those about literature. Once those readers are engaged with the text in a way that seems nonthreatening, protean metaphor comes into play—undergoing changes, moving implied readers through various stages, as if through the stages of an argument. At each new stage, belief-bridging again engages the implied readers. By the final stage they are persuaded of beliefs that would have disconcerted them if presented suddenly at the beginning. What belief-bridging and protean metaphor have in common is their emphasis on how reading *changes* readers, a point that tends to be neglected by many reader-response critics.

Belief-Bridging

I would like to create an explicit theoretical framework for something that many of us already intuit: it makes no sense to try to persuade someone with whom you have nothing in common. In order to put forward a new belief, such as admiration of feminism, belief-bridging links it with an old belief already held by implied readers, such as respect for heroism. The device involves implied readers by means that seem safe and familiar, for tying an unfamiliar belief to pre-existing ones makes the new one seem trustworthy, like the friend of a friend, until finally, no longer needing that mediation, readers form their own direct ties to the new belief.[1] Since utopian novels in general offer especially salient examples of persuasion, they offer especially suitable places to study belief-bridging; and since pragmatic utopian novels in particular need to be persuasive each time they introduce readers to a new stage, they present still more compelling instances of the technique. Although this book will concentrate on novels, further study may well reveal belief-bridging to be a very fundamental device that fuels all persuasive discourse.

To give a more formal definition: *belief-bridging is a persuasive technique by which new beliefs are made attractive as the implied author associates them with old beliefs, already held by readers.*[2] The assumption being made here is that, other things being equal, the more two people's beliefs already overlap, the more likely one person is to succeed in convincing the other to adopt a new belief originally held only by the first person. The initial overlap helps build trust, making the new belief seem less alien than it otherwise might. With belief-bridging in literature, implied readers first learn that some of their pre-existing beliefs coincide with certain beliefs supported by the text; the implied readers then discover that the text links the shared beliefs with the new ones, such as feminism. Because the text has created a bridge from the existing to the new, readers are encouraged to view the new more favorably. In Lessing's *Marriages,* for instance, readers are invited to think well of feminism because it is associated with the heroine, who is kind and talented.

Taking a more extended example: in nineteenth-century England some real readers of George Eliot's *Adam Bede* were inclined to view Methodism with a wary eye, but the text made possible a more tolerant response by embodying the minority religion in Dinah Morris, a serenely beautiful woman who devoted herself to the welfare of others. In this example, the values shared by the text, the implied readers, and many real readers are serenity, beauty, and selflessness, which together make Methodism more palatable.

The implied author did not necessarily insert Dinah in the novel for the purpose of promoting Methodism; the claim made here is simply that tolerance of that religion is one of the effects on the implied reader. Nor is the novel making some grand proclamation that all Methodists are serene, beautiful, selfless, and therefore admirable. Rather, the text resembles a spider spinning out one delicate thread linking a few points. In fact, the thread is a construct that need not have a counterpart outside the text: whether or not any real Methodists are serene, beautiful, or selfless does not substantially alter the effectiveness of the technique, for it can succeed even if those three qualities and Methodism are not necessarily clustered with each other anywhere besides Eliot's novel. For the device to function, what matters is that within the novel the new value, Methodism, be associated with readers' old values. The four traits must at least be compatible, though; if by definition Methodists were never serene, the bridging would not work. While in this example from *Adam Bede,* the beliefs concern evaluation, belief-bridging can also include beliefs about a state of affairs. Most of my examples will, however, involve value since the evaluative strand of the persuasive process has special importance for feminist persuasion.

Belief-bridging should not be confused with the reduction of literature to a sugar-coated pill, the concept of hiding an unpleasant or difficult lesson under the ornamentation of literature—in short, of hiding the instructive in what is pleasing.[3] Nor should my ideas of belief-bridging and matching be confused, although they are related and both involve overlap. Each can occur without the other. In belief-bridging, implied readers (and, it is hoped, real ones) overlap with the implied author in terms of pre-existing beliefs; in matching, implied readers overlap (in beliefs or other characteristics) with real readers.

Belief-bridging may seem simple, but some of its complexities can be uncovered by returning to *Adam Bede* for a look at Dinah's kinswoman, Hetty Sorrel. The technique can function in a negative sense: an implied author who wants to warn readers away from a new value can make a bridge from it to old values that readers already reject. Hetty, for instance, is willing to engage in sex outside of marriage, and, according to this book, such a woman is the kind who, in a panic, abandons her baby in a field. The text clusters nonmarital sex with the abandonment of a baby—an act likely to offend readers' pre-existing values. The particular circumstances in which Hetty leaves her baby show that she possesses little serenity or selflessness, further threatening to offend readers' old beliefs. By clustering Hetty's sexual attitudes with values that the implied reader already condemns, the implied author urges condemnation of the sexual attitudes as well.

Hetty's story also introduces another facet of the technique: the effect of weighting. Hetty is even more beautiful than Dinah, yet implied readers' admiration of her beauty still will not lead them to admire her sexual attitudes, for a small number of traits in one group (in this case appealing) are outweighed by more numerous traits in another group (in this case unappealing). Similarly, a single belief held strongly by readers can outweigh a single weaker one, and a belief central to readers' concerns can outweigh a marginal one.[4] (Note that in a complex novel, especially one such as *Adam Bede* that emphasizes sympathy, the rejection of Hetty's sexual practices need not entail a rejection of everything about her: the wrenching scenes of her trial and its aftermath still call on the implied reader to sympathize with her.)[5]

Another complexity of belief-bridging involves distributing the labels "old" and "new." In discussing Dinah, I said that the old values of beauty, selflessness, and serenity made the new one of Methodism attractive. If readers instead admire beauty, selflessness, and Methodism, then *Adam Bede* could convince them to develop a new admiration for serenity. The text normally tells us only between which beliefs the implied author has constructed a bridge—not which are meant to be new or old, nor which direction we should travel on the bridge.

Indeed, the technique does not even tell us whether the beliefs in a given cluster are to be regarded as appealing or repellent, only that they are to be regarded together. If a real reader for some reason hates beauty, serenity, and selflessness, *Adam Bede* can turn that person against Methodism. The unlikelihood of such an event stems, not from the cluster itself, but from the fact that most people in our culture, like Eliot's readership, hold beauty, serenity, and selflessness in fairly high esteem. These issues affect the way in which I approach the three novels to be discussed in part II. I talk about *Marriages* as if the text is advocating the new value of feminism by linking it to the old one of kindness, but theoretically the text could be advocating kindness by linking it to feminism or could even be denigrating the new value of feminism by linking it to the already despised value of kindness. Knowledge of societal values, however, means that we can weed out cases that are theoretically possible but highly improbable.

The Problem of Disengaged and Resisting Readers: Negatively Implied Mismatched Relationships Involving Beliefs

Having an understanding of the part that beliefs play in successful persuasion, we can now examine their role when persuasion fails. This analysis requires a return to the notion of matches and mismatches, since beliefs constitute one of the key traits in terms of which the real and implied readers can succeed or fail in matching. For a specific real readership in a given time and place, the possibility of overlap with an implied reader is riddled with difficulties—depending, for instance, on overlap in cultural codes and historical moment. Some twentieth-century feminists might actually find Dinah Morris's selflessness pitiable or irritating, with the result that the new value—tolerance of Methodism—might seem less attractive than it would to a nineteenth-century reader, who would be more like the implied reader.

Such mismatches occur when a real reader corresponds not to the implied one, but to what was defined above as the negatively implied reader. The twentieth-century feminists just imagined match *Adam Bede's* negatively implied reader more closely than they match its implied reader. When a mismatch involves beliefs—as opposed to some other trait, such as real readers' inadequate vocabulary or lack of prior knowledge—we can make a further distinction within the group of negatively implied relationships. They range along a spectrum that stretches from the *resisting*

Table 3.1

Possibilities for Feminist Persuasion of Real Readers Whose Old Beliefs Match or Do Not Match Those of Implied Readers

Relationship between beliefs of real and implied readers	Result
Match	
Real and implied readers have matching relationship; they share old belief.	*Real reader ends as feminist, whether started as one or not.*
Mismatches	
Real and implied readers have arbitrary relationship; implied reader's belief is irrelevant to result.	Real reader's reaction cannot be predicted from text.
Real and implied readers have negatively implied relationship; real reader is unmoved because matches negatively implied reader who is disengaged (indifferent to old belief).	Real reader stays as is (feminist or not).
Real and impied readers have negatively implied relationship; real reader is annoyed because matches negatively implied reader who is resisting (opposed to old belief).	Real reader ends as non-feminist (whether started as one ot not).

reader—who disagrees with the implied reader's beliefs—to the *disengaged reader*—who simply does not care about them.[6] Someone appalled by Dinah's selflessness matches the resisting reader, whereas someone bored by it matches the disengaged reader. A negatively implied relationship can actually be so annoying to a resisting reader that the persuasion backfires, leaving the real reader with disdain rather than admiration for the belief being put forward by the implied author; thus, some of Norman Mailer's works might unintentionally convert certain real readers into feminists.

In short, a negatively implied reader may be indifferent to a belief, may actively oppose it, or may occupy any point on the continuum between the two positions. Table 3.1 shows that, no matter where negatively implied readers stand along this spectrum, they end up unmoved by, or even rejecting, the new belief to which the implied author is trying to direct approval.

Like the previous table, this one must simplify, as when it refers to only one old belief and one new belief (feminism). To underscore the importance of belief-bridging, the table assumes the implied and real readers match in all other ways.

The Solution: Literary and Narrative Belief-Bridging

Our introduction to the risk of mismatching has revealed the vulnerable point in much belief-bridging: the perfect implied reader cannot be constructed, since authors can never wholly anticipate the majority of their real readers' existing beliefs. The best solution lies in a particular kind of belief-bridging, that which I identify as *literary*. Here a text associates the new beliefs with the beliefs that readers are most likely to share—those relating to the literary text as text. A poet, for example, may have no clue as to whether poetry readers will admire lawyers but can safely guess they will care for poetry. In other words, a poem about a feminist lawyer will be less likely to make feminism appealing to readers than a poem about a feminist poet, such as Elizabeth Barrett Browning's Aurora Leigh.

Because my study deals with novels, the type of literary belief-bridging that is relevant here is *narrative belief-bridging*, which makes certain beliefs attractive by linking them to narrative values. We can generally assume that readers of narrative like the genre (though perhaps we must except students trudging through a fiction course to satisfy a distribution requirement). Most readers of narrative are kindly disposed toward the categories to which narrative belongs, if not toward every individual member of those categories, and so such readers have a certain admiration for art in general, language, storytelling, novels, books in general, heroines, heroes, and narrators, unless by specific signals a text proves one of those to be unworthy, in which case it can seem all the less worthy.[7] Thus, no matter how much readers of narrative vary in other ways, they are a self-selecting group of people who do share some beliefs.

In the opening of Charlotte Brontë's *Jane Eyre,* for instance, the Reeds' harshness toward the young protagonist seems all the more egregious because she is absorbed in reading a book (rather than in some other activity) when John Reed interrupts her and because, when he causes her to fall and cut her head, he does so by hurling the book at her (rather than throwing some other object). As this example shows, narrative belief-bridging need not involve the precise genre to which the text belongs: Jane is reading nonfiction when John interrupts her, but like a novel it belongs to the broader class of books. Narrative belief-bridging frequently enhances persuasion in the feminist utopias this study will discuss. Wittig's utopian lesbians, for example, write in and read from a book much like *Les Guérillères* itself, a practice that weaves their feminism into a fabric likely to please readers who value literary art. *Jane Eyre* and *Les Guérillères* point readers toward values, such as female independence, that are held by the characters associated with narrative values.

In sum, during the persuasive process belief-bridging makes new beliefs, such as those about states of affairs and values, attractive by linking them to ones already possessed by the implied reader. Since real readers are most likely to share a belief if it is literary, some novels construct an implied reader with such beliefs and then connect new beliefs to those. Belief-bridging in general and the narrative sort in particular play on cultural codes to engage readers with narrative fiction: they are invited to place themselves at a comfortable spot in the text and then to stretch out to reach other places nearby.

Protean Metaphor

In the three novels studied here, geography represents the sexes: a female place is a figure for women, a male place is a figure for men, and, most importantly, the relationship between the two places is a figure for the relationship between women and men—for instance, a patriarchal or feminist power relation. Although it would be an exaggeration to say men are from Mars and women from Venus, the metaphor of geography for sex does permit these three texts to experiment with the idea that members of one sex feel members of the other are alien, as if they were foreigners or even extraterrestrials. In particular, the metaphor enables the novels to explore how patriarchy makes women into exiles, experiencing both the suffering and the enhanced perspective that such a situation entails.[8] And, because in most cases inhabitants of the different lands literally speak different languages, the novels can prompt readers to play with the notion that, outside the text, women and men figuratively speak different languages or literally use language somewhat differently.

The average narrative does not necessarily even need to describe its setting, much less go further and create a setting that is thematized, much less metaphorical. Utopian narrative is different, however: a "utopia" may be "no place" in our world, but it certainly occupies imagined space, and so setting matters deeply in all utopian narratives. In the three feminist utopias studied here, as in a number of others, setting takes on still more importance, since it also serves as the vehicle of a metaphor whose tenor is sex. In these books, for example, a female land is not just a place appropriate for women; it is also a semantic substitution for them, so that what happens in that country and to it is also meant to be read as commentary on women's condition. So, while protean metaphor generally resembles any other metaphor in its wide range of possible tenors and vehicles, it is no coincidence that these particular texts, being feminist, have sex as the tenor and, being utopian, have setting as the vehicle.[9]

Most intriguing, though, is the metaphor's protean nature. Geography continues to represent sexes throughout, but each book passes through various stages in which it further complicates the meaning of "female" and "male" place, and, for that matter, the very meaning of "place" itself. As a result, each book evokes a series of increasingly nuanced ways of considering the relationship between women and men. Thus, as places and the relationships between them become more complex, so do the sexes and the relationships between them.

More generally, the second major technique that I have identified in feminist narrative persuasion is *protean metaphor: a type of metaphor, found in narratives, that undergoes a series of changes that take readers step by step through a persuasive process as an argument would.*[10] Ordinary metaphors sometimes undergo changes as well—some of Shakespeare's come to mind—but only the protean sort undergoes this specific, systematic kind of transformation.[11] Protean metaphor, while not appearing in every narrative, is well suited to the dynamics of the genre: although lyric is conventionally claimed as the most appropriate genre for metaphor, recognition of the protean kind reveals narrative as a genre that deserves more appreciation, for protean metaphor thrives on movement, on transformation.[12] Because the relative stasis of the lyric moment cannot accommodate such changes, the protean type of metaphor appears almost exclusively in narrative. While belief-bridging permeates discourse, both within literature and outside it, protean metaphor appears less commonly, in more specialized contexts. In this study, however, the two techniques merit equal attention, for both deeply color the persuasive process in the novels under discussion.

Protean metaphor is significant because of the way its transformations can affect implied readers and the real readers who match them; only reader-response theory offers an adequate means by which to grasp it. The temporal sequence of reading, underscored by theorists such as Wolfgang Iser and Stanley Fish,[13] means that readers encounter each stage, each transformation of the metaphor, in turn.[14] The story can carry readers along, consciously or not, through a series of stages that will ultimately affect their beliefs. All readers encounter each stage in order as they progress through the book, incrementally learning more, though not every reader takes away the same thoughts and feelings from the encounter with a given stage. In addition, some readers re-encounter the stages, in a much less predictable order, if they go back and think more deeply about the implications of what they have already learned.

Insofar as time and change are the lifeblood of narrative—as opposed to lyric—the very structure of narrative lends itself well to another dynamic structure, the stages of an argument. In certain narratives, that argument takes the form of protean metaphor. The sequential nature of protean metaphor is crucial because it enables the metaphor to move readers step by step as an argument would, though of course in a manner more literary than rigorously syllogistic. Beginning in a form that implied readers can easily accept, the metaphor next prompts them to take a slightly different position, then urges them to stretch to adopt a more difficult one, and so on, until the readers have gradually been persuaded of a point that they might have rejected if it had been presented in a lump at the outset. Like an argument, protean metaphor gives the greatest weight to its final stage, representing the belief of which readers are ultimately to be persuaded. Herein lies the power of protean metaphor—*it unites narrative and argument by using the temporality of narrative for persuasive purposes.*

Persuasion also works in a less obvious but more interesting way in protean metaphor: as in some arguments, the journey rivals the destination in importance. In the novels examined here, for instance, a character's trip from one *pays moralisé* to another can cause readers not only to critique the first country in light of the second but also to meditate more generally on crossing boundaries and accepting otherness. By following a metaphor through various metamorphoses, implied readers learn a certain *process* of thinking and may eventually be able to anticipate what stage will come next. When the process is compatible with the beliefs being learned, then the process powerfully reinforces them, since the readers engage in the process being advocated instead of just reading about it.

For instance, a protean metaphor in what Susan Rubin Suleiman calls authoritarian fictions could act by accretion, with each stage adding to the previous one instead of questioning it.[15] The argument would proceed teleologically, with a monolithic revelation at the end. In addition to inculcating authoritarian beliefs, such a novel would influence implied readers through its very process, teaching them that it is presenting the absolute truth in easy stages because they are incapable of appreciating it all at once. I shall be discussing novels that, in contrast, teach implied readers a pragmatic way of thinking. Although protean metaphor can appear in novels that lack pragmatism, it is particularly compelling in pragmatic novels, especially in those that advocate what I have defined as "pragmatic feminism," since they encourage readers to learn how to think critically about their own and others' ideas. Indeed, the process is so anti-authoritarian that the pragmatism sometimes attacks the novels themselves, as we shall see in my discussion of Wittig's *Les Guérillères*. While different types of novels teach different processes—authoritarian, pragmatic, and other kinds, the common point is that protean metaphor fosters in implied readers not only the belief represented by its final stage but also the thought process set in motion as the metaphor moves from stage to stage. Texts threaded through with protean metaphor thus have enormous persuasive potential, a factor of special importance in feminist utopias.

In the most technically challenging novels, such as those discussed here, the pattern is somewhat dialectical, in that each stage represents refinements of, not total rejections of, those that have come before. Such instances of protean metaphor enable a novel to encourage complex, multifaceted beliefs. In the most challenging novels, the pattern is also somewhat deconstructive in that the pattern is skeptical, with each stage revealing a blind spot in the previous stage.

Joseph Conrad's *Heart of Darkness* typifies the novels whose protean metaphor follows a dialectical and deconstructive pattern. In his text, color represents degrees of civilization and morality. It seems in the first stage that white, or light, represents all that is civilized and good—all that is enlightened, while black, or darkness, seems to represent all that is barbaric and evil—all that is benighted. White Europeans initially perceive themselves as superior to black Africans. The novel then passes through a series of stages that complicate the meaning of "civilization" and "morality," so that Marlow's final act—his lie to Kurtz's fiancée—calls for, yet stubbornly resists, classification in those terms. At the same time, the meanings of "white" and "black" also waver. White, for example, is the color of the skulls on stakes around Kurtz's hut.

The transformations of Conrad's metaphor are dialectical in that each stage shows some trace of those that have preceded it; the trace of the quest for enlightenment, though sobered by doubt, persists till the end. The metaphor's transformations are also deconstructive. For instance, after the metaphor is established, readers learn of Marlow's hypocritical Belgian employers and are tempted simply to reverse the metaphor: the "whited sepulchre" of corrupt Brussels is dark inside, while the interior of darkest Africa is whitened by Kurtz's ivory and his uncanny integrity. But a reversal would be too simple, for Kurtz may be the most corrupt character of all. As the white/black, civilization/barbarity, and good/evil oppositions are deconstructed, so is the opposition between inside and outside that has been intimately connected with all three. With the final words of the novella, implied readers who considered themselves safely outside the text are drawn inside, into the "heart of an immense darkness," and must also look inside themselves for their own heart of darkness.

Other texts offer similar examples of dialectical protean metaphors that deconstruct binary oppositions: witness the role of the page in Isak Dinesen's "The Blank Page" and of castration in Honoré de Balzac's "Sarrasine."[16] Sometimes the protean metaphor oscillates in the liminal space between the poles of several oppositions, as does the wallpaper in Charlotte Perkins Gilman's "The Yellow Wallpaper." Often the oscillation occurs between the natural and the supernatural (as in the title character of Toni Morrison's *Beloved*) or between the natural and the artificial or human (the creature in Mary Shelley's *Frankenstein,* the garden in Nathaniel Hawthorne's "Rappaccini's Daughter," or the werewolf in Angela Carter's "The Company of Wolves"). As these examples suggest, protean metaphor is by no means limited to geography and sex, though those are the elements that predominate in the novels on which this book concentrates. In all protean metaphor, the figure metamorphoses as the narrative progresses, leading implied readers through stages, like those of an argument; not only does the text invite readers to travel from a more familiar to a less familiar location, but it also urges them to adopt a new means of travel.

Although feminist narrative persuasion inevitably employs other techniques in addition to belief-bridging and protean metaphor, I emphasize these two because they are important and have not yet received the critical attention they deserve. I concentrate on feminist narrative literature (specifically utopias), but we have also observed that belief-bridging and protean metaphor can flourish in texts that foster other beliefs, such as religious tolerance. Moreover, the two techniques are not confined to literary narratives: protean metaphor can appear in narratives that are not literary, and belief-bridging can appear in discourse that is neither literary nor narrative. While the two devices need not appear together, they exert an especially strong persuasive pull when acting in concert. Protean metaphor carries us to increasingly new places, and belief-bridging encourages us to appreciate what we find there.

CHAPTER 4

Feminism as a Rejection of Patriarchal Patterns

I myself have never been able to find out precisely what feminism is: I only know that people call me a feminist whenever I express sentiments that differentiate me from a doormat or a prostitute.

—Rebecca West (219)

Introduction

By no means are we in a "post-feminist" time: Western feminism may be said to be in its Third Wave, while the waves of feminism elsewhere in the world are also surging—in a different order and in different directions. Feminism is a vital, changing force that calls out for further study.

Since *Politics, Persuasion, and Pragmatism* is about novels of feminist utopian persuasion, I have sketched out what I mean by "utopian" and "persuasion," especially in novels, and now turn to what I mean by "feminist," the particular kind of beliefs these novels are putting forward. This chapter and the next explore the term "feminism"—the current chapter exploring what feminists have in common, with the next one tracing what they disagree on. Because I believe that what unites feminists is their rejection of "patriarchy," this chapter goes into some detail about that term as well. Inspired by the work of Luce Irigaray, these chapters present a number of different patterns both as an aid to understanding each persuasive stage in each novel and as a contribution to feminist theory more generally. Because part II presents literary examples in depth, the examples in these two chapters are largely nonliterary.

I'd like to explain briefly why, in an era that mistrusts definitions, I feel justified in proposing one. This in turn requires justifying the activity of generalization, because laudable respect for the specific or concrete has spawned a phobia about identifying commonalities at all. In short, the generalization baby has been thrown out with the totalization bathwater.[1] Thus, a number of theorists have given up on defining feminism, as when Rosalind Delmar asserts that the "fragmentation of contemporary feminism bears ample witness to the impossibility of constructing modern feminism as a simple unity in the present or of arriving at a shared feminist definition of feminism" (8).[2] In response to such sentiments, Sylvia Walby persuasively argues that while postmodernists have responded to simplistic modernist explanations of the world by rejecting the goal of explanation altogether, we should instead aim to find better explanations, ones that take complexity into account. And Susan Stanford Friedman sensibly calls for "a new singularization of feminism that assumes difference without reifying or fetishizing it" (4). For instance, while it is imperative to note that feminism may take different forms in different cultures, it is equally necessary to realize that *something* must unite the different forms if they are all to be called feminist. My definition may not apply perfectly in all times and places, but I do believe it will work beyond the cases to which it is applied here, and perhaps other scholars will test it in other contexts.

In order to account for a range of different, specific patriarchies and feminisms, the following discussions are complex. In novels, as in life, the patterns exist in a swarm of contradictions and conflicts; to unravel such tangles, one must approach them a strand at a time. In particular, we need to revise existing definitions of feminism because often they have only one dimension or they have more than one but fail to examine the implications of that multidimensionality.[3] My basic definition of feminism is flexible in that it consists of four dimensions (four beliefs), to be explained in detail below. Two beliefs concern the nature of patriarchy, and two concern responses to patriarchy. Feminists believe at least one of the four.

Such a multi-part definition is required for full awareness of the motley textures in the novels discussed in this book, since complex metaphors of patriarchy and feminism structure the persuasion in all three. In Lessing's novel, for example, Zone Three represents women, Zone Four represents men, and the relation between the two is of the sort I will be defining as "different power." Sometimes even a single place is feminist, such as Zone Three, or patriarchal, such as Zone Four. Being protean, the metaphor takes readers on a journey from one patriarchal or feminist pattern to another, at each stage of which they encounter persuasion through belief-bridging.

My definition concentrates on belief rather than activism or any other kind of action because mental state—conscious or unconscious—is fundamental to feminism. Although I prefer feminist action to inaction, my definition does not require such praxis. Instead, I stress belief because it gives action its meaning: we could not label an act "feminist" unless it seemed to express or promote feminist ideas and values. Even in the rare case where the person taking action does not actually possess such beliefs, our very ability to describe that exception derives from our notion of what feminist beliefs are. Conversely, feminists who fail to act on their beliefs may be powerless, cowardly, or hypocritical, but they are still feminists; not every feminist, after all, is a wholly admirable person. For these reasons my definition is built on belief.

So many different forms of feminism exist that they can hardly be united in a tidy package. What does unite diverse feminists is their rejection of patriarchy; they agree on the problem, not on how to solve it. We must therefore begin our encounter with feminism by way of an understanding of patriarchy. I define *patriarchy* as *the subordination of women* and *a patriarchal society* as *one in which such subordination predominates.*[4] Among the myriad specific instances of patriarchal subordination, there are two salient traits that usually occur together: *dominant male power* and *dominant male focus.* For the moment we can think of "dominant male power" as the privileging of men in the material realm and "dominant male focus" as the privileging of norms related to men in the conceptual realm.

This chapter defines individual terms that contribute to my definition: sex in contrast to gender, and power in contrast to focus. Finally, using these terms, I unfold the four feminist beliefs.

An Acquaintance with Terms

Sex and Gender

In the last twenty-five years terms relating to sex and gender have blossomed to reveal new complexities. As Elaine Showalter says,

> Within Anglo-American feminist discourse, the term "gender" has been used for the past several years to stand for the social, cultural, and psychological meaning imposed upon biological sexual identity. . . . Thus "gender" has a different meaning than the term "sex," which refers to biological identity as female or male, or "sexuality," which is the totality of an individual's sexual orientation, preference, and behavior. While a traditional view would hold that sex, gender, and sexuality are the same—that a biological male, for example, "naturally" acquires the masculine [male-associated, in my terms] behavioral norms of his society, and that his sexuality "naturally" evolves from his hormones—scholarship in a number of disciplines shows that concepts of masculinity [male-associated gender, in my terms] vary

widely within various societies and historical periods, and that sexuality is a complex phenomenon shaped by social and personal experience. (Introduction, 1–2)

There exists no foolproof way to define these concepts; what follows is just a set of serviceable distinctions. Slightly modifying the liberal feminist convention exemplified above, I use *female* and *male,* as well as *women* and *men,* to refer to the inborn anatomical traits of *sex;* I use *female-associated* and *male-associated* to refer to the acquired traits and common activities of *gender.*[5]

These concepts rest on the probability that particular traits will cluster: for instance, concerning sex, if you have certain chromosomes, you are overwhelmingly, though not totally, likely to have certain hormones and organs at a given time in your life; concerning gender, in a society such as ours, if you wear a dress and have a child, you are overwhelmingly, though not totally, likely to be the partner who cares for that child. Note that neither sex clusters nor gender clusters need take the form of binary oppositions: an intersexed person, for example, might have male chromosomes but female external genitalia. In fact, though, people do strongly tend to group at the endpoints of the sex and gender spectra. Much of what I say below, therefore, concentrates on the two main clusters on each spectrum, though we should not forget the rest.

The distinction between sex and gender matters to feminists because it separates the (basically, though not absolutely) unchangeable—sex—from the (basically) changeable—gender: a key move if patriarchy is to be challenged. Around the question of how sex relates to gender swirls much debate, hinging on two questions.

The first is, "Of the traits that *can* be acquired, are gender traits among those that *should* be acquired?" Many feminists, particularly in the United States, would say no, while a more complicated stance is taken by feminists who value sex difference, such as cultural feminists and French feminists such as Hélène Cixous. They doubt the value of some traditional gender conditioning, such as the stigma on women's writing, but conceivably might approve of a nontraditional form of gender conditioning—perhaps encouraging women to write in a nonlinear style—as a means to increase difference between the sexes.[6]

The second question is, "Which traits are the inborn ones of sex and which are the (potentially) acquired ones of gender?" Although almost everyone agrees that *some* traits are acquired, there is little agreement on their number and nature. This question has fueled some of the hottest battles against and within feminism. Patriarchal belief tends to hold that a good deal is inborn, but many feminists, going back at least as far as Mary Wollstonecraft, tend to attribute most of such traits to gender indoctrination. Even the inborn sex differences that do exist need not have the last word, since acquired traits can and sometimes should soften the effect of innate sex differences. Conversely, acquired traits can create even physical differences between the sexes in addition to their inborn distinctions; Ruth Hubbard says that the sexes will differ "biologically as well as socially" if girls, unlike boys, are subjected to diets, restrictive clothing, and taboos on vigorous activity (69). Under my definitions, such bodily traits possessed by only one sex still come under gender since they are not inborn.

To situate myself in terms of current controversies: I assert we can at least sometimes tell sex from gender. Studies of different cultures can help sort out what is inborn, which almost never varies cross-culturally, from what is acquired, which often varies.[7] Some recent scholars emphasize that distinctions between sex and gender are difficult, while I emphasize that they are possible.[8] I stress how similarly the privileging of inborn, anatomical traits occurs in disparate cultures. I stress also the empirically verifiable facts that underlie many of those similarities. Among all the variegated traits of humanity, then, societies tend to select certain ones (those I call inborn and anatomical) and group them into two clusters (those I call female and male). Thus, theorists who despair of distinguishing between innate and acquired need to explain why people, even those from very different cultures, would tend to agree much more on the relevance of observing that only some people have vaginas than on the relevance of observing that only some people wear dresses.

It might be objected that some cultures apply the labels *innate* and *acquired* differently than I do: for instance, in traditional Zuni culture it was believed that, by massaging an infant, a midwife could influence the child's sex, a belief I regard as mistaken (Roscoe, 342). Admittedly, the *interpretations* and *consequences* of sex as well as of gender vary tremendously across cultures, and those practices should be understood and respected.[9] However, not all the interpretations necessarily deserve equal endorsement, which in any case would be impossible, since some contradict each other. I am claiming that my notions of sex and gender offer a helpful way to grasp what is going on in a number of cultures, even though some of those cultures would disagree. The thoroughness of gender conditioning in most if not all societies has made it impossible, at least so far, to prove where to draw the ideal line between sex and gender, but we do know something about both, and it is irresponsible to claim otherwise.

Power and Focus

When feminists reject patriarchy, they are doing so on two planes: that of power and that of focus. One or the other of these realities underlies most feminist thought: for instance, much Marxist feminism stresses the necessity of gaining power, while a good deal of cultural feminism stresses that of shifting focus, as to nurturing. *"Power" refers to the material realm of how much one can do and how much one controls or is controlled by others.* Inequities in women's education and employment are examples of dominant male power. *On the other hand, "focus" refers to the realm of thought—to norms, to values and concepts. The object of focus is what people consider visible or valuable.*[10] An example of dominant male focus would be labelling of only paid work as "work," considering a homemaker to be someone who "doesn't work." In the terminology employed here, while "female power" means power exercised by women and "male power" means power exercised by men, a member of either sex can have a "female focus" or a "male focus" and can focus on "female norms" or "male norms." A female homemaker, for instance, may describe herself as "not working."

In patriarchies, dominant male power and dominant male focus tend to occur together and to reinforce each other; each can affect the other; and occasionally it proves tough to decide whether to classify something in one category or the other. Nonetheless, significant differences distinguish the two levels. The realm of power relations is basically material and related to praxis, while the realm of focus is basically that of belief (about what to focus attention or esteem on).

Another crucial distinction divides the two notions as well. If feminist goals were defined in terms of power but not focus, feminists would risk seeing women merely as more or less lacking something that men have, merely as victims of or coveters of men's power. By including female focus, I am concerned more with women in relation to each other and to female norms—a perspective that has value in general and is particularly necessary for understanding the feminism of lesbians, women-identified women, and separatists. As Alison M. Jaggar noted in 1990: a number of feminists "have begun to look at difference in a more woman-centered way, not just as evidence of women's weakness but as a possible source of women's strength" (248).[11]

The idea of focus undergirds a good deal of feminist thought but is lacking in many actual definitions of feminism, in which the other three elements of my model (power, the awareness of patriarchy, and the possibilities of resisting patriarchy) are often present either explicitly or implicitly.[12] A number of other definitions do include something akin to focus but do not explore what happens when certain dimensions of feminism are present while focus or some other such dimension is lacking.[13] Finally, those definitions that do approach the idea of multidimensionality do not break focus down specifically by object (sex or gender) or by pattern (singularity, centrality, duality, and multiplicity). The concepts of power and focus structure this chapter and the next one, which flesh out the concepts with specific examples.

The Nature of Patriarchy

Belief One: Advocacy of Female Power and Critique of Dominant Male Power. The Patriarchal Pattern of Power, Inequality: Inequality (Dominant Male Power)

Women should have the power they deserve; dominant male power (the privileging of men) is undesirable because it is unjust.

Power relations in patriarchy are characterized by inequality, specifically by *dominant male power.* I describe male power as "dominant" because most feminists do not reject the idea that men should have any power at all, just the idea that men should have dominant power. This dominance takes vastly different forms, depending on specifics such as culture, historical period, sexual orientation, and class. We can, however, make some generalizations.

"Dominant male power" refers, in the first place, to men's systematic power over women—the most obvious way in which men subordinate women. Men's control over women's bodies, their economic resources, their access to knowledge, their energies, their words: these are all among the examples, too common to need elaboration, of the varied ways in which many men exert power over many women. A less-recognized but perhaps more tenacious facet of dominant male power is men's systematic possession of more power than women have: not power over women as such but over other possible objects of power, such as money or other resources. For instance, in some cases where a man earns more than a female co-worker (even though he may have no direct power over her), if the disparity reflects a systematic, sex-based power differential, it is a case of dominant male power. Feminist persuasion regarding these issues typically encourages an audience to notice an instance of male power or to observe its systematic nature.

In this dimension of feminism, more ethically oriented than the other three, feminists condemn dominant male power because it is unjust.[14] Belief One holds that many women should get more power but does not have to mean that every acquisition or exercise of power by a woman is necessarily just and therefore feminist: when a female slaveholder in the antebellum United States exerted power over a male slave, her act was not a feminist one. Feminist persuasion in this realm often involves convincing an audience that a specific instance of male power is unjust or that particular female power is just. Another reason I include justice in this definition is to emphasize that feminists want power for women as a group. As Barbara Smith says, "Feminism is the political theory and practice that struggles [*sic*] to free *all* women: women of color, working-class women, poor women, disabled women, lesbians, old women—as well as white, economically privileged, heterosexual women. Anything less than this vision of total freedom is not feminism, but merely female self-aggrandizement" (49). Without this sense of women's structural subordination, if a woman fights dominant male power only because it threatens her as an individual, or only because it threatens her particular group, then she, like the Marquise de Merteuil, in Pierre Choderlos de Laclos's *Dangerous Liaisons,* is not really fighting for justice.

Belief Two: Respect for Female Focus and Critique of Dominant Male Focus

Introduction to Patriarchal Patterns of Focus
Female norms should be visible and valued as much as or more than others; dominant male focus (the privileging of male norms related to sex and gender) is undesirable because it neglects significant norms; female sex and gender should not be viewed as deviations from male norms.[15]

Feminists reject "dominant" male focus, but most of them do not reject male norms altogether; they just refuse to place them at the center of human concerns. *Dominant male focus,* which has a good deal in common with androcentrism and phallocentrism,[16] means *privileging male norms, not only members of the male sex but also what a culture links with them: gender traits and behavior found usually in men but sometimes in women. Feminists reject patriarchal focus, which is dominant male focus.*

Writing of American society, Catherine A. MacKinnon vividly paints the effect of what I call dominant male focus: "Men's physiology defines most sports, their health needs largely define insurance coverage, their socially designed biographies define workplace expectations and successful career patterns, their perspectives and concerns define quality in scholarship, their experiences and observations define merit, their military service defines citizenship, their presence defines family, their inability to get along with each other—their wars and rulerships—define history, their image defines god, and their genitals define sex" (219).[17] Focus entails value or visibility: in a society with a dominant male focus, sometimes men and things male are regarded as more valuable than their female counterparts, while at other times men and things male are simply more visible and get more attention—their female counterparts are just not regarded at all.

While dominant male power directly benefits only the male sex, dominant male focus can benefit both the male sex and the male-associated gender. Most basically, although factors such as class and sexual orientation cause advantages to be reaped unequally, at the focal point are men. For instance, studies have shown that male students tend to receive much more attention than female ones—from teachers of both sexes (Hall and Sadler). Or the focal point may consist of gender: traits and activities that a particular society associates with men because within that society men ordinarily, though not exclusively, acquire those traits and perform those activities. Consider, for example, the many pages that U.S. newspapers addressing readers of both sexes devote to professional sports in contrast to the few pages about childrearing.

The notion of focus helps account for the pervasive problem of *otherness* that women face in patriarchy, for dominant male focus defines man as self (however complexly constructed), defines woman as other, and then distributes specific traits as needed.[18] Woman is not necessarily relegated to the gutter, for she may be placed on a pedestal, but in either case she is the exception, not the norm—the marked case, not the unmarked one. In this way patriarchal society can avoid having to accept women's detailed specificity. In patriarchy, as long as man is self and woman is other, particular traits can appear in either one of the categories and can even shift from one to another, as we shall discover.

Adding focus to power as a tool to aid analysis thus can help explain why women who are struggling for power in patriarchal society often feel that, as soon as they touch what they have been striving for, it crumbles away. For example, in the nineteenth century most clerical workers in the United States were men and received a good deal of respect; now, for complex reasons, most clerical workers are women and receive little respect. Women won the right to such jobs, but the work changed gender, and so their very success caused the disappearance of some of the advantages they had sought.[19] Identifying and understanding dominant male focus, with its many mutations in specific cultural situations, helps account for what would otherwise seem inexplicable inconsistencies.

The Patriarchal Patterns of Focus: Singularity and Centrality, the Types of Dominant Male Focus

The most extreme pattern of dominant male focus is *male singularity, the notion that the male norm is, in effect, the only norm—at least the only one worthy of notice.* Only one norm is visible, and so only one is valuable. Examples include economists who study only paid work and anthropologists who study only male rituals in the society they are visiting.[20]

Of course, even the most patriarchal society cannot remain totally oblivious to the existence of female sex and gender. But the specificity of that existence is sanitized, recuperated—as if a man were to look at a woman but see only his own image, as if he had looked in a mirror instead of at her. Luce Irigaray draws on the mirror analogy to structure an entire book, *Speculum of the Other Woman,* which has inspired my explanations of all the kinds of focus discussed below.[21] Irigaray critiques the patriarchal insistence on oneness, identity, and unique truth, signified by the phallus. The mirror reflects the self, not the other, as male singularity absorbs the other into the self. Sensitized by Irigaray's analogy, one can find many examples of how the other collapses into the self's solipsism, as in the supposedly generic use of "man,"[22] as in the Freudian notion that the active sexual drive is masculine,[23] as in the long-standing principle of English common law by which marriage rendered the husband and wife one person and that person was the husband.[24]

A less extreme pattern of dominant male focus is *male centrality, the notion that there are two norms but the male one is worthier.* Two norms are visible, but only one is truly valuable; the self notices but does not esteem the other's difference, what Simone de Beauvoir calls "the second sex."[25] As constructed by male centrality, female inferiority serves a patriarchal purpose, for it can act as a foil and confirmation for men's superiority. The attitude is typified by Sigmund Freud's view of the clitoris as an inferior penis. It would seem that only one norm matters and women simply do not measure up to it—for instance, in height, in the ability to lead armies, or—as Aristotle would have it—in the possession of intrinsic heat.[26] Some women react to male centrality by attempting to prove that they can indeed measure up; as the example of clerical work illustrates, however, such efforts can never fully succeed if dominant male focus persists.

Oddly enough, male centrality can do more harm than male singularity: women can be better off when left to themselves, as in James Tiptree, Jr.'s "The Women Men Don't See." At other times both kinds of focus do the same amount of harm: some medical researchers omit women from studies simply because females are ignored (singularity), while others omit them because their fluctuating hormones would complicate the results (centrality) (Litt, chap. 14). Whether women are granted low visibility or low value, they end up being prescribed medicines that have been tested only on men (Conway, 12–13).

One type of male centrality may be called pseudo-duality. Duality can obviate some of the problems caused by male singularity and male centrality. And, as the next chapter explains, one feminist response to dominant male focus is indeed dual focus, in which both female and male norms receive equal respect. Yet genuine duality is elusive, for, as Jacques Derrida and the civil-rights movement have shown, "separate but equal" dualities tend to be hierarchies (e.g., Derrida, "Signature, Event, Context," 195; "Limited Inc abc . . . ," 211, 236). I use the term *pseudo-dualities* for such *hierarchies disguised as dualities,* which pervade Western thought from Pythagoras through Carl Gustav Jung.[27] According to a number of French feminists, these concealed hierarchies are at the root of women's subordination, since Western societies often link male norms with the self, the mind, and the subject, while connecting female norms with the other, the body, and the object.[28] In my terms, the focus on male and female often functions as a pseudo-duality: the two sets of norms may appear equally valid, but society in fact grants female focus less validity, so that the pattern is actually a version of male centrality.

Particular instances of such pseudo-duality abound. A Freudian example is the pair penis/vagina, which avoids reducing the clitoris to an inferior penis but succumbs to another kind of male centrality, since Freud sees the vagina as lack. Pseudo-dualities are epitomized by the doctrine of separate spheres, which, despite its liberatory potential, was often employed by the Victorians to buy off the middle-class woman (Showalter, "Feminist Criticism in the Wilderness," 198). Complementarity is a type of duality especially vulnerable to becoming pseudo-duality. Yin/yang and other instances usually define female and male norms as not just different from each other but as mutually exclusive, a pattern that need not slide into male centrality but often does. As we have seen, in patriarchal society the male norm takes precedence, becoming in effect the self that defines the other—as its opposite, in the case of complementarity. In such a model the other is implicitly contained in the self. Patriarchal complementarity is typified by the notion of the vagina and uterus not as lack but as a concave, empty space for the penis.

Responses to Patriarchy

The preceding discussion has developed a definition of patriarchy as two traits, ordinarily found together: thus, *dominant male power and dominant male focus define patriarchal society, and patriarchal belief can be defined as belief in the desirability of patriarchal society.* Yet most systems are riddled with fissures and cracks; from within such anomalies in patriarchy some people eschew dominant male focus and criticize dominant male power, even if they are subject to it. Since feminists reject patriarchy, *feminist society is defined by the just distribution of power between women and men (the absence of dominant male power) and by the appropriate visibility and valuing of female norms (the absence of dominant male focus).* One might expect *feminist belief* in turn to consist simply of belief in the desirability of these two goals involving power and focus (i.e., the desirability of feminist society), but feminism needs two more elements than its patriarchal counterpart: because cultures around the world are by and large patriarchies, feminists need both to recognize and to resist much of the status quo.

Belief Three: Awareness of Patriarchy

Instances of patriarchy have existed and still exist; feminists recognize patriarchies.

The third element of feminism is that feminists believe dominant male power and dominant male focus have existed and still do. People lack this element if they think patriarchy in general is still a problem but fail to recognize an actual instance or if, out of fear or self-interest, they are unwilling to admit to recognizing it. Thus, feminist persuasion sometimes consists of convincing a person to see, or to acknowledge seeing, an example of patriarchy. It is important to distinguish the third dimension from the first two; nonetheless, the third tends to accompany the other two. When a novel, for instance, draws readers' attention to the existence of patriarchy, usually the text also presents patriarchy as being rooted in dominant male power and focus.

The recognition of patriarchy usually includes certain nuances, for the type of patriarchy and the degree to which an individual woman is affected by it can vary greatly, depending on her specific place in a specific culture. Moreover, feminism does not require the belief that all men subordinate all women. Sometimes other forms of domination, such as racism, outweigh patriarchy, as when white women subordinate Asian men. A defining characteristic of patriarchy is, however, that on average within a given race (or class or other grouping) men tend to subordinate women.

Belief Four: The Possibility of Successfully Resisting Patriarchy

Individuals or groups can successfully resist patriarchy.

Feminists go beyond the mere wish or hope that change *might* be possible, for they believe some change *is* possible, even if they themselves do not enact it. If patriarchy were invincible, criticizing it would be as futile as criticizing the weather; instead, the fourth element gives my definition its political edge, which has particular significance in feminist utopias. Feminists may or may not believe long-lasting, widespread change can occur. But, since the personal is political, if a woman gets her husband to stop expecting her to pick up his socks from the floor, she *is* resisting patriarchy; three hundred and sixty-five pairs of socks per year matter.

This fourth element is intended to exclude people who think that patriarchy exists but that weakening it is impossible. An obvious example of such people would be the kind of sociobiologist who believes patriarchy is preordained by baboon behavior. This fourth dimension of feminism even excludes people who object to women's subordination but believe patriarchy is invulnerable. Addressed to such people, feminist persuasion would take the form of an effort to instill confidence in the possibility of change, on however small a scale.

The resistance element of my definition grew out of a particular, much-debated question—is Doris Lessing a feminist?[29] More specifically, is the implied author of *The Golden Notebook* a feminist? Awareness of the importance of the fourth feminist belief helped me understand that the critics debating the implied author's feminism have not really been disagreeing: some are applauding the presence of the first three feminist elements (the novel eloquently presents the women characters' values and problems), while others are lamenting the lack of the fourth (the novel often resorts to fatalism about the human inability to solve those problems). Analyzing this debate helped me realize the need for a multidimensional definition, so that one could ask about each specific dimension rather than simply asking, "Is the novel feminist—yes or no?"

Consequences of This Definition of Feminism

I hope to have sketched out a definition that will include most people considered by themselves or others to be feminists, and that will exclude most people considered neither by themselves nor others to be feminists. To enrich my notion of feminist persuasion, I have attempted to nuance the definition of feminism, as in distinguishing between power and focus. Most importantly, as in Ludwig Wittgenstein's notion of family resemblances, there is no essence, no single characteristic whose presence or absence determines the presence or absence of feminism (31–32). We cannot search for only one element and then label a given text, much less an oeuvre as a whole, still less an actual person.

As we have seen, this multidimensionality makes possible analysis of problematic cases, such as *The Golden Notebook,* for in the beliefs of a given person (or of a given text's implied author) all, some, or none of these four dimensions may be found. A person who possesses none of them is not a feminist, but I consider someone possessing even one of them to be a feminist. It might make sense to measure degrees of feminism, but I leave such measurements, should they seem useful, to others. My claim is that, instead of asking, "Is this person feminist or not?" we should be asking, "Does this person have any of the four feminist beliefs? If so, which one or ones?" These last two questions, by evoking specific answers, can stimulate further exploration.

Some critics concerned about diversity may object that the definition can apply only to my own culture, that of the United States in the early twenty-first century. Probably the definition does most comfortably fit people whose subject position closely resembles my own. Nevertheless, by devoting part II to trying out the definition on women writers who, though apparently all of one race (white), have different sexual orientations and come from three countries, I hope to suggest its broader scope. In addition, one of the novelists is of particular multicultural interest:

Lessing has roots in Asia, Africa, and Europe and cannot be tidily confined in any single one of the cultures that contributed to forming her. If the definition proves to offer a fruitful set of questions for approaching the implied author presented by such a multicultural writer, it may show promise for other contexts as well. What is more, the definition itself draws on more than one tradition. Among its elements, it is true that the fourth evokes the beliefs behind the activism that has historically pervaded United States feminism. But this belief in change also draws on the Marxism that so strongly characterizes British feminism, and the rejection of dominant male focus springs from French feminism.

Finally, the definition, while explicit on certain points, leaves open others, such as sex, ethnicity, and sexual orientation. And separatists, postmodernists, liberals, radicals, Marxists, and other kinds of feminists can also be accommodated. The definition further leaves room both for feminists who merely hold certain beliefs and for those who also act on them; for feminists who conceive of change narrowly and for those who conceive of it broadly; and for feminists who emphasize power and those who emphasize focus.

As for the three novels themselves, evaluation has a place, and one could evaluate a text according to its degree of feminism, just as one could evaluate it according to the quality of its metaphors. But my goal is not to assign each novel a score according to political correctness; instead, I want to ask, "Exactly where and how is the text feminist?" And, whether one is glad or sorry to find that a text has a feminist streak, such a text deserves study because of its potential for persuasion, for exerting a political influence on readers. Even antifeminist critics must, in order to examine these writings thoroughly, ask whether feminism appears in the text. In the spirit of examining the writings thoroughly, my aim here is more descriptive and analytical than evaluative, though my own preference for feminism is obvious.

CHAPTER 5

Diverse Patterns of Feminism

My candle burns at both ends;
It will not last the night;
But ah, my foes, and oh, my friends—
It gives a lovely light!
                    —Edna St. Vincent Millay (9)

Having observed what links feminists together, we can now explore what differentiates them from each other. Although every political belief system attracts more than one sort of adherent, feminism is particularly distinguished by diversity—not surprising within a group concerned with improving the lot of so many. The previous chapter defined feminism by what it is not—describing feminist belief as the rejection of patriarchy and describing feminist society as the absence of patriarchal society or the absence of dominant male power and focus—but this definition leaves open a wide range of possibilities for what specific incarnations feminism might take. One reason I defined feminism in terms of a problem instead of a solution was my desire to accommodate different sorts of feminism. We have already noted that feminists can differ according to which of the four basic beliefs they hold; they can also differ in what they propose as an alternative to patriarchy. This chapter presents some of those alternatives, in terms of the notions of power and focus previously outlined.

A major purpose of this classification scheme is to make it possible to situate different types of feminists in relation to each other. If feminism as a whole resembles a round loaf of bread, then traditional classifications grab one hunk from here and another from there, whereas I slice the loaf more systematically—along parallel lines, in terms of power, or radially, in terms of focus. In mapping out a range of feminist patterns and how they relate to each other, I do not aim to tout one particular brand as the best. While it is the failings of patriarchy to which feminist patterns address their most forceful responses, each kind of feminism can also be interpreted as responding to the inadequacies of others; I shall therefore be laying out the various patterns in an ongoing dialectic.

Feminist Patterns of Power: Inequality (Dominant Female Power), Equality, and Difference

Within the realm of power, there can exist *unequal, equal,* or *different* relations between the sexes. Of the three, inequality and equality deal with the degree of power, whereas difference deals with the kind of power. This classification, as we shall find, helps solve the problem of equality and difference that has long beleaguered feminist theory. As we have observed, the only patriarchal pattern of power is inequality—specifically, dominant male power. Feminist power relations, however, can take any of the three forms.

The feminist version of *unequal* power is in most ways the reverse side of the patriarchal version. *Dominant female power* thus entails both *women's systematic power over men* and *women's systematic possession of more power than men have.* Among the advocates of dominant female power early in the Second Wave of feminism were Elizabeth Gould Davis, Valerie Solanas, and Mary Daly. Since I have described feminists in general as people who condemn dominant male power for being unjust, it may seem surprising that I nevertheless include dominant female power among the varieties of feminism. Yet unequal power is not necessarily unjust, for it can be based on genuine superiority in some relevant area. So feminists who believe women to be superior to men find it fair for women to enjoy dominant power. (A similar claim can be made for dominant female focus.) Nonetheless, the female pattern of inequality cannot escape its entanglement in similarities with the male pattern; there exist, however, other feminist patterns that avoid this disadvantage.

The first of these more original patterns is *equality of power,* in which *women and men have equal power.* In the equality pattern, while particular power differences can be found between individual women and men, on a structural, society-wide scale neither sex has power over the other and neither has more power than the other. Liberal feminists, particularly in the United States, exemplify those who work toward equal power, such as equal pay for equal work.

Even in the United States, though, feminists have had to admit the existence of smudges on the ideal of equal power. The notion of equal pay for equal work functions well within certain contexts, but striving for fully equal power can prove daunting because, as Moira Gatens points out, "liberal society assumes that its citizens continue to be what they were historically, namely male heads of households who have at their disposal the services of an unpaid domestic worker/mother/wife" (124). The notion of equal pay for equal work also proves inadequate in the face of sex-segregated occupations such as those of child-care workers and truck drivers. Although one answer to these problems is to determine comparable worth, even this move beyond equality still sometimes proves insufficient or procrustean.

The pattern of feminist *difference of power* can be a stronger response to the weaknesses of feminist equality. In this pattern *women and men have different power from each other.* Inequality signifies only a contrast in the *degree* of power held by each sex, whereas difference means a contrast in the very *kind* of power, as when Hélène Cixous urges that women exercise uniquely female faculties, metaphorically writing in white ink—the milk of their breasts ("The Laugh of the Medusa," 251).[1] The need for different power is illustrated in a more everyday example, the problem of parental leave: granting the parents of a newborn leaves of equal length will either shortchange the mother or give the father more time than he needs.[2] Feminists in western Europe often recognize the necessity of going beyond the equality pattern and of emphasizing difference instead.[3]

Ann Snitow has written an insightful review of how equality and difference have strained against each other throughout the history of Western feminism. She explains how this pair corresponds roughly to others: for example, radical feminists (stressing women's shared oppression) versus cultural feminists (celebrating being female), social constructionists versus essentialists, and so-called "American" versus so-called "French" feminists. Keeping in mind the slipperiness of these categories and the impossibility of labeling either equality or difference as definitively more desirable, she sums them up as follows: "Do women want to be equal to men (with the meaning of 'equal' hotly contested), or do women see biology as establishing a difference that will always require a strong recognition and that might ultimately define quite separate possibilities inside 'the human'?" (52). As Snitow's essay explains, equality and difference have indeed served a function as terms for the aims of two types of feminism that are frequently placed in opposition to each other. Yet, rather than setting feminist equality in opposition to feminist difference, perhaps we should oppose feminist equality to feminist inequality: we cannot conceive of one without the other (see Offen, "Reflections," 54).

Inequality and equality occupy two poles of the same scale, while the idea of difference lies in some barely comparable space.

In short, the pattern of different power for women and men has its attractions: if dominant female power risks just flipping the same old coin of patriarchal inequality to the other side, and if equality just balances the coin precariously on edge, then difference goes much further: it sets the coin in motion and rolls it away. Of the three patterns of power, difference may also sound like the most highly evolved and therefore the most desirable, partly because I have saved it for last in this discussion. Yet feminists might become understandably nervous about the championing of difference as a feminist pattern when it leaves behind the whole question of equal and unequal power. They might wonder whether, in attempting to transcend that question, the pattern of difference only evades it, leaving patriarchy largely unchallenged. An emphasis on difference may indeed run the risk of conjuring up the old stereotypes of separate spheres, so often invoked to women's detriment. Thus, appealing as difference may be, a comprehensive definition of feminism needs to retain the option of equality—and, according to some, even inequality—along with difference.

Feminist Patterns of Focus

Feminist focus is any focus other than patriarchal focus, thus any focus other than dominant male focus. The focus may be on sex or gender. For example, a person with a feminist focus might concentrate on the female sex by researching women's health, or might concentrate on female-associated gender by engaging in peace activism, given that for millennia women have participated little if at all in armies.

In response to dominant male focus, some feminists propose placing female norms (of sex and gender) at the center of human concerns, while others propose doing so only as a temporary measure to compensate for centuries of dominant male focus, and still others jettison the concept of privileging either sex by placing its focus alone at the center. In any case, feminists tend to agree that society has neglected female norms and should no longer focus mostly on male ones.

Occasional feminist statements may, however, be misinterpreted as endorsing patriarchal values. A subtle example of feminist focus is the stance many feminists take toward silence, a female-associated trait. Since they decry the oppressive silencing of women, it may at first be surprising that silence can count among the female traits for which feminists urge respect. In doing so, however, they are not saying that men should silence women but rather that silence can in some contexts merit as much respect as speech. Thus, although all feminists oppose the oppressive silencing of women, not all simply oppose silence per se or want women to eschew silence by taking on male-associated gender attributes, by out-talking other people. Feminist focus involves a more thoroughgoing transformation of norms, since some female-associated gender features have been too hastily denigrated; perhaps *both* sexes should engage in certain types of silence.

In short, feminist focus rejects patriarchal focus (dominant male focus). By drawing attention to the female sex and its gender, feminist focus undermines the privileging of the male sex and its gender. A trait is not exalted simply because it ties in with the female sex or its gender, nor is such a trait belittled simply because it is also considered desirable in patriarchal terms.

Singularity and Centrality (Female Patterns)

Of the four types of feminist focus—singularity, centrality, duality, and multiplicity—the first two correspond roughly to patriarchal counterparts: *female singularity and centrality make up dominant female focus.* Like dominant male focus, it privileges the self rather than encouraging openness to otherness.

Female singularity is the notion that the female norm is, in effect, the only norm—at least the only one worthy of notice.

Admittedly, women in our society can hardly avoid noticing men and their norms, and anyone immersed in the reality of patriarchy may find it hard even to imagine a pattern in which female norms would loom so large that male ones could be ignored. Some women's music festivals and lesbian separatist communities may, however, be said to possess a focus of female singularity at certain moments, and, as we shall find in *Les Guérillères,* an experimental, fantastic novel can—if only in part of the text—create such a focus as well.

Female centrality is the notion that there are two norms but that the female one is worthier.

This pattern is more easily imagined, since it involves devaluing male norms rather than remaining oblivious to them. Susan Moller Okin attributes what I call female centrality to such feminists as Mary Daly, Susan Griffin, and Mary O'Brien in the United States, along with Hélène Cixous, Xavière Gauthier, Claudine Herrmann, Luce Irigaray, Annie Leclerc, and others in France. Summarizing some norms that predominate in what I call female focus, Okin explains that these French thinkers believe: "Women's language and thought are distinct and superior—more concrete, more focused on the contingencies of life, more emotional, less preoccupied with domination over others or over nature" ("Thinking Like a Woman," 152–53).[4]

Duality

Female singularity and centrality cannot help recalling their male counterparts, with their elevation of self over other. But feminism also embraces patterns that split more decisively from patriarchy. The other two types of focus—duality and multiplicity—include both male and female and so belong to neither male nor female focus alone. The varieties of *feminist* focus thus include not only the two patterns of dominant *female* focus but also duality and multiplicity.

In duality two norms, female and male, are accorded equal respect. Feminists who support duality endorse the visibility and value of the female sex and its gender along with their male equivalents, as when Carol Gilligan urges that we listen to "a different voice" that expresses the traditionally female-associated attentiveness to relationships. These thinkers want us to respect female norms in addition to, not instead of, male ones.

An attempt at dual focus can give rise to certain difficulties, however. As noted in the description of male focus, what at first seems duality often turns out to be nothing but pseudo-duality (in patriarchal society, usually male centrality). The problems of pseudo-duality are avoided, though, by genuinely dual focus, in which both norms are accorded the same visibility and value. Such genuine duality can take the form of *complementarity, similarity, or incomparability.*

Complementary Duality: The Example of Androgyny
While complementarity (in which each half has what the other lacks) is particularly susceptible to sliding into pseudo-duality, one can still conceive of complementarity that would remain truly dualistic and thus truly feminist. As Karen Offen recounts, "[T]hroughout the nineteenth century and well into the twentieth, French feminists, like the surrounding

French high culture in which these ideas were elaborated, not only accepted but insisted on physiological dualism between the sexes and on female
experience as mothers as grounds for the project of emancipating women,
even demanding a redistribution of political and social power on their
behalf. In France notions of complementarity of the sexes and 'equality in
difference' were fully elaborated" ("Feminism and Sexual Difference,"
17).

Complementary duality—in its weaknesses as well as its strengths—is
exemplified by androgyny.[5] Androgynous focus means not only focus on
complementary norms, both female and male, but, in particular, focus on
the two in combination. That combination of complementary traits,
whether combined in individuals or in society as a whole, itself becomes
a norm, implying metaphorically that the equal mixture of female and
male *within* an individual or society can contribute to equal power
between the sexes.

Yet the pattern of complementary duality also has flaws, as typified by
those of androgyny, which Mary Daly calls "misbegotten—conveying something like 'John Travolta and Farrah Fawcett-Majors scotch-taped together'"
(xi). Daly's objection would have little force if she were just criticizing a straw
opponent, androgyny of *sex;* instead, she is objecting to androgyny of *gender,*
which in practice proves especially liable to slip into pseudo-duality.[6] Beyond
such practical issues lies a graver problem, inherent in the very definition of
the androgynous norm. As Mary Anne Warren says: "[I]t is itself formulated
in terms of the discredited conceptions of masculinity and femininity which
it ultimately rejects. . . . We are still taking the two constellations of human
traits and establishing them as polar opposites" (23, 25). The norm of
androgynous gender thus remains mired in the very opposition (between
"male-associated" and "female-associated," to use my terms) that it seeks to
avoid. Furthermore, androgyny is conservative insofar as it merely combines
formerly female-associated and male-associated characteristics, whereas some
of them, such as dominance and servitude, should be dropped altogether
(Raymond, 60). So the norm of androgynous sex makes no sense as a feminist goal, while the norm of androgynous gender—if it escapes falling into
male singularity or centrality—ironically stays locked in the traps of opposition and dominance that it was meant to escape.

Similar Duality
Two things may be not opposite to each other but similar. Although our
society associates certain attributes and activities with each sex (intuition

and child care with women; rationality and playing football with men), one can choose to note the commonalities—after all, child care and football both require intuition and rationality. Anatomical similarities can also be stressed: for example, men have a pair of rounded organs—testicles—that could easily be compared to a female pair, such as ovaries or breasts.[7]

In "When Our Lips Speak Together," an essay of lesbian erotics, Irigaray plays with what I am calling similar duality. Neither lip complements or is opposed to the other; nor does either have priority as the singular, phallic original of which the other serves as a mere reflection or imitation. And the doubleness of the lips is itself double, for Irigaray is referring to lips of both the oral and the (female) genital sort. The imagery is problematic, however. Her reference to genital lips in addition to oral ones excludes men; since she elsewhere associates male genitals with the phallic oneness that she is criticizing, this exclusion elevates women over men, at least in this construction. Paradoxically, to value duality over singularity, and therefore, in this context, to value women over men, is thus in itself an example of pseudo-duality, not duality.[8]

Incomparable Duality

The final type of duality involves not opposition or resemblance but difference, indeed incomparability. For example, one can think about many of a society's typically female- and male-associated activities in a variety of ways to which the models of opposition and sameness are both irrelevant. Cooking dinner and repairing a car hardly form a tidy binary opposition; nor do they closely resemble each other. Anatomical distinctions can also be imagined in incomparable ways. When Irigaray discusses the uterus per se instead of the empty space it encloses, it ceases to be a female space that complements a male entity, and so ceases to risk becoming the negative that would so neatly complement and defer to a positive (*Speculum,* 227–40). The penis and the uterine walls are both entities, very different entities.

Multiplicity

"The dream . . . is to get beyond not only the number one—the number that determines unity, of body or of self—but also beyond the number two, which determines difference, antagonism, and exchange conceived of us [*sic*] as merely the coming together of opposites. . . . [The dream] embodies . . . a desire for both endless complication and creative movement" ("The Politics and Poetics of Female Eroticism," 136).

Susan Rubin Suleiman accompanies this observation about multiplicity with references to the theories of Beverly Brown, Parveen Adams, Jacques Derrida, and Hélène Cixous, then traces this dream of multiplicity through a novel, *The Passion of New Eve,* by Angela Carter. Exploration of multiple focus is also at least nascent in the theory of some other thinkers such as Joan Scott, Jane Flax, Marjorie Garber, and Judith Butler; in the work of more popular writers such as Phyllis Burke; in the practice of certain transsexuals; and in some science fiction. But such multiplicity is still new and rare; the very strangeness of its geometry requires that I write about it at some length and in a manner that is evocative and speculative rather than definitive. This strangeness also means that, when feminist utopian narratives attempt to represent multiplicity in an appealing way, their persuasive techniques must rise to the challenge.

Multiplicity constitutes the final pattern of feminist focus, a type in which *more than two norms are accorded equal respect.* This focus most radically challenges the binary opposition female/male. The duality of the sexes needs to be interrogated because of impasses concerning its significance—over how it feels, over which of its aspects matter. And the significance of the sexes' duality extends beyond them, to gender. The concept of multiplicity provides a powerful way to carry out this interrogation.

Focus on more than two norms means respect for norms based on more than two sexes. By "multiplicity" I mean the fraying of duality, the angles of view from which two-ness is not as clear-cut as some would assert, the ways in which two slip away from the paradigm of two discrete, opposite, tidy ones. I want to deconstruct the sexes' duality, proposing a variety of subtle but telling manners in which it is fractured. Multiplicity is itself multiple—we can find no one or two models that sum it up. This section begins by unpacking the notion of how we can think of sex and gender as multiple in the first place. Then, after describing the norms based on multiple sex and gender, I will suggest how taking multiplicity more to heart in the future could alter society, by challenging patriarchy and other belief systems.

Multiplicity of Sex
Although I believe there are basically two and only two human sexes, my use of the word "basically" signals a certain doubt about whether there are only two. Some utopias and science fiction suggest that in other places and other times sexual arrangements could diverge widely from our own. In John Varley's series about the planet Gaea, for example, there are only two sexes, but each of the planet's centaur-like inhabitants has both female and

male equine genitalia, plus either female or male human genitalia, all of which can be involved in fertilization, so that twenty-nine "sexual ensembles," involving one to four Gaeans, are possible.[9] Vonda McIntyre's *Dreamsnake* posits three sexes (287), and, as we shall find, in *The Left Hand of Darkness* the sexes need not be present in twos. Even today on Earth our culture gives the occasional nod to the multiplicity of sex—for example, in MUDs (Multi-User Domains or Multi-User Dungeons), a sort of ongoing psychodrama on the Internet. First-time MUD participants need to create characters for themselves, and doing so usually involves specifying one's sex, if only so other participants will know how to refer to the newcomer. One such MUD offers ten possibilities, each with its own set of pronouns (Rosenberg, 4–7). While some of these do not represent a sex in the fullest sense, the existence of so many choices hints that at least some participants find the standard options too constraining.

In more ordinary contexts as well it makes sense to conceive of the sexes along a continuum, for women and men are not as mutually exclusive as they seem, even in terms of sex traits.[10] They are inadequately represented by the classic binary opposition that completely separates female from male. To begin with, such an oppositional model obscures the traits normally shared by members of different sexes. Sexual characteristics aside, women and men share many other innate traits, both having organs such as the pancreas, and both having body parts such as nipples whose commonality is less acknowledged. In addition, there are innate traits such as one's skin color; any given color is possessed by approximately equal numbers of women and men. Just because our culture is obsessed with sex duality, that does not mean such binarism necessarily deserves to be exalted above the third category, the myriad nonsex features innate to humans. Each pole, female and male, does not differ totally from the other.

Conversely, as thinkers such as Audre Lorde and Elizabeth V. Spelman have explained, the people at a single pole do not totally resemble each other. The dualistic model tends to obscure differences between the members of a single sex, whereas feminists in recent years have become increasingly aware of women's diversity, even in terms of inborn characteristics. The skin color with which an Asian woman is born and that with which a white woman is born can sharply separate the two in spite of their shared sex traits. If each pole is in itself multiple, then sex duality fragments into multiple sex dualities: for instance, Asian women/Asian men, Asian women/white men, and so on.

One reason the sexes do not divide as absolutely as they seem to is that some sex characteristics, such as body hair or height, differ only in degree, not kind. Most women do have some body hair, albeit usually a smaller quantity than most men. Supposing that all women had the same small amount of body hair and all men had the same large amount, the fact that both sexes had some would still make this sex difference one of degree. And of course the amount actually varies among women and among men, making it still more evident that the characteristic differs only in degree, not kind. Cultural practices often magnify the appearance of such degree-based differences so much that the trait in one sex almost seems to differ in kind from that in the other sex—as when women in the United States accentuate their relative paucity of body hair by shaving their legs and underarms (see Rhode, "Theoretical Perspectives," 6).

The notion of a continuum becomes still more compelling when our discussion, most of which has so far concerned the majority of cases, now turns to the minority. Nonsex traits are not the only ones that can be shared: even when sex attributes actually do differ in kind, those that usually appear in one sex and those that usually appear in the other can at times combine in a single person, such as a hermaphrodite (see Baker). According to developmental geneticist Anne Fausto-Sterling, who has written authoritatively on multiple sexes,

[B]iologically speaking, there are many gradations running from female to male; and depending on how one calls the shots, one can argue that along that spectrum lie at least five sexes—and perhaps even more.

[T]he standard medical literature uses the term *intersex* as a catch-all for three major subgroups with some mixture of male and female characteristics: the so-called true hermaphrodites . . . , who possess one testis and one ovary . . .; the male pseudohermaphrodites . . . , who have testes and some aspects of the female genitalia but no ovaries; and the female pseudohermaphrodites . . . , who have ovaries and some aspects of the male genitalia but lack testes. Each of those categories is in itself complex; the percentage of male and female characteristics, for instance, can vary enormously among members of the same subgroup. . . . I suggest that the three intersexes . . . deserve to be considered additional sexes each in its own right. Indeed, I would argue further that sex is a vast, infinitely malleable continuum that defies the constraints of even five categories. (21)[11]

In some earlier societies, intersexed people were more acknowledged, if not necessarily more accepted, than in our own (23). Because intersexed possibilities are unusual and not obvious to the casual observer, most people in current Western society remain unaware of them. Despite the lip service paid to the glamour of gender ambiguity, cases of actual sex ambiguity tend to be concealed. In this culture people born with traits of both sexes (if not "corrected" at birth) usually want to, or are pressured to, consider one sex their "real" one and to suppress the other, even surgically (Kessler). Such desires and beliefs cannot obliterate the fact that certain people indeed have a mix of female and male sex traits.[12]

Multiplicity of Gender

Gender offers still richer possibilities of multiplicity than sex does. If everyone belonged to one and only one of the two genders, people in both groups would still have a good deal in common because of the many other acquired traits shared by members of both groups: in this country, both genders are equally likely to have a taste for reading. And, conversely, the people at a single pole differ among themselves. In the United States, for instance, child rearing has for centuries been a female-associated gender trait, but other non-innate traits produce enormous diversity among those who rear children. A mother with a low household income often longs to spend less time at a paid job and more at home with her children, while, at least until very recently, a mother from a more affluent household often yearned for the reverse.

The observations just made would hold true even if its poles were mutually exclusive—whereas actually they are not. To begin with, some gender characteristics differ in degree but not kind. The fact that men do perform some child care means that male-associated gender is marked only by a lesser degree of participation in child care, not by its utter absence. As with some sex differences, certain gender differences in degree are accentuated by cultural practices that make them seem differences in kind. The notion of a female computer nerd, for example, sounds like a contradiction in terms because the culture of the computer world renders almost invisible the few women programmers—nerds among them—who can indeed be found. In short, though many an acquired characteristic is gendered—occurring more often or more strongly in one sex—nevertheless, many such traits are not mutually exclusive and do appear in both sexes.

Until now my comments about gender have roughly paralleled those about sex. Because gender is not innate, however, it also offers potential for multiplicity that sex cannot: for instance, gender systems can vary widely between cultures and between time periods. The West usually assigns merchants to the male-associated gender, but in the Jewish shtetl such business was generally women's work. Similarly wide variations occur in a single culture over time, as when clerical work slid from men to women, in the United States and elsewhere. And features gendered in one time or place might not be gendered at all in another. Furthermore, even in cultures that condone only a distinct gender for each sex, some individuals have managed secretly to pass as members of the other sex by adopting its gender role, as when women in Europe and the United States disguised themselves as male soldiers. In other cultures, each of two genders may be seen as distinct but not absolutely tied to the associated sex—as in the Balkans, where until recently some women "assumed the male social identity with the tacit approval of the family and the larger community" (Grémaux, 242).[13] In other cultures it is possible to mix traits of both genders, as some transgenderists have done in recent years (Bolin). And some cultures make available a gender that can be distinguished in at least some respects from both the female- and male-associated ones, as when "in some [Native American] tribes male berdaches dressed distinctly from both men and women" (Roscoe, 335).

In these ways gender, more than sex, is permeated by flexibility that at times reaches multiplicity. While human sex does consist of multiple traits, by definition the number of traits has so far remained the same in different times and places, and no innate trait has gone from sex to not or vice versa, though of course human understanding of the categories has wobbled a good deal. In contrast, gender not only consists of multiple traits—multiple continua—but has taken on multiple configurations in different times and places, including instances in which an attribute that was gendered in one milieu became ungendered in another or vice versa. Gender morphs much more than sex.

How Multiplicity of Sex Interacts with Multiplicity of Gender

In order to tease apart the intricacies of multiplicity, I have been analyzing sex and gender separately, whereas in reality they usually interweave in an extremely complex manner. When sex and gender interact, each pole is further complicated—for instance, the female sex divides by gender, and people with female-associated gender traits divide by sex. Each sex pole is overlaid still more by various acquired traits, such as class status, while each gender pole is similarly overlaid by various innate traits, such as skin color. One more complication is added by another set of factors: those that give rise to controversy about whether they are innate, acquired, or some combination of the two. People argue, for example, about the origin of sexual orientation, and they have not even agreed enough on the definition of ethnicity to argue convincingly about its origin. When such factors interact with sex and gender, the very notion of dual norms fragments. Finally, neither sex nor gender actually consists of mutually exclusive poles; each stretches along multiple continua made up of multiple points.

Multiplicity of Sex, Multiplicity of Gender, and Multiplicity of Focus: Their Significance

In all these ways, multiplicity already roams the edges of sex and gender, but without being widely recognized. If fully acknowledged, the awareness of duality's fragility could fundamentally transform our focus on gender and sex norms and, beyond that, our patterns of thinking about other subjects. The utopian possibilities, for feminism and beyond feminism, are profound.

When only the two conventional genders are conceivable, then people are urged to adopt one cluster of characteristics or the other, but a focus on multiple genders would explode the groupings: someone who wore dresses might or might not rear children or keep house. Society could profoundly reconceive which gender traits should be encouraged in which sex and which traits should or should not be considered gendered in the first place. Multiple focus could enable different people of the same sex to enjoy different sorts of conditioning or freedom from it—some men might be brought up to be aggressive while others might not. We could come to doubt more deeply whether we should define the genders as opposites and whether we should squeeze each person into only one gender. Although one cannot ignore conventions, full awareness of the luxuriant gender multiplicity in various cultures and periods induces a healthy type of relativism, liberation from taking gender strictures as natural, including those in one's own time and place.

We can go further and imagine a culture in which no characteristics would be gendered: nothing about a person's activities and acquired traits could be predicted by knowing the person's sex. Notions such as cross-dressing or gender ambiguity in general would have no meaning, because no one can violate a gender convention that doesn't exist in the first place. To my knowledge, such a culture flourishes only in nonrealist fiction like the Chronicles of Tornor series, by Elizabeth A. Lynn, where one's role is decoupled from one's sex.[14] Touches of genderlessness can actually be felt in our own world—for example, in the elements of traditional Yorùbá culture that have survived colonial forces (Oyěwùmí, 34 and passim). Genderless ways of clustering people, even into mutually exclusive groups, need not all be dualistic once they are no longer based, as gender ordinarily is, on the basically dual nature of the sexes. At times it makes sense, say, to think of people in groups according to how much money they earn or what languages they speak. In a genderless society, the number of possible ways a person could combine traits would be huge, while the number of genders would be zero—the term would be drained of meaning. Genderlessness could also alter thought more generally: such a society, though still composed of inhabitants basically belonging to two sexes, could, in comparison to our society, be freed to think more in terms of multiplicity and less in terms of duality.

While gender, as I have explained, can be deconstructed by going beyond two, beyond many, to zero, sex—perhaps fortunately—cannot go quite so far. It can go beyond two to many, but within current biological conditions it cannot disappear altogether. Recognizing sex multiplicity can nonetheless have profound effects. First of all, intersexed people could live very differently from the way they do today. Fausto-Sterling says, "[H]ermaphrodites would be concerned primarily not about whether they can conform to society but about whether they might develop potentially life-threatening conditions . . . that sometimes accompany hermaphroditic development. In my ideal world medical intervention for intersexuals would take place only rarely before the age of reason" (24).

For society more broadly, acknowledging multiple sexes could open up a rich lode of thought, particularly in terms of focus. Patriarchy has relied for millennia on singularity or centrality of focus, and duality certainly challenges patriarchy but is vulnerable to slipping into pseudo-duality. Multiplicity offers a stronger, more radical challenge to patriarchy. Recognizing sex multiplicity not only can challenge patriarchy but, by analogy, can challenge other habits of thinking as well in situations where sex, duality, and especially sex duality offer an inadequate conceptual framework. Feminists such as Hélène Cixous, for instance, have asserted that sex dimorphism has laid the foundation of dualities like nature/culture that structure much Western thinking ("Castration or Decapitation?" 44). Whether or not that is historically true, a feminist challenge to the sex pair can inspire questioning of the others. For example, feminism can contribute to upsetting the object/subject dichotomy, and so can spark a re-evaluation of much of Western metaphysics. Binary thinking certainly has its place, but it provides a better model for the operation of a computer than for the more complex relationships in the rest of the world.

In fine, given the phallic singularity and centrality of patriarchy, one feminist alternative is duality, but multiplicity offers another alternative, one that goes beyond duality. Multiple focus, while recognizing the physical distinction between the sexes, also points out their ambiguities and denies the dualistic notion that nonsex traits must necessarily divide along sex lines. Such focus brings not only the recognition of female norms but also the recognition that each sex, like each gender, forms a heterogeneous group. Multiplicity avoids offering any unified, internally consistent system to replace that of duality.

One being less than two, and two being less than many, my readers may have hoped that multiplicity, as the feminist pattern that the West has most recently developed and that I have described last, would prove to be the ideal one, but it, too, has flaws. In its deconstructive power lies its danger as well as its appeal. Just as the deconstruction of power by difference could provoke uneasiness among liberal feminists, so the deconstruction of focus by multiplicity could trouble other feminists, such as U.S. cultural feminists and some French proponents of *écriture féminine:* they may detect one more attack on female specificity in the deconstruction of sex and gender. Such feminists might ask, if there are multiple sexes, why does it feel as if men are subordinating women? If there are multiple genders, why is it so likely that the spouse wearing the dress is the one who takes care of the child? A partial answer to such objections lies in Audre Lorde's dictum that the master's tools will never dismantle the master's house. Multiple focus enables us to imagine new tools.

The Patterns and the Novels

Much of the feminist theory I am developing could be adapted to groups subordinated on grounds other than sex. One could, for example, talk about singularity and centrality as patterns that characterize focus on a dominant group other than men, with singularity, centrality, and multiplicity characterizing focus on subordinate groups other than women. Duality also could be adapted to nonfeminist theory, particularly given the duality of self and other, subject and object.[15]

Strangely enough, it is hard to rank these feminist patterns according to which a society would be created that would be most free of patriarchal subordination, for traces of it haunt each pattern. Dominant female power and focus seem conservative because they mirror patriarchal patterns of dominant male power and focus. Yet a society governed by dominant female power and focus in fact would contrast so vividly with our present one that so far it can be met with only in faint memories of long-dead matriarchies and in science-fiction visions of the future. Meanwhile, equal power and dual focus sound conservative in their own way because they allow at least some of the male power and norms of patriarchy to survive. Equality and duality do, however, swerve dramatically from patriarchy in refusing its obsession with oneness. Finally, different power and multiple focus in their turn appear conservative in detouring around the issue of power, in multiplying the issue of focus until it blurs. But those same deconstructive gestures, by refiguring the terms in which we think, can open up our imaginations to real innovation.

While I do not want to flatten out or condescend to the disputes that divide various groups of feminists, I do believe that some of the conflicts between them arise less from actual disagreements than from differences of emphasis, such as realistic versus idealistic goals. As for my personal preferences: I lean toward equal power, and in the everyday world I advocate the realism of dual focus, but my dreams go in two other, conflicting, idealistic directions—toward multiplicity and toward female centrality. The dreaming part of me, the part that reads science fiction, is enchanted by the multiplicity of *Dreamsnake*'s three sexes and by the female centrality of the bumper sticker that reads, "It will be a great day when our schools get all the money they need and the Air Force has to hold a bake sale to buy a bomber."

The patriarchal and feminist patterns of power and focus described above pervade the novels discussed in part II; reading that discussion, and especially reading the novels themselves, should bring to life the patterns I have been introducing more abstractly. Indeed the plots of the three narratives consist of movement from one pattern to another, though in different rhythms and orders, depending on the specifics of each text. Each pattern develops dialectically into the next. Such movement, generating the novels' persuasive energy, evocatively represents patriarchy and various forms of feminism, leading readers from one to another. This chapter has given particular attention to the delicate relation between duality and multiplicity because each novel both honors and goes beyond dualities. By not only defining feminism but also distinguishing various kinds within it, I hope to help readers of these novels not only to decide *whether* a text is engaging in feminist persuasion but also to determine *in what way* it is doing so.

Table 5.1
Patterns of Power

Inequality	Equality	Difference
1) Men have dominant male power (patriarchal)	Sexes have equal power (feminist)	Sexes have different kinds of power, which cannot be compared (feminist)
2) Women have dominant male power (feminist)		

Table 5.2
Patterns of Focus

	Singularity	Centrality	Duality	Multiplicity
Dominant male focus	1) Male only (patriarchal)	1) Male at center (patriarchal)		
Dominant female focus	2) Female only (feminist)	2) Female at center (feminist)		
More than one focus			Female and male foci (feminist)	More than female and male foci (feminist)

PART II
Readings of Feminist Utopian Narratives

The theories of utopia, persuasive techniques, and feminism from part I braid together in the examples in part II. In this part are presented readings of texts typical of those that go beyond stasis by leading readers from one patriarchal or feminist pattern to another.[1] In these three novels the patterns form in various literal and metaphorical ways, since characters and places can be female, male, feminist, or patriarchal, and relations between characters or between places can be feminist or patriarchal. In addition, because the inhabitants of some of the different lands literally speak different languages, the novels can plumb the conceit that women and men figuratively speak different languages or literally use language somewhat differently.

Being protean, the geography/sex metaphor undergoes changes that feed the texts' dynamic pragmatism. Although the pragmatic process can have myriad manifestations, in these particular books it takes the form of four stages that set up binary oppositions, particularly between the sexes, and then challenge those oppositions.[2] These stages are categorized as putting sex on the map, a remapping, another remapping, and, most extremely, a different remapping. Belief-bridging directs implied readers' beliefs at each stage of the process; this book reveals how each novel attempts to persuade readers differently, as the texts differ in novelistic genre and as their implied readers differ in political belief. Rather than following the order in which the novels were written, part II begins with the novel that most clearly exemplifies the theories put forth in part I and then moves on to novels that more tantalizingly challenge them.

CHAPTER 6

Doris Lessing's *The Marriages Between Zones Three, Four, and Five*

> I shall ride my heart thundering across the plain,
> Outdistance you all and leave myself behind—
> —Doris Lessing (*Marriages,* 227)

Introduction

Doris Lessing's novel *The Marriages Between Zones Three, Four, and Five* at first may seem a puzzling example for a study of feminist persuasion, since, instead of culminating in a feminist utopia, the book begins with one but then proceeds to criticize it. We will find, however, that the novel's feminism takes subtler forms: although the multiple implied readers are initially directed to the static utopian feminism of one country, protean metaphor then carries them to other lands, and belief-bridging (especially the narrative sort) inclines these readers to new values, ultimately those of pragmatic utopian feminism. Lessing's novel indicates the stages of its argument with special vitality, in part through the text's affinities with fantasy and allegory, which enable the phases of argument to stand out in high relief.

This chapter begins by sketching Lessing's vexed relationship with feminism and summarizing the novel's plot, then concentrates on the stages of mappings that, supported by narrative belief-bridging, transform the protean metaphor of geography and sex. The chapter goes on to describe how three genres—fantasy, allegory, and realism—combine to reinforce the persuasion, and it concludes with an account of how the novel inspires feminist pragmatism.

Lessing's Feminism

Doris Lessing is a contemporary British writer, best known as a prolific creator of novels and short stories. She was born, of English parents, in Iran (when it was called Persia), grew up in Zimbabwe (when it was called

Rhodesia), and has spent most of her adult life in Britain. Although she detests labels and has a truly original mind, it is fair to say that her writing has been influenced by Marxism, by Jungian psychology, and by Sufism, a form of Islamic mysticism. Apparently heterosexual, she rarely writes about homosexuals; her lesbian characters tend either to be marginalized, as in *The Diaries of Jane Somers*, or to come across as pathetic neurotics, as in *The Good Terrorist* (see Bulkin). Her writing style ranges from realism, through fantasy and space fiction, to more experimental forms. Carey Kaplan and Ellen Cronan Rose have said: "More than any other major twentieth-century writer—excepting, possibly, D. H. Lawrence—Lessing challenges her readers and changes them; alters their consciousnesses; radicalizes their sexual, personal, and global politics" ("Lessing and Her Readers," 5).

The nature of Lessing's feminism is notoriously elusive. In fact, at times she and her fiction seem not to be feminist at all; this feminist reading of *Marriages* might well irritate her, particularly given her contempt for academics in general. Furthermore, Lessing's beliefs conflict with each other, they conflict with those of her implied authors, and those of her varied implied authors conflict with each other as well.[1] We can make generalizations, though. Of the four feminist criteria, the one that best characterizes Lessing is the second, the rejection of dominant male focus, since her writing so often accords women's issues a central place. On the other hand, as we have observed about *The Golden Notebook,* in notable instances her writing lacks the fourth feminist element, the belief that individuals or groups can successfully resist patriarchy.[2] Yet the other three elements sometimes prompt a feminist response in real readers anyway.[3]

This chapter will make it clear that *Marriages* is a strongly feminist novel, having a greater proportion of feminist elements than any of Lessing's earlier—or, probably, later—novels. Even if she herself merely intended *Marriages* to present women's subordination as an example of subordination in general, the text manages to avoid diluting the specificity of women's issues. This book's feminism is by no means simple: given the problematic complexity of Lessing's beliefs and those of her implied authors, it is not surprising that *Marriages* presents various kinds of feminism, each in dialectic with the others, in a dynamic that leads from static utopianism to the process of pragmatic utopianism.

The Plot of the Novel

Marriages is the second in Lessing's *Canopus* "space fiction" series.[4] The series describes three galactic forces: the good empire Canopus, its well-meaning but shortsighted ally Sirius, and the criminal planet

Shammat in the evil empire Puttiora. Sirius and Shammat do not overtly appear in *Marriages,* but the novel does suggest that the beings it calls the Providers are those known as Canopeans in other volumes of the series. The action of *Marriages* takes place not on Earth but in concentric shells called zones that lie above our planet (*Shikasta,* 7). Starting closest to the earth's surface, the countries in the *Canopus* series range from Zone Six—which is lowest not only in altitude but also in level of civiliza-tion—all the way up to Zone One, which is so exalted that Lessing bare-ly mentions it. *Marriages* is narrated by Lusik, a Chronicler from Zone Three, which is a mountainous region located high above Zone Four. As readers progress through the book, they follow the travels of various char-acters, starting in static utopian Zone Three, then descending in turn through Four and Five, and finally ascending to Zone Two.

The story begins when Al·Ith, queen of utopian feminist Zone Three, is ordered by the semidivine Providers to marry Ben Ata, king of patriar-chal Zone Four. At first both deeply resent the forced marriage. The rulers come to understand, however, that their union is intended to fuse "the imaginations of two realms" (35), which suffer from insularity. The Providers tell Al·Ith at what times she should live with her husband in his zone and at what times she should return to her own. The alternation of distance and closeness occurs not only in the geographical sense but also in the personal sense, even when the queen and king are in the same place. Although their relationship remains complexly ambivalent, they do begin to love one another, and they have a son.

Soon the Providers send new orders: Al·Ith must return home and Ben Ata must marry Vahshi, queen of Zone Five. He and his new wife have a daughter. Meanwhile Al·Ith's sister Murti· has begun to rule Zone Three, and the former queen has almost become an outcast. Her husband, her son, and her friend Dabeeb come from Zone Four to visit her on rare occasions. She makes repeated trips to mysterious Zone Two and finally does not come back. As the story ends, the zones are going through an exciting, if discomfiting, time of exchange and renewal.

Mappings

Space Fiction as Fiction about Space

Lessing's work provides a good starting point for studying utopian exam-ples, since utopia is built on *topos* and place is a central motif in her oeu-vre. When she refers to *Marriages* and the rest of the Canopus series as "space fiction" in the sense that might be summed up as *unscientific fiction about outer space* (see Braudeau), we must also attend to the richer resonance of the term's wider sense, *fiction about space and place in general.* That wider meaning matters because the central protean metaphor of *Marriages* involves geographical space: rugged mountains and soggy plains, a desert wilderness and a crystalline place so alien it can hardly be described.

Lessing's earliest work concentrates on the space of rooms, houses, and sometimes cities.[5] Then in 1971 *Briefing for a Descent into Hell* carries the epigraph: "*Category:* Inner-space fiction. For there is never anywhere to go but in" (7). Yet the movement inward is accompanied by a movement outward into outer space, for creatures who resemble the Canopean Providers appear in that book. *The Memoirs of a Survivor* (1974) returns to the space of rooms but expands their possibility. At the end of the book characters travel through a wall, from the confining room of reality into a larger space that is open to various interpretations, including the possibility that it represents fantasy, into which Lessing's work was gradually moving at the time. Lessing's movement from rooms to inner and outer space has special meaning for women: discussing *The Four-Gated City,* Elayne Antler Rapping says that the men "have been able to transform their fantasies into public projects for which they are rewarded. . . . [Women] too long for escape but for them the only free space is inner space" (38).

In the *Canopus* series, Lessing is claiming outer space for the woman writer. Public space on Earth may still belong almost exclusively to men, but women are staking a claim to what is larger and what is smaller, to outer as well as inner space. Moreover, because Lessing's fictions create a continuity between macrocosm and microcosm, certain meanings persist through the changes of scale. Even in the wide spaces of *Marriages* the different zones can represent different parts of a single human spirit; conversely, the individual represents the collective in a smaller space.

As the title suggests, in *The Marriages Between Zones Three, Four, and Five,* geographical space has especially great significance, the zones being almost protagonists. The sexes are mapped onto female and male spaces by the central protean metaphor. Furthermore, since in fact both women and men live in most of these countries, feminism and patriarchy are signified in various relationships—between women and men living in a single zone, between women and men living in different zones, and between zones that metaphorically represent women and men. Therefore, the geography/sex metaphor functions in a very complicated way: for instance, one zone is both male and patriarchal, while another is both female and feminist. Sometimes the male/female nature of the two comes to the fore, as in the concept of marriage between the two lands; at other times their patriarchal/feminist nature stands out, as in the contrast of the relations between the sexes within each of the two zones.

The protean movement of metaphor in *Marriages* takes the form of deconstructing the binary opposition between spaces and thus between sexes.[6] As will be elaborated below, the first stage sets up an opposition, albeit a precarious one, between the two sexes by opposing the female country, a feminist utopia, to the male country, a patriarchy. The next stage undercuts that opposition by revealing that the two poles are not entirely distinct, for the feminist one contains flaws, including a trace of patriarchy. Then the opposition is further undermined by introduction of a third country—both female and male, but with a difference. In the final stage a fourth, extremely different country breaks down the notion of opposition altogether.[7]

Stage One: Putting Sex on the Map

The first stage of the feminist argument in *Marriages* sets up the protean metaphor in its initial configuration, connecting Zone Three with women and feminism, and Zone Four with men and patriarchy—a binary opposition familiar to many real readers and thus an easy starting point.[8] Rather than complementary duality the relation is actually one of pseudo-duality, for female Zone Three comes across as far superior, through the belief-bridging that connects it with admirable values.

Marriages associates each of the two main characters with one of these lands: Al·Ith with Zone Three, Ben Ata with Zone Four. Especially in the beginning the two zones are embodied by these exemplary rulers, who devote their lives to their countries (45). As commander of the army, Ben Ata occupies the pinnacle of his zone's militaristic, rigid hierarchy. Though neither imaginative nor reflective, he is conscientious. The best soldier in a land of soldiers, he is strong, brave, and obsessed with order and orders. Al·Ith and all she represents are a "landscape that he had never even imagined" (77), her traits quintessentially those of highly civilized Zone Three—rationality, intuition, subtlety, contentment. Like her compatriots, she is not limited by what most readers would see as the inevitable boundaries of identity. Rather than locating the queen at the peak of this egalitarian society, it is more appropriate to place her at its center. Although both sexes live in both realms, the queen's Zone Three focuses on female norms, while the king's Zone Four focuses on male ones.[9] In fact, women characters in his country feel so deeply that Zone Three is female that living in their own land feels like exile (220). The text's construction of norms is sometimes reinforced by analogies to our society: by acting as mother to a number of orphans, for example, Al·Ith melds her role as ruler with that of nurturer, the latter seeming familiarly female-associated to our society.

Patriarchal Zone Four is a place of dominant male power as well as focus. The crown and control of the army are passed down from father to son. For most contemporary readers the land's total orientation towards war makes it male-centered, since most real armies are largely male in composition and wholly male in focus. In Zone Four only men can serve in the army, and all fit men do so, which means that any other sort of effort is despised as "women's work" and is allotted few resources. Al·Ith explains that the resulting poverty leads to hierarchy (75), and her friend Dabeeb laments that the system divides the sexes: " 'The boys are brought up by women. . . . Boys have to turn against women when they have known nothing but women, in order to become men at all'" (203). Al·Ith notes that the women in turn treat men "'as if they were . . . enemies, or idiots [the women] can't trust or small boys'" (177). Ultimately, though, Zone Four is hierarchical—dominated by the Father in particular and by men in general.

In all these traits it differs from Zone Three. First, the queen's zone is democratic, for Al·Ith rules only through her sensitivity to the people's concerns. Second, the pattern of male focus on a single, dominant Father does not exist in Zone Three, where the sexual double standard is unheard of and each child has several carefully chosen fathers—a Gene-Father and several Mind-Fathers. Such customs fly in the face of the patriarchal obsession with establishing paternity, an obsession thought by some to lie at the historical origin of women's oppression in our world.[10]

A third difference between Al·Ith's land and her husband's is the pattern of power, for her society resembles a utopian feminist dream of equality of power. Women as a group apparently enjoy no privileges denied to men, and labor is not divided according to sex—though during the time described in *Marriages,* Zone Three is ruled by women. Zone Four's perfunctory sexual practices may satisfy only men, but, as Ben Ata learns, Zone Three's art of lovemaking can bring pleasure to both sexes. Even the biological mandate that women have closer contact with a developing fetus is partially balanced by the influence of the Mind-Fathers during pregnancy.

In most ways Al·Ith's zone directs its focus so exclusively toward female norms, such as valuing lovemaking rather than stark sex, that it follows the feminist pattern of female singularity, rendering male norms invisible. One exception is noteworthy, though. The society prizes multiplicity—not particularly in terms of sex-based norms but in general. Comparing the landscapes of the two zones, for example, shows a contrast between variety and uniformity, movement and inertness. The narrator explains: "Everywhere you look, in our realm [Zone Three], a wild vigour is expressed in the contours of uplands, mountains, a variegated ruggedness. The central plateau where so many of our towns are situated is by no means regular, but is ringed by mountains and broken by ravines and deep river channels. With us the eye is enticed into continual movement. . . . But [in Zone Four Al·Ith] looked down into a uniform dull flat, cut by canals and tamed streams that were marked by lines of straight pollarded trees, and dotted regularly by the ordered camps of the military way of life" (23). Zone Four's hierarchy, despite its minute distinctions of rank, ironically proves to be a kind of uniformity, for the army makes "individual wills . . . cease to be entirely, absorbed in [a] larger, terrifying will" (238); everyone uniformly grovels in front of superiors and bullies inferiors.[11] Conversely, Zone Three is not homogeneous, despite its egalitarianism, for its people eschew rank but not the "real faculties of discrimination" (144).

Thus, the two countries contrast sharply. In patriarchal Zone Four the men overwhelm the women (dominant male power), and male norms render female ones practically invisible (male singularity), while in feminist Zone Three the sexes exercise the same amount of power (equality), and the society's focus is almost entirely on female norms (female singularity), except for the prevalence of multiplicity, another feminist pattern. While no one zone can simultaneously please all feminist readers, for those who admire equality of power and female singularity of focus, Zone Three is a utopia.[12]

Having determined how the geographical protean metaphor, in its first form, sets up two zones, we can now observe how it relates them to each other. From the start, the novel avoids creating a completely airtight opposition. In terms of power, the dominant male pattern of Zone Four is not simply mirrored by a dominant female pattern in its neighbor; instead, the existence of equal rather than unequal power within the queen's land means that the power relation between the two countries is one of difference. The telepathic abilities of Al·Ith's land can hardly be measured against the military strength of Ben Ata's. Indeed, the question of which land has more power cannot be settled; the inhabitants can barely breathe each other's air, much less conquer each other's country.

Meanwhile, in terms of focus, implied readers are nudged toward feminism because of female centrality: belief-bridging places Al·Ith and her female, feminist homeland higher than Ben Ata and his male, patriarchal one, even in altitude. Al·Ith never loses all her independence, but she becomes a victim worthy of sympathy in that she is dominated by Ben Ata and the bond she feels with him more than she is influenced in any of her relationships at home. The couple's closest moments display asymmetry: "[S]he *clung* to him, *feeling* that without him she couldn't be *anything*. And he *held* her, *thinking* that without her he would be only *half* himself" (emphasis added; 150). The queen learns less from her husband than she teaches him; she must live in his land most of the time they are together; and, significantly, their union brings forth a male child. Nothing in the novel makes the dominance by male power seem fair, and so, for the many readers who believe in fairness, that existing belief serves to support the new belief that the heroine deserves sympathy.

Al·Ith's victimization has implications beyond her individual plight, for she becomes a victim not because of unique circumstances but largely because marriage in a patriarchal land must take on patriarchal qualities; her subordination to her husband resembles that of women to men throughout Zone Four. By tying the asymmetries experienced by the queen to others in her husband's realm, the text encourages readers to recognize structural imbalances in their own societies. And, by evaluating along with describing, by presenting such subordination as unjustified, the text urges readers to critique Zone Four in particular and patriarchy in general.

There is another reason, still more compelling than her victimization, for implied readers to feel empathy with Al·Ith: the text links her to a number of worthy values, making her superior to her husband. Most importantly, she is the one who first realizes that the true purpose of their marriage is to cure the sterility of their zones (42). Meanwhile, Ben Ata's adaptation to his wife's ways is made to seem more desirable than her adaptation to his, because the novel debunks much of what the Zone Four military establishment prides itself on. For instance, *Marriages* undercuts the men's illusions of power and freedom by disclosing their "obligatory" nature, fostering the anti-essentialist feminist belief that sexual behavior is not some natural force exempt from cultural conditioning: "[Ben Ata's] tent flap was pulled back, and a couple of soldiers who had been on a raiding party thrust into the tent a young woman. . . . The soldiers were grinning, as was obligatory. They stood with arms folded just inside the tent flap, waiting for him to be pleased with them. He put a smile on his face, thanked them, added some of the necessary winks, leers, and knowing looks, and tossed them some coins he had in his robe's pockets for just such occasions" (205–6).

To criticize the male country, the novel cleverly plays off of societal conventions with which Western readers are familiar, such as the presence of men in almost every occupation. In Zone Four, since "men's work" is restricted to fighting, Ben Ata is incredulous when his wife says that a man can do any type of work (99)—a reversal to which humor gives added force. Here belief-bridging acts negatively: *Marriages* discredits his belief by linking it to one that implied readers regard as false in their own world. Readers may go on to note that in a different sense his society also resembles their own: both divide labor by sex and belittle women's work. Laughing at Ben Ata's attitude causes the more thoughtful implied readers to notice the absurdity in their own society. They are incited to observe other absurdities in their own patriarchies by the employment throughout of a narrator from the feminist utopia; when he expresses amazement over aspects of patriarchy that implied readers take for granted, he makes the familiar strange, in the enlightening sense intended by Viktor Shklovsky and Bertolt Brecht.[13]

In such ways, belief-bridging in the first stage associates Zone Three with positive values by presenting Al·Ith's victimization as undeserved and by presenting her and her zone as admirable through their links with common values, such as self-awareness. Readers are encouraged to identify with the queen and to feel an affinity with the higher land, and thus with women and feminism. So, although the first stage sets up a binary opposition, even at this early point the opposition is tippy, since the female-centered focus upsets the balance. At this point the relation between the zones, and metaphorically between the sexes, is binary but not in every way an opposition.

Stage Two: A Remapping

The second stage in the novel's feminist progression refines the first by moving away from a focus of female centrality and moving toward, though not reaching, duality between the female and male zones. As Ursula K. Le Guin says in a review of *Marriages,* we discover, "gradually, guided gently by our author, what [is] wrong with the utopian Zone

Three, that now quite familiar country where nobody is possessive or destructive or has bad taste in furniture" ("Marriages," 35). The stage begins when AlIth gets to know her husband's country and views her own with new eyes, causing implied readers to see that seemingly flawless Zone Three does not tower as far above Zone Four as they thought, for the smug female land is as insular as the male one. The second stage even exposes patriarchal elements at the feminist pole: Zone Three is not so greatly different from Zone Four. From this stage on, the novel's feminist strategy draws less on static utopianism and more on the process of pragmatic utopianism.

Laziness, complacency, and forgetfulness have prevented the inhabitants of Zone Three from looking beyond their borders. While rejoicing at multiplicity among their own people, they are as suspicious of outsiders as their patriarchal neighbors are. What is more, self-satisfied Zone Three ironically starts to acquire some of the very defects for which it feels contempt: when Zone Four's influence disturbs the utopia, its inhabitants, who had been living peacefully and happily, prove to have no foolproof way of guarding against discontent, aggressiveness, and even a bit of militarism.

Zone Four, however, is not the original cause of the changes, for it begins to influence its western neighbors only when their queen marries, and the marriage has in turn been ordered by the Providers in response to a problem that was already looming—the decline in fertility and in the will to live. The physical and mental sterility afflicts all the zones equally, for it results from their parochial stagnation. Al·Ith's "Descent Into the Dark" (57), her catabasis into the underworld of the lower zone, with the pain and self-questioning it causes, serves as an emblem of the suffering all the zones must undergo to shake them out of complacency. Al·Ith helps her husband see that their marriage, which they at first regarded as the beginning of their problems, has in fact been the first step in solving the more serious problem of provincialism to which they had been oblivious.

The feminist country has not only some of the same flaws as the patriarchal one but also, more disturbingly, some additional ones. Because the utopians have been living narrow lives that lack the darker emotions, they do not know the complete range of human potential and in a sense are also weak, for they have not developed the strengths that adversity can call forth. Al·Ith needs contact with otherness, and although Ben Ata takes more from her than he gives, he does bring her some of that contact. The imperfections of Al·Ith and her people show up with particular distinctness in her encounters with the subordinated and fearful patriarchal women of Zone Four, most notably Dabeeb. The women have something to teach the heroine and, through her, readers who have so far been led to identify with her.

One of Dabeeb's sighs tells Al·Ith everything she needs to know about women in the lower zone: "Resignation. Acceptance. *Humour.* And always a pull and a tug from within these armours of watchfulness, patience, humour, of a terrible need" (64). The representation of these women's subversive acts exemplifies the principle that political effect depends as much on how a novel presents events as on what events it presents. A patriarchal book could evaluate these women as culpable schemers, but feminist *Marriages* shows how the struggle for survival makes their secret codes and deceptions necessary and admirable, if largely ineffectual. The women teach Al·Ith about the kinds of solidarity and resilience that grow in spite of—and because of—adversity. By creating a bridge between the Zone Four women and such admirable values, the text shifts implied readers' sympathies toward the women, offering them not as an alternative preferable to life in Zone Three but as a corrective to the complacency in the utopian zone *and* to the patriarchal attitudes in societies like our own.

In addition to learning from the Zone Four women's strengths, Al·Ith learns from their weaknesses, especially when she realizes that her sojourn in their land has produced the same vulnerabilities in herself, formerly the epitome of a Zone Three woman. The queen, and implied readers along with her, realize that much of her past freedom resulted from the supportive conditions of her homeland. This acknowledgment of the force of culture has various anti-essentialist feminist corollaries—among them the understanding that women who lack freedom may lack it because of societal conditions, not because of some inborn incapacity. Another corollary involves the resistance element in my definition of feminism: by not citing fixed nature as the cause of the heroine's new pleasure in submission, *Marriages* leaves open the possibility that she can resist such feelings, if only by going elsewhere.

Since the feminist land's very superiority has now revealed cracks, Stage Two has cast doubt on the focus of female centrality that privileged the utopia (the power relation between the zones remains unchanged, though). Insofar as the two lands still differ a good deal in characteristics, if no longer so much in value, the focus becomes a bit like complementary duality. Furthermore, because some of the utopia's newly disclosed faults are shared with the patriarchy, the two zones no longer remain in sharp opposition. The rulers' exogamous marriage, opening up to otherness, even represents a tentative step toward a focus of similar duality; at first the newlyweds have nothing in common, but they gradually influence each other. Ben Ata begins to question the value of constant warfare, while his wife makes a "descent into possibilities of herself she had not believed open to her" (58). And the more the monarchs are influenced, the more their zones are. For instance, members of both sexes become more warlike in Zone Three, more prosperous in Zone Four. In this way a society with some traits of both sorts develops *within* each land.

By creating an admirable feminist utopia and then questioning it, the text may seem to be moving away from feminism. Yet on a deeper level the movement is a feminist strategy, for it undercuts some of the scaffolding that upholds dominant male focus: uniformity, obsession with self, and lack of imagination. Nor does the novel bring the zones to total symmetry. It brings the female zone down to the male level in one respect, in uncovering Zone Three's complacency, but never presents the patriarchal land as preferable or even equally impressive. Just as the Providers never appear in a blinding flash to offer explicit instructions on every subject, so *Marriages* never neatly abandons one position to give total allegiance to another. Instead Stage Two goes dialectically from female centrality to not-quite-duality, from static to pragmatic utopian feminism, not a place but a way of thinking. By placing Zones Three and Four in an asymmetrical relationship and then remapping them closer to symmetry, *Marriages* chooses continued questioning over an inert answer—even a feminist one—and continued motion over an appealing moment of rest—even a feminist one.

Belief-bridging is employed to win over several different types of implied readers (this novel addresses no single type). With feminist ones, Stage One builds a rapport through the familiar beliefs of Al·Ith's utopian homeland; then Stage Two introduces less familiar beliefs, so as to turn those readers away from the rigidity of any settled solution and toward pragmatic feminism. Meanwhile, the novel also gains the trust of patriarchal implied readers who were impatient with the feminism of Zone Three. If they have made it to Stage Two instead of simply ceasing to read, then they feel relief upon leaving the queen's country for the more familiar values of Ben Ata's. It seems only right to them that, during Stage Two, Al·Ith should learn from her husband's realm. Ironically, though, what she learns is not patriarchal values but pragmatic values like self-critique. The patriarchal reader is urged to adopt these unfamiliar beliefs because a bridge links them to familiar ones, such as the value of questioning a feminist utopia. In short, belief-bridging urges feminist readers to question Zone Three for the inertia of its utopianism, while suggesting that patriarchal readers ought not to throw out the baby of feminism with the bathwater of Zone Three.

Stage Two draws in another type of implied reader as well—the one who is put off by a vehement degree of persuasion. Such a reader has been wincing during the almost caricatured first stage, when Zone Four can do almost nothing right (even the animal that its soldiers kill to eat is a deer, not a less Bambi-esque beast such as a boar). If such readers manage to keep going as far as the more nuanced second stage, then they find it more persuasive, as it discloses merits in Zone Four and defects in Zone Three. Here and in later stages, some of the most alienated readers may be deftly recaptured, since the text not only endorses ongoing self-critique but also, through pragmatic questioning, performs it.

Stage Three: Another Remapping

Up to this point, the novel has merely pointed out the vices, such as complacency, that virtue can entail; from now on, though, *Marriages* casts doubt on the very categories by which utopia has been defined. And now the breakdown of binarism itself begins.[14] The Providers take the radical step of challenging the married twosome they have created: they introduce "a tertium quid, startling and inevitable," by ordering the marriage between Zones Four and Five (Le Guin, "Marriages," 35). Ben Ata is to marry Vahshi, the magnificent, unself-conscious queen of the wild desert land that borders his; and Al·Ith is to spend half of each year in her homeland and half down in her husband's land. Their son will stay in Zone Four.

The order for the second marriage does not come until three-quarters of the way through the novel; by that time Al·Ith and Ben Ata love each other deeply and are stricken when they hear the order about the new marriage. The decree jars implied readers as well. Even those who do not identify with the protagonists and their dismay are surprised by the violation of literary convention: after a couple goes from squabbling to affection, the two are not supposed to break up again. Although some readers no doubt remember that the title mentioned Zone Five, they probably have not imagined its marriage in this particular form. The shock occasioned by the second marriage encourages pragmatism by preventing implied readers, like characters, from slipping into unthinking contentment with things as they are. Yet *Marriages* lessens the risk of alienating implied readers, for the novel has devoted greater attention to the more conventional romance than it will to what follows. In addition, dashing, howling Zone Five starts to become captivating in its own right, its insouciance refreshing implied readers after the earnestness of previous zones. The country is viewed largely through Ben Ata's eyes, and, as he is touched by the heedless charm of Vahshi and her country, so, too, are implied readers won over, made receptive to entertaining the beliefs represented by the third stage.

In terms of power *within* Vahshi's realm, it is difficult to determine the relations between the sexes, since aside from her the female citizens are rarely mentioned. Power relations *between* zones are more identifiable: the whirlwind force of Vahshi's land proves as incommensurable with the powers of Zones Three and Four as theirs are with each other. Just as difference (rather than equality or inequality) characterizes the power relation between female Zone Three and male Zone Four, so difference defines the power relation between each of those countries and female/male Zone Five.

As to focus *within* Vahshi's land, it is dualistic, combining traits of the other two zones, often in a complementary way. Zone Five's bellicosity might make its norms seem wholly male, but its guerrilla anarchy differs sharply from male militarism as defined in Ben Ata's country. This queen laughs at the predictability of her husband's soldiers, and he learns "that the discipline, order, martial correctness of his army provoked nothing but derision in his opponents who, in their own eyes at least, did exactly as they liked and when they liked" (208). Since the novel has already established flexibility as a female norm in Al·Ith's country, the guerrillas' female-associated flexibility balances their male-associated norm of combat. As in Zone Three, the ruler here is female, and this marriage even brings forth a female child. Yet Vahshi lives by largely male norms, and it is her father who receives mention, not female relatives. Her ascendancy comes from combat, a conventionally male-associated activity, and most of her warriors are men (203). The text itself balances the time it devotes to each sex—giving the most attention to the charismatic queen, then giving next highest priority to her male warriors.

Meanwhile, the pattern of focus *between* zones has become that of multiplicity, since the third stage has gone beyond dualism by introducing a third monarch, a third realm, and a third way of thinking, which combines female and male norms. Because the multiplicity consists of only three terms, I call it "mild," in contrast to the "strong multiplicity" we will find in Stage Four. Transforming the tidy binarism of the earlier stages, Stage Three's almost Hegelian synthesis of female and male jolts implied readers into remembering that more than two polarized possibilities exist. Moreover, Zone Five unsettles the previously established oppositional poles not only by synthesizing female and male traits, but also by throwing into question which traits should be classified with which sex in the first place. Since the king's zone lies between those of his two wives, barbarian Vahshi's zone is located closer to Ben Ata's than to Al·Ith's, and indeed Vahshi has more in common with the man than with the other woman. In Ben Ata's second marriage he ironically fills some of the roles played by Al·Ith in his first marriage (215): more civilized than Vahshi, he is the one who teaches more and learns less. The third stage discourages essentialist notions of female and male that readers may have developed during the first two stages.

In all these ways the marriage between Zones Four and Five serves to loosen the binary opposition created by the earlier union. Vahshi's land is a place of feminism—not in the static sense of petrified perfection but in the pragmatic sense of dynamic questioning. It is tantalizing, frustrating, and appropriate that the text devotes fewer pages to the third stage than to the preceding ones; providing no ideal answer, Zone Five only shakes up the patterns that have come before.

Stage Four: A Different Remapping

Finally, in the fourth stage, the initial opposition of Zones Three and Four is more radically undone: Al·Ith makes repeated trips over the pass to Zone Two, a place of extreme difference, and ultimately does not come back. Later, some other characters follow her there. Reminiscent of the heroine in Kate Chopin's *The Awakening,* the queen ends by traveling beyond Zones Three, Four, and Five, possibly toward her demise.

Enigmatic Zone Two differs so much from the others that it is almost impossible to see, get to, or describe. To see it from the capital of the next lower zone, characters must climb the highest tower; to enter the land itself, they must ascend a steep, little-used road and must labor to breathe the thick blue air. Al·Ith "thought the blueness was only the underground of something different, as yellow flames have a blue base to them. The blue was only what she could see" (192). On her first trip she loses her senses and awakens on a vast plain: "She did not know this earth—if it was earth, this crystalline yet liquid substance that held her on its surface, while it was able to move and slide and resist. . . . Yet . . . she was at home, even while she recognised nothing at all" (193). Ironically, a person who seeks otherness can feel at home only in a place where nothing is familiar.

Unlike the zones that marry, Zone Two is accorded few pages in the text and does not appear in the book's title, since its strangeness makes it almost unrepresentable. To refer to a "marriage" between Zones Two and Three would be inappropriate, for instance. First of all, it is possible that Zone Three, or at least Al·Ith, is destroyed by Zone Two. Moreover, to use the term "spouse" for the flame-like beings of the northwestern land is to anthropomorphize them misleadingly (194). Considering the precedent of alternation between the other zones, readers might expect this one to have a man as ruler, but they are shown no ruler, no men, and no humans at all. It is truly different. Like the close, erotically charged friendship between the queen and Dabeeb, the existence of Zone Two works against the heterosexism that might result if the book presented either of the previous marriages as its culminating ideal. The very issue of sex, not to mention gender, seems incongruous here, as would the association of specific sexes or even specific answers of any sort with such a mist-shrouded land, and so the fourth stage represents extreme pragmatism, questioning the clear-cut static utopian terms with which the book began.

Since Zone Two has no sexes we can recognize, it would be meaningless to ask about the relations of power between the sexes within that country. Nonetheless, it still makes sense to comment upon power relations between Zone Two and other countries: it neither dominates another nor is dominated, nor does the concept of equality suit the relationships between such disparate places. If any zone has different power from the others, it is this one. With regard to focus, it is again difficult to decipher any pattern within the country, but in relation to the other lands the pattern is strong multiplicity. As bizarre as the land of the Houyhnhnms in *Gulliver's Travels,* Zone Two has gone beyond the female norms, male norms, and dual female/male norms of the other lands, for it has introduced something, or some things, other than the two human sexes and the three configurations in which they have previously been presented. The protean metaphor has undergone its most drastic transformation, the binary poles that—separately or in combination—identified the other three zones having now given way to multiplicity, far from the insularity with which the story began. In fact, by the fourth stage, some multiplicity tinges all the zones, for people from one country are sometimes willing, even eager, to travel to another, sharing culture and customs.

As the pinnacle of the book, in altitude and otherwise, Zone Two runs the risk of seeming overblown and thus estranging readers who find its belief-bridging overdetermined in its degree of vehemence. Several strategies are employed to ward off such a reaction. For example, by setting the story in zones above Earth instead of in recognizable countries and by invoking the genres of allegory and fantasy in addition to realism, *Marriages* is better able to accommodate Zone Two's exorbitance than a wholly realistic text could.

By culminating in Zone Two, the novel appears to fall into two traps, however. First, by valuing different power and multiple focus, and in a land with no sexes, the novel may be charged with going so far beyond its initial feminist utopia that it has gone beyond feminism altogether. Nevertheless, as we noted above, while difference and multiplicity may run certain poststructuralist risks, they still belong in feminism. But a second trap remains: to make difference the single highest pattern of power, and multiplicity the single highest pattern of focus, is ironically to celebrate inequality and centrality and so to neglect difference and multiplicity. A similar difficulty pervades the role of the Providers: even though they order characters to question authority, as authorities themselves they cannot avoid traces of paternalism, if not patriarchy (see, e.g., Kaplan, "Britain's Imperialist Past"). Yet elevating certain feminist patterns inevitably entails downplaying others. At least the patterns privileged in Zone Two favor inclusiveness and thus in a paradoxical way permit acknowledgment of others. What is more, the novel's pragmatism means that no pattern is absolutely dismissed; Zone Two's patterns are put forward as the best ones, not the only ones. Since any persuasive text must offer its alternative as superior to others, the contradiction in *Marriages* is inevitable. If readers triumphantly pounce on the contradiction, at least they are employing the same pragmatic critique that the novel is recommending.

Belief-Bridging

How Narrative Belief-Bridging Supports the Mappings

Al·Ith feels deep love for her horse, Yori, which will cause some real readers to esteem her all the more but will irritate resisting readers and strike disengaged ones as merely silly. While it is hard to guess what reaction horses will evoke in real readers, it is more probable that they will share a belief in the value of novels and such related media as literature in general, other arts, and other forms of communication. Indeed, an implied reader with such beliefs is the addressee for whom a good part of the belief-bridging is intended in this very self-reflexive text, with its copious references to narratives and art.[15] The full title itself mentions narration: *Canopus in Argos: Archives. The Marriages Between Zones Three, Four, and Five (As Narrated by the Chroniclers of Zone Three),* and the text begins and ends with references to songs and tales.

Narrative belief-bridging builds rapport between implied readers and the book as a whole, for this entire book calls out to people who love language and communication in general.[16] Such concerns resonate throughout: the narrator and the other characters are obsessed with language and silence, constantly thinking and talking about them; at first different dialects estrange one zone from another, and those differences both cause and result from profound gaps between the countries' attitudes; and later, when influences start to waft between zones, it is often in language that the most striking changes occur.

More specifically, narrative belief-bridging, like ordinary belief-bridging, invites readers to each of the four stages in turn. Although most of the zones use several forms of communication, each country has its characteristic form, uniquely combining either words or their absence with sound or its absence. Readers learn, for example, that the inhabitants of female, feminist Zone Three can commune by silent thought or feelings, using neither words nor sound. Stage One sets all this in direct opposition to the communication of male, patriarchal Zone Four, which is typified by speech, using both words and sound.[17] Even when Zone Three does use speech, it does so very differently from its neighbor: just as Al·Ith cannot bring herself to refer to "having" another person sexually, her husband cannot accept that the men she was "with" at home were neither "husbands" nor "lovers" (102, 99, 94).

The language difference underlines the foreignness of each sex to the other: even speaking two dialects of a single language, the female and male countries have a good deal of trouble communicating. The relationship between women and men in some patriarchal societies, like that between the speakers of two dialects, has a deceptive appearance of closeness—at the very least, everyone has a parent of the other sex. Such close contact can mask the extent to which women and men are foreign to each other. By giving characters a single language but giving different dialects to the female and male lands, the novel represents the close contact while accentuating the foreignness.

Like Al·Ith's realm as a whole during the first stage, Zone Three's means of communication at first seems vastly preferable to that of her husband's homeland. Compared to her nearly telepathic abilities, his more mediated efforts seem clumsy, and the queen experiences her descent to Zone Four as a fall into language—and into the concomitant possibility of lying (107). But communication benefits from otherness; just as contrast is needed to make black print legible on a white page, so in dim light a black horse can be seen only when standing close to a white one (38). As the novel moves to its second stage and begins to cast doubt on the utopia, Al·Ith finds that the patriarchal land's very imperfections have some advantages, that words can be "right, and necessary" (64). She learns that signification can serve certain purposes, as when Ben Ata prevents bloodshed by concentrating on creating a military force that *signifies* power rather than one that *is* powerful (237).

Her husband's zone is marked not only by mediation in general but by metaphor in particular. The narrator, being from Al·Ith's zone, implicitly criticizes Zone Four when he proudly notes that *his* zone's ballads lack "the inversions, the ambiguities, that are always bred by fear of an arbitrary authority" (27). Judged from another angle, however, the censorship in Zone Four means it is a place where figurative language flourishes. For instance, while Zone Three songs tend to describe the marriage with literal truth, a Zone Four song says that Al·Ith has died, which on a deeper, metaphorical level does accurately describe the wrenching change in her life. In a sense the linguistic and figurative inclinations of Ben Ata's country ironically make it a more artistic realm than Al·Ith's.

In Zone Four, conflict, too, can have a positive narrative result, by encouraging drama in daily life. In contrast, when Al· Ith explains that her territory has no weapons, its lack of conflict bothers Ben Ata: "'The animals are our friends,' she said, and saw the incredulity on his face. Also, he found her account lacking in drama" (98). His reaction brings up a genuine problem with Zone Three. Because it lacks the dependence on language, on metaphor, and on conflict that typifies the patriarchal country, her static utopia generates less narrative energy; it is no coincidence that so much of the novel is set in patriarchal Zone Four. Its imperfections give it greater narrative interest and make it a more fertile ground for language and figuration, all of which are narrative values that, in the second stage, function through belief-bridging to encourage doubts about female centrality.

Then in the third stage, when female melds with male in Zone Five, readers find that its style of communication combines traits from Al·Ith's and Ben Ata's lands. Its people ululate, laugh, and shriek—using sound but no words. Lastly, the beings of Zone Two recombine the traits another way when they communicate through dreams. Like the inhabitants of Zone Four, they use words, and, like the inhabitants of Zone Three, they send the messages without sound. With every country, a different type of communication has been introduced, each with its own advantages, so as to help readers appreciate each zone in turn.

Another prominent kind of narrative belief-bridging in *Marriages* takes place through the narrator, Lusik, who is also a minor character in his own right. Since narrators generally have more authority than most other characters, assigning that role to an official Chronicler from the most recognizably feminist zone reinforces the novel's feminist persuasion. Meanwhile, being a character enables Lusik to evolve, unlike the average undramatized narrator.[18] He sets an example for readers: like Al·Ith, he begins by unquestioningly endorsing the ostensibly perfect utopian feminism of his homeland but gradually comes to renounce chauvinism and cherish otherness, disagreeing with complacent majority opinion.[19] His development appears sometimes in explicit statements, sometimes in narrative choices such as diction. Thus, as a character, Lusik can change his mind as he goes through the four stages of the text's feminist argument; as the narrator, he can authoritatively persuade implied readers to change along with him.

His subtlest, yet perhaps most compelling transformation occurs on the technical level of point of view. In Gérard Genette's terms, the answer to the question "Who speaks?" is always Lusik, whereas the answer to the question "Who sees?" (focalization) becomes increasingly variable, corresponding roughly to the text's four stages (186).[20] For almost three-fifths of the book Lusik tells of Al·Ith's journeys, leaving her perspective only briefly. Next the position of "who sees" is occupied more by Ben Ata alone than by Al·Ith alone. After the king marries Vahshi, when women from his zone try to travel to Al·Ith's, dualism has dissolved far enough for substantial attention to go to characters other than Al·Ith and Ben Ata. The queen can no longer be the one "who sees," for her eyes are filled more and more with the blue mists of Zone Two, a sight that can barely be narrated. In the last fourteen pages of the book the narrator sees through the eyes of a diverse range of characters. The ultimately variegated focalization corresponds to the difference and multiplicity that are valued in the culminating fourth stage. In these ways the text's very structure causes implied readers, during the reading process, to experience the patterns toward which the feminist argument is leading them.

How Genre Supports Belief-Bridging: Fantasy, Allegory, and Realism

The novel's three main genres are allegory, fantasy, and realism, and in order to grasp how belief-bridging contributes to the feminist persuasion in *Marriages,* we need to examine how the book braids those three together.[21] Allegory makes meanings clear through its unflinchingly explicit metaphors, at times giving *Marriages* the force of a fable or a Sufi teaching tale.[22] For instance, the rigidity of patriarchal Zone Four is betokened by the heavy helmets with which it punishes citizens who try to raise their eyes to the heights of the next zone. Such techniques are interlocking parts of a system that structures the whole narrative, rendering it especially suitable for persuasion.

As for fantasy, among the various types in *Marriages,* the most prominent is "space fiction." With its disregard for scientific credibility, this novel indeed has been called "more Sufi than sci fi" (Abley, 52).[23] Space fiction and the other fantasy elements ensure that, when the text sets out to persuade us to believe something about one of the zones, the belief is painted in bold strokes. For example, Zone Two's flame-creatures, unfamiliar to readers and inexplicable by rational means, help the zone epitomize difference and multiplicity.

Allegory and fantasy, however, in the very process of making clear the implied author's beliefs, can interfere with belief-bridging by failing to link them to real readers' pre-existing beliefs. *Marriages* solves this problem by including the strand of realism. For example, the novel displays much of the psychological insight and attention to personal relationships that mark realistic novels of character. Such devices can remind Western implied readers not only of realism in other novels but more importantly of practices in their own lives, such as the subtle ebb and flow in a "marriage mood" (96). Because the novel links some of its descriptions to implied readers' pre-existing beliefs about psychology and relationships, those readers feel more inclined to credit other, perhaps less familiar, beliefs that the novel presents, such as those about feminism. Similarly, *Marriages* avoids the facile wish fulfillment that sometimes plagues fantasy, for the text plausibly, pragmatically shows life full of doubts and slow, partial achievements rather than resounding triumphs and defeats. In these ways, the novel's blend of genres supports persuasion. In *Marriages* allegory and fantasy help clarify the implied author's beliefs about feminism; realism helps make those beliefs convincing by linking them to other, more familiar beliefs; and all three contribute to the technique I call "exemplarity."

Exemplarity is a key technique of persuasion, especially in feminist utopias: the individual stands for the collective, so that individual characters and events have meanings that ripple out beyond themselves.[24] Lessing's very title refers to marriages between zones, not individuals, and the first page calls the marriage of Al·Ith and Ben Ata "exemplary." Each of the book's three chief genres contributes to this effect: allegory is by definition exemplary; fantasy permits Lessing to employ a sort of magical exemplarity, by which the rulers' experiences not only represent but also mysteriously influence their entire realms; and her realism is characterized by fascination with the Balzacian "type."

Lennard Davis has complained that most novels either fail to present successful collective action or do so but become tedious in the process (119); Lessing's combination of the collective with the individual addresses that problem. Increasingly recognizing how tightly the individual and the collective intertwine, she has said that the way to deal with the problem of "subjectivity" is to see the individual "as a microcosm and in this way . . . [to make] the personal general, as indeed life always does" (Introduction, *The Golden Notebook* xiii). In *Marriages* exemplary characters such as Lusik and the monarchs both symbolize and catalyze change. By presenting characters with aspects of both the one and the many the novel makes its persuasion more likely to move implied readers to act: *Marriages* not only avoids letting attention to the individual become solipsistic or escapist but also avoids letting attention to the collective deprive the individual of responsibility. While every exemplum asks its readers to follow or shun the example of at least one of its characters, this book is unusual in asking its characters to do the same. The people of each zone are to pattern themselves after their monarch; for example, the drumbeats during the "exemplary" marriage so the populace can "share in the marriage, in thought, and in sympathetic support—and, of course, in emulation" (69). Gayle Greene says: "As elsewhere in Lessing's fiction, it is the process of thinking it out . . . that is instructive: and what the characters do in the novel mirrors what the reader does in relation to the novel" (*Doris*

Lessing, 183). In this exemplum about exempla, readers are offered models of model-following—self-reflexivity that feeds narrative belief-bridging.

How Belief-Bridging Supports Feminist Pragmatism

Marriages displays all four elements in the definition of feminism. The praise of various feminist patterns and the critique of Zone Four's dominant male power and dominant male focus mark a forceful condemnation of patriarchy, and the process of recognizing patriarchy is modeled—from outside it by Al·Ith and from inside it by Ben Ata. The novel also offers the possibility that individual and group action can resist patriarchy and other problems: through the hard work of deep thought, honest self-criticism, and, most important, the acceptance of responsibility, characters and entire societies undergo profound changes.

This fourth element—so often problematic in Lessing's work—requires a bit more discussion. Sometimes she indeed retreats into despair or mysticism, but critics who accuse her of altogether rejecting science, politics, or religion fail to notice that she rejects them only in their traditionally limited and factional forms.[25] It is noteworthy, moreover, that this book—unlike most of the *Canopus* series—takes the human point of view. Thus, even if the progress will not last eons, it does have a tremendous effect during the lifetimes of the characters we care about. And, even if the changes occur as the result of orders by the Canopean Providers, humans are still needed to carry out the orders, which are in fact minimal—humans must think the rest out for themselves (42).[26] Admittedly, the presence of the Providers in *Marriages* does complicate the notion of human responsibility, but the novel remains one of the Lessing texts that are most encouraging about progress, including feminist progress.

Marriages suggests that pragmatism, a technique employed by both characters and implied readers, can prove an effective resource for change and resistance.[27] Having explored the novel's four stages, we can now look back over them as over a strand of beads and find out more about the string that links them: the pragmatic questioning that moves from one stage to the next. We have observed how belief-bridging invites readers to the beliefs represented by each of the four stages; now we can inquire into how it nudges them to value movement between stages, asking them to practice pragmatism while reading, not just later.

The chief way that belief-bridging fosters feminism in *Marriages* is through the exemplarity mentioned earlier. Specifically, moving toward new attitudes about unfamiliar zones represents moving toward new attitudes about unfamiliar beliefs, with belief-bridging supporting both kinds of pragmatic movement. Sometimes the examples demonstrate what not to do, as in the first time Al·Ith crosses the pass into Zone Two (194). But as the years go by and she becomes more deeply imbued with the higher zone's influences, she manages to progress farther and stay longer each time she goes there. The novel offers optimism about pragmatism if it avoids rashness.[28] As illustrated in Al·Ith's successful passage to Zone Two, the positive examples are often linked by belief-bridging to her, for she possesses many admirable qualities and, as the boldest pragmatic questioner, the one who first attempts Zone Two, she follows the literary convention of the quester.[29] Her humility can teach readers not to lapse into thinking that they have all the answers, while her persistence can teach them not to lapse into the "pleasurable luxury of despair" about ever doing anything to change their lives.[30]

Another quality exemplified in Al·Ith is openness to otherness in general, a trait relevant to pragmatism, which requires openness to new beliefs in particular. As the solipsistic countries learn that they need foreignness, so individual characters such as the queen learn that the self needs the other. Indeed, the movement toward otherness can be traced through gradual changes in the use of "self," a word that the text uses many times.[31] Beginning with a concept of the self as a unitary and valued entity, the book moves toward difference and multiplicity, with a single "real" self coming to seem less possible and less desirable. Individuals and countries grow less self-centered and in doing so provide a pragmatic model for readers. Yet the search for otherness should not be equated with mindless preference for the new. To a great extent the zones once knew but have now forgotten how to live as the Providers would wish. Because much of what characters seek lies in the undervalued past and in its neglected remnants such as old songs, cognition often takes the form of re-cognition. In a related way, pragmatism means thoughtfully reforming old beliefs, not rejecting them out of hand.

Implied readers also are warned that pragmatism can be arduous. Struggling against insularity can bring great hardship, for the increasing permeability of the borders between the zones leads to revolutionary, often overwhelming changes in the characters' lives. Coming from Zone Three, with its appreciation of multiplicity, Al·Ith is comparatively well prepared for the exogamous leap from self to other. But then Lessing, her

own life haunted by exile from various countries,[32] makes Al·Ith the ultimate exile and confronts her with more devastating forms of otherness:
the crudeness of Zone Four and the extreme, perhaps deadly, otherness of
Zone Two. Similarly, implied readers find it easy to nod cheerfully at the
notion of the other when it appears in the sparkling utopia of Zone Three,
but otherness becomes more harrowing when it takes a form that the
novel itself defines as inferior or totally alien, as in the other zones.

Some readers may consider the feminist argument in *Marriages* labored.
If it seems to take a position only to doubt it later, that is because the
novel includes a number of feminist patterns and must confront the conflicts that arise between some of them. Judith Stitzel remarks that "if
Lessing forces us to entertain the possibility that the truth cannot be
known, it is because this possibility is the precondition for radical questioning of what and how we know . . . and why" (502). The conflict with
the greatest potential to bother readers is that between static and pragmatic utopian feminism, between the lessons of Zone Three and those of
movement through the other zones. No matter how much Zone Three
appeals to some feminists, its very solidity calls forth the doubts of pragmatic feminists. By definition no single answer, no matter how good, can
fully satisfy them.

Herein lies much of the novel's brilliance. Instead of culminating glori-
ously in a feminist utopia, it begins with such a utopia, then takes the risk
of daring readers not only to savor places that are more impoverished, barbaric, or puzzling, but, more importantly, to appreciate the taxing process
of shedding parochialism. Furthermore, instead of simply presenting persuasion toward a course of action to follow later, the novel, through the
protean quality of the geography/sex metaphor, draws implied readers
into engaging in the process about which they are reading.[33] Ursula K. Le
Guin testifies to having such an experience in the process of reading
Marriages. She says that she distrusts Zone One (which is barely mentioned), "fearing that it will turn out to be not simply better, but perfectly good, and therefore longing to find something wrong with it: just as we
discovered, gradually, guided gently by our author, what was wrong with
the utopian Zone Three" ("Marriages," 35). The book's skepticism about
Zone Three has taught her to be skeptical of Zone One. Instead of establishing a unified origin, Zone One—by its absence—simply indicates the
inexhaustible pragmatic process of approaching otherness.

By the time readers reach the end of *Marriages,* they have traveled through four zones: female Zone Three presents a static utopian feminist answer to women's problems; male Zone Four presents the patriarchal problems themselves; female/male Zone Five mixes feminism with patriarchy; and Zone Two transcends the very terms of all the others. Readers have encountered four stages of feminist argument: that a feminist utopia is admirable; that even a patriarchal dystopia can expose the static complacency of a utopia; that the oppositions between female and male and between feminist and patriarchal need not be so polarized; and that pragmatic feminism means moving beyond binary oppositions altogether. At each stage, the metaphor undergoes a protean transformation, which appeals to readers through belief-bridging, especially the narrative sort. No stage utterly rejects the sex/geography metaphor of the preceding one, but each stage renders the metaphor more refined and complex. One source of complexity is the fact that *Marriages* includes all three patterns of power and all four patterns of focus, with the final stage of the book, by introducing the patterns that characterize barely imaginable Zone Two, leading implied readers to value difference of power and multiplicity of focus.

Travel through the stages entails continual questioning and the pragmatic imagining of provisional goals. Because the novel makes its argument in stages, rather than presenting feminism in a daunting lump, the text teaches the dynamics of pragmatic utopian feminism along with specific feminist beliefs. By the end of the book, implied readers have traveled from a static *place* to a pragmatic *process* that questions any individual place.

CHAPTER 7

Ursula K. Le Guin's *The Left Hand of Darkness*

The king was pregnant.

[T]he whole tendency to dualism that pervades human thinking may be found to be lessened, or changed, on Winter.
—Ursula K. Le Guin (Left Hand 100, 94)

Introduction

Ursula K. Le Guin's novel *The Left Hand of Darkness* (1969) bases its feminist persuasion on unconventional narrative techniques and, more strikingly, on the imaginative resources of science fiction. Although the book presents a moving story of love, betrayal, loneliness, and political intrigue, it is best known for being set on a planet where sexuality differs dramatically from that on Earth. Most of the time the planet's inhabitants are neither female nor male, but occasionally they take on one form or the other. (I follow the author in referring to Gethenians as males, a fraught practice to be examined below.) The resulting freedom from gender roles makes the planet in some respects a feminist utopia, one meant to motivate readers to appreciate particular types of feminism. Of course without drastic physical changes, readers on Earth cannot reach these ideals in the same way Le Guin's aliens do. Yet, because the novel offers pragmatic feminism as a way of thinking, readers may learn to develop their own paths to feminist goals. Through belief-bridging and protean metaphor, the book strives to encourage such thought, particularly in its main implied reader, the ordinary male science fiction reader in the United States of 1969, who is urged to identify with Genly, a visitor from Earth.

The implied reader is coaxed away from patriarchal patterns toward feminist ones and ultimately toward multiplicity, a focus reinforced by the novel's structure, which consists of a variety of narratives by different narrators, working in a range of genres.[1] Multiplicity characterizes the alien sexuality as well, for there is no one correct way for Genly or us to classi-fy it. The Gethenians experience different phases of their own sexuality, and the implied reader, like Genly, must keep coming up with different models of it, thereby engaging in pragmatic thinking.

After introducing the author's feminism and the novel's plot and nar-rative structure, this chapter explains the Gethenians' unusual sexuality. Next are described how *Left Hand* maps out various patterns of focus and power and how, despite the virtual absence of men, the novel nonetheless constructs a male orientation. The chapter concludes with remarks on how the science-fiction genre relates to pragmatism.

Le Guin's Feminism

Before turning to the feminism of Le Guin in particular, a few comments are in order concerning the growing number of feminist science-fiction writers in general. For years science-fiction ("SF") writers showed little trace of feminism; the genre was largely of, by, and for men, though a few excep-tions existed.[2] Since the 1960s, especially in the United States, more women have started reading and writing SF, and female characters have become more numerous and less narrowly presented. Although some women writ-ers differ little from their traditional male counterparts, a feminist sensibil-ity has been brought to the field by other women, such as Joanna Russ, and by a few male writers, such as Samuel Delany and John Varley. Along with the fiction there has arisen a body of feminist commentary on it, increas-ingly informed by feminist theory, as pioneered by Marleen S. Barr.[3]

Science fiction has special potential to contribute to feminist utopian persuasion, for in recent decades the genre has been starting to live up to its claim of open-mindedness and to its potential for exploring possibili-ties of social change. In one of the first essays to delve into these issues, Joanna Russ proposes science fiction as one of several literary realms more promising than most others. Certain didactic modes, including SF, "all carry a heavier intellectual freight (and self-consciously so) than we are used to. . . . All imply that human problems are collective, as well as indi-vidual, and take these problems to be spiritual, social, perceptive, or cog-nitive—not the fictionally sex-linked problems . . . with which we are all so very familiar" ("What Can a Heroine Do?" 19). Pamela Sargent makes a key point: "*Only sf and fantasy literature can show us women in entirely new or strange surroundings. It can explore what we might become if and when the present restrictions on our lives vanish, or show us new problems and restrictions that might arise*" (lx).

Le Guin has long been a leader among those science-fiction writers who are women and, more recently, among those who are feminists. She probably first gained an awareness of outsiders and a respect for cultural diversity through her father, the anthropologist Alfred L. Kroeber, and her mother, Theodora K. Kroeber, who also wrote on anthropological subjects. A contemporary U.S. author, Le Guin writes essays, poems, and short stories; she is best known, however, as a novelist, particularly as a writer of science fiction and fantasy. In recent years she has moved more into experimental fiction.

Le Guin has shown a profound interest in politics, but, true to her anarchist inclinations, she is basically "not a joiner" (McCormack and Mendel, 40).[4] Her political interest springs from her abiding preoccupation with ethics, which she sometimes finds in conflict with her aesthetics; she has said, "A story inevitably makes a moral point, but at least you try to shove it under the carpet—even if the carpet moves a little" (Lecture). Political concern appears, if under the carpet, in much of her fiction, most obviously in *The Dispossessed,* "an ambiguous utopia." Ambiguity in that novel and others comes partly from the tension between Le Guin the optimistic moralist who stresses choice and responsibility and Le Guin the stoical Taoist who believes in the permanence of evil.[5]

Women's issues did not always occupy a major place in Le Guin's ethical and political awareness, but she is now a dedicated feminist, and the implied authors in her fiction have developed along similar lines. (Apparently heterosexual, she does not devote much attention to other sexualities but has moved away from the homophobia of *The Dispossessed*.) While her earliest work evinced sympathy with women's issues, it did not concentrate on them or on women; then, though much of her writing continued that first trend, books like *The Dispossessed* (1974) took a new tack by introducing some characters who explicitly discuss the female condition and relations between the sexes. The novella "The Eye of the Heron" (1978) begins by alternating focalization between two people who fall in love, but then the man dies, after which the woman and the story carry on; this novella, while continuing the second trend, also started a third one, in which the attention turns toward women themselves.

Like most of Le Guin's early fiction, *Left Hand* does not belong to the third, woman-centered group. Because of the peculiarities of Gethenian sexuality, however, the novel does belong to the second group, as a work that gives attention to women's issues. In 1976 the author laid out her thoughts about *Left Hand* in an essay entitled "Is Gender Necessary?," which she rewrote eleven years later, as "Is Gender Necessary? Redux," because, being a pragmatic feminist, she had evolved her thinking over the years. "Redux" shows her modifications in bracketed italics. Explaining the novel's genesis, the author says that, when the women's movement began its groundswell, "I began to want to define and understand the meaning of sexuality and the meaning of gender, in my life and in our society. . . . *The Left Hand of Darkness* . . . is the record of my consciousness, the process of my thinking" ("Redux," 8). Le Guin adds: "The most it says is, I think, something like this: If we were socially ambisexual, if men and women were completely and genuinely equal in their social roles, equal legally and economically, equal in freedom, in responsibility, and in self-esteem, then society would be a very different thing. What our problems might be, God knows; I only know we would have them. But it seems likely that our central problem would not be the one it is now: the problem of exploitation—exploitation of the woman, of the weak, of the earth" ("Redux," 16).

The Plot of the Novel

It is A.D. 4870 and Genly Ai has come to the planet Gethen, called "Winter" in his own language because of its Ice Age climate.[6] He is the Envoy representing the Ekumen of Known Worlds—a federation of eighty-three planets, including his home world, Earth (known as "Terra"). *Left Hand* consists of Genly's report to this federation on his efforts to convince Gethen to join it.

The first nation he visits is a metaphorically female one called Karhide. Its prime minister, Therem Harth rem ir Estraven (known as "Estraven"), has supported Genly's efforts to persuade the country to join the Ekumen, but Genly distrusts him for a variety of reasons. The paranoid king, Argaven XV, exiles Estraven as a traitor and rejects the idea of joining the Ekumen, though he allows Genly the freedom to roam about Karhide. The Envoy leaves the capital and journeys to the interior of the country. There he visits a community of Foretellers, who belong to an unusual sect called the Handdara. Meanwhile, exiled Estraven has fled to Orgoreyn, the metaphorically male nation that borders Karhide. Although the planet has never before known war, Orgoreyn is gaining in power and may be preparing to invade its neighbor. Back in Karhide, Estraven's rival and successor as prime minister tries to inflame passions against Orgoreyn. At last Genly, frustrated at the Karhiders' indifference to his mission, leaves for the male country in hope of a better reception.

On Genly's first night in Orgoreyn, Karhiders raid the town he is visiting. Orgota officials at first lock him in a cellar with other refugees but then take him to the capital city. There, although Genly awakens some interest in the Ekumen, he is eventually arrested and sent to a prison farm, from which Estraven rescues him. The two realize that, to get back to Karhide without being caught, they must cross the Gobrin Ice-Sheet against almost impossible odds. They make the journey and along the way come to trust and love one another, though they never make love. After they return to Karhide, Estraven's presence is betrayed, and he is killed as he tries to cross the border into Orgoreyn again. Genly is devastated by his friend's death, but their goal is finally realized when Gethen joins the Ekumen.

Narrative Structure

Left Hand's movement toward multiplicity is powered in part by the mixed nature of its unusual narrative structure. The plot just described is, properly speaking, only the main one, for interspersed with its chapters are others containing an Ekumenical report on Gethenian sexuality, a myth, tales, and a religious text. The main plot is told (in chronological order) by Genly and through Estraven's journal, but the other chapters have other narrators. What can be called the "interpolated chapters" are tied ambiguously to the main ones as if by delicate, multicolored threads: some provide parallels, others contrasts, still others explanations. Several deserve study as stories in their own right, but I shall concentrate on the main plot.

In tension with this multiplicity is the fact that *Left Hand* is dominated by a single voice, Genly's. To begin with, implied readers identify with him: he is usually the only non-Gethenian in sight, and as he learns about the alien planet, so do they. He is brought up short by the same kind of shock that would disconcert them, as when the masculine Shusgis, "a hard shrewd jovial politician," mentions having been pregnant (118). In addition, through belief-bridging Genly earns implied readers' admiration, for he is thoughtful and ready to risk everything for his ideals. Yet the implied author carefully underdetermines Genly's heroism—he makes mistakes that are serious enough for him to seem believable, someone with whom readers can identify, though the errors are understandable, so that he still deserves esteem.

By inviting this balance of empathy and respect for the Envoy, the novel renders more palatable the ways in which he differs from the old-fashioned science-fiction hero. With strength coming not from violence or trickery but from verbal persuasion, he arrives on Gethen without a military force. And he arrives alone, embodying the Second Wave feminist adage that the personal is political (293). Genly resembles the traditional science-fiction hero enough to create a rapport with implied readers who are like the genre's average 1969 real reader, but he veers from the norm enough to coax them to broaden their horizons. By the time he starts his gradual glide toward feminism, the implied readers trust him enough to move along behind him.

His change is constructed so as not to scare them off by seeming too sudden or too thorough. For example, even after changing many of his opinions on sex and gender, Genly nevertheless says Estraven's child "had a girl's quick delicacy in his looks and movements, but no girl could keep so grim a silence as he did" (299). The off-worlder is still judging Gethenians at times by his old standards and is continuing to apply the standards to non-Gethenians as well, for it does not occur to him that on Earth girls might be silent and boys delicate. Genly's comment has been perceived by Jewell Parker Rhodes as a flaw in the book, but I read the comment as an example of how skillfully the text has underdetermined his transformation (119).

In addition to the authority the Envoy possesses as a character, he is further privileged as a narrator, since his voice dominates the narrative structure: having narrated half the chapters, he also pulls all of them together for his report to the Ekumen. As Susan Sniader Lanser says, "If the persona uttering a given stance is in a position of dominance in the narrative structure, then his or her ideology carries more authority than it would carry if expressed by a subordinate personage" (*The Narrative Act,* 220). Genly "Ai" is both the chief "eye" who sees and the chief "I" who speaks: his chapters, more numerous than anyone else's, enclose the others, comprising the first one and the last three, in addition to some other chapters. Moreover, since the whole book consists of his report to the Ekumen, his narration occupies a higher level than everyone else's: although he and Estraven mostly describe the same set of events, the Envoy is telling the outer story, while his friend and all the other narrators are telling the stories within it. Genly has selected all the chapters, decided where to interpolate tales within the main plot, added the appendix, and presented the whole to the Ekumen.

Since he reports facts accurately and makes most judgments by standards considered ethical and reasonable in our culture, he manages to retain the authority granted by default to a largely reliable narrator, especially an extradiegetic one. At first the implied author does, however, present Genly as unreliable in one realm—his patriarchal beliefs. As he gradually lets go of those beliefs, his judgments are presented as more trustworthy, a process epitomized in his relationship with Estraven. Genly's major mistake is his initial tendency to believe in everyone but Estraven, the one person who completely trusts him and deserves his trust (198–99). Admittedly, since the political situation would seem confusing to any outsider, this is one of the misperceptions that is forgiven him by the implied reader. But the text is constructed so that the more insightful Genly's perceptions become the more he recognizes the trustworthiness of Estraven, who, as we shall see, is linked with the novel's feminist values. Thus, narrative belief-bridging makes these values appealing by linking them to Genly's increasing reliability as a narrator.

Other Sexuality

Gethenian sexual arrangements require separate discussion because they are so odd, at least to Terrans like us, and are so fundamental to the novel's feminist belief-bridging. The story being set on Gethen, readers must be able to tolerate the planet in order to keep reading, to remain receptive to the novel's persuasion. Moreover, openness to Gethen is also needed because the planet sometimes serves specifically as a metaphor for women. Not only must implied readers accept Gethenian sexuality in these general ways, as part of accepting the planet as a whole, but they also need to be open to two particular aspects. So, after describing Gethenian sexuality, this section analyzes how *Left Hand* invites readers to respect the society's physiologically based absence of gender and to appreciate the otherness of the inhabitants' sexuality. For all these reasons, if readers are to be persuaded by *Left Hand*'s feminism, they must both understand Gethenian sexuality and accept it.

Gethenian Sexuality

It may seem odd to talk of feminist implications in a work whose plot can be summarized without a mention of any female characters, making the novel sound like conventional male-oriented science fiction. But *Left Hand* adds a twist that differentiates it from traditional science fiction: although no major characters are women, none is a man either, with the exception of Genly. An account of Gethenian sexuality will answer the riddle of how such a situation is possible.

Each inhabitant of Gethen can be considered to be of each sex in turn, of both sexes simultaneously, of neither sex, and even of some other sex or sexes. Gethenians alternate between a twenty-one- to twenty-two-day period of latency called "somer" and a four- to seven-day period of "kemmer," a time of extremely intense sexual desire akin to estrus. Ekumenical Investigator Ong Tot Oppong, whose landing party studied Gethen secretly before Genly arrived openly, reports:

> A Gethenian in first-phase kemmer, if kept alone or with others not in kemmer, remains incapable of coitus. . . . When the individual finds a partner in kemmer, hormonal secretion is further stimulated (most importantly by touch . . .) until in one partner either a male or female hormonal dominance is established. The genitals engorge or shrink accordingly, foreplay intensifies, and the partner, triggered by the change, takes on the other sexual role (? without exception? If there are exceptions, resulting in kemmer-partners of the same sex, they are so rare as to be ignored)[7]. . . . Normal individuals . . . do not know whether they will be the male or the female, and have no choice in the matter. . . . Once the sex is determined it cannot change during the kemmer-period. . . . [Afterward,] if conception has not taken place, the individual returns to the somer phase within a few hours . . . . If the individual was in the female role and was impregnated, . . . [during gestation and lactation] this individual remains female. . . . [T]he mother of several children may be the father of several more. (90–91)

During kemmer females and males in a group may have sex with each other in a kemmerhouse, but the "furthest extreme from this practice is the custom of *vowing kemmering* . . ., which is to all intents and purposes monogamous marriage. . . . [O]ne can only vow kemmering once" (92).

There are occasional exceptions to the physiology just described: for instance, a few people are born as "perverts"—people who are always in kemmer and always just female or just male. Women and men from other planets, including Earth, seem like perverts to Gethenians.[8] Although most critics speak of Gethenian sexuality as a single entity, it actually differs from ours in two ways—its somer/kemmer alternation and its female/male variation. Since in effect the implied readers themselves are always in kemmer, somer is the phase that is hardest for them to imagine.

Some of the society's sexual practices suit the novel's emphasis on openness toward the other and on the interdependence of all things. Because one person in kemmer cannot develop sexually without another, masturbation is presumably less feasible. The stress on otherness is also represented in the (modified) prohibition of incest between siblings, who may have only a temporary relationship and may not keep kemmering after one bears a child (92).

How Belief-Bridging Makes Gethenian Sexuality Acceptable

Surprisingly—given all I have just described—one way this physiology is made acceptable is by its very familiarity, for it cannot be dismissed as totally alien: Gethen's sexuality recalls Earth's in that at most two sexes can participate in intercourse at once; only two kemmering sexes exist in the first place; and those two are female and male. Many other Gethenian traits are unfamiliar, though, and require more belief-bridging.

A major technique for appealing to the novel's implied readers is the construction of Gethenian sexuality in such a way that it solves problems that currently bedevil the sexual attitudes of many people on Earth, particularly in the Western world. The somer/kemmer cycle dissociates sexual activity per se from guilt, for instance; Oppong, the Ekumenical Investigator, explains that "no one, whatever his position, is obliged or forced to work when in kemmer" (93). Another Earth problem that Gethen escapes is rape, which the somer/kemmer cycle makes impossible (when just two people are present), since only mutual attraction can bring on the culminant phase of kemmer (94, 157).[9] Nor do Gethenians suffer from frustration of the sexual drive, for the drive is satisfied if a person finds a kemmering partner, and in any case frustration ends when kemmer does (95). Readers might fear a lack of frustration would mean a lack of motivation, but the off-world Investigator eventually concludes that Gethenians are "not castrate, but latent" (96). *Left Hand* thus undercuts the Freudian theory of sublimation, for the book presents characters who, while in somer, manifest as strong a desire for achievement as people on Earth.

Gethen also avoids another problem that bothers many people in our society, the wide gulf between women and men. One way to describe the Gethenian solution is simply to say the planet has no women or men and thus no gulf. Another way is to call the inhabitants androgynous, as Oppong does when she describes the Gethenian in somer (91); although, as I have pointed out, androgyny has its flaws, it can also captivate readers (Hayles, 99; Brown). Whether Le Guin's readers imagine the Gethenian as androgynous or in other terms, they will in any case find no disturbing chasm between women and men.

How Gethenian Sexuality Goes beyond Gender

Having reviewed some of the ways *Left Hand* forestalls objections to

Gethenian sexuality, we can explore why that belief-bridging matters so much. A paramount reason is that the inhabitants' sexuality ensures the absence of gender: by making the former appealing, the implied author is making the latter attractive as well. Obviously Gethenians in somer are free of gender. Though the novel never shows two Gethenians together in a fully aroused state, in kemmer the difference between female and male genitalia presumably dictates some minimal difference in *sex* roles, but we have no direct evidence of different *gender* roles. The people in kemmer shown making sexual advances happen to be female—implying that if kemmer does have gender conventions, they at least differ from ours.

Le Guin calls *Left Hand* itself a "thought-experiment" in which she "eliminated gender, to find out what was left. Whatever was left would be, presumably, simply human" ("Redux," 9, 10).[10] Although not all feminists object to gender distinctions per se (cultural feminists, for example, welcome some gender difference), all feminists object to patriarchy's enforced gender distinctions, and so Gethen's freedom from such distinctions contributes to its status as a feminist utopia, with a profoundly feminist distribution of power: the novel makes literal the anti-essentialist idea that particular genitalia do not render a person more or less fit to run a household or to run a country. The vital point is that anyone "can turn his hand to anything. . . . The fact that everyone between seventeen and thirty-five or so is liable to be . . . 'tied down to childbearing,' implies that no one is quite so thoroughly 'tied down' [on Gethen] as women, elsewhere, are likely to be—psychologically or physically. . . . Therefore nobody here is quite so free as a free male anywhere else" (93–94). These arrangements, of course, will be unappealing to some readers' tastes, especially to male self-interest, but through multifarious belief-bridging, the novel strives to overcome such obstacles.

The planet will also seem distasteful to some readers because of Gethen's indifference to progress, a feeling that Le Guin's essay attributes to the inhabitants' weaving together of traits that patriarchy sunders into two genders:

> The Gethenians do not rape their world. They have developed a high technology . . . , but they have done so very slowly, absorbing their technology rather than letting it overwhelm them. They have no myth of Progress at all. Their calendar calls the current year always the Year One. . . . In this, it seems that what I was after . . . was a balance: the driving linearity of the 'male,' the pushing forward to the limit, the logicality that admits no

boundary—and the circularity of the 'female,' the valuing of patience, ripeness, practicality, livableness." ("Redux," 12)

Anyone who might object to the slow rate of technological progress finds that slow development has certain advantages, such as avoiding "the price that Terra paid" for its industrial revolution; in any case, the slow pace may result from the planet's cold climate rather than from its inhabitants' sexuality (99). In addition, Gethen's limitations on "driving linearity" may be a virtue insofar as they have discouraged full-scale warfare (96). This relative peacefulness, whether caused by climate or sexuality, does help make the planet utopian.

Other possible objections to Gethenian sexuality and lack of gender are also answered. If people were always in somer, that phase would not lose its feminist advantages, but those might be ignored by readers who found somer too unfamiliar or considered orgasm the only path to excitement. The novel's addition of kemmer to Gethenian life not only provides an extra form of desire to help propel the narrative, but also intensifies the feminist persuasion: implied readers who worry that life without gender would be dull even in kemmer find instead that kemmer is more unabashedly sexy than most people's own lives (and that people in somer also feel other passions). *Left Hand* thus dilutes the possibility that it might be accused of feminist puritanism.

Yet the absence of gender may be hard for non-Gethenians—whether readers or characters—to grasp. When Genly notices himself wrongly thinking of a Gethenian as simply female or simply male because of some trait, readers who find themselves doing the same thing are encouraged to interrogate their own tendencies to assume, for example, that a bluff, tough politician must be a man. This process typifies how the novel softly prods readers to become conscious of their own preconceptions. Even when off-worlders understand that a Gethenian does not belong just to the female-associated or just to the male-associated gender, they may nonetheless perceive him as possessing both genders. I have mentioned that Oppong writes of the Gethenian as androgynous in sex, and that Le Guin says she was trying to balance "the driving linearity of the 'male,' . . . and the circularity of the 'female.'" Technically, however, Gethenians are not androgynes; from their point of view, the concept makes no sense.[11] Thus, though androgyny is endorsed by many well-meaning feminists—including the real author in statements like the one just quoted—the implied author moves beyond androgyny, and beyond gender altogether.

How Gethenian Sexuality Privileges Otherness by
Going beyond Dominant Male Focus

Left Hand's attempt to make Gethenian sexuality admirable is part of the novel's description and positive evaluation of otherness in general, particularly sexual otherness: the implied reader is urged to become, through pragmatism, more receptive to the other and variety, less mired in the self and sameness. In particular, because *Left Hand*'s main implied reader is patriarchal and male, this change means a move beyond male singularity and centrality. If Genly and the implied readers learn to accept the sexual otherness of the Gethenians, it can help them accept a kind of sexual otherness closer to home: that of women, whom patriarchy defines as other. The kinds of otherness celebrated in *Left Hand* include racial and national otherness, but the most salient and probably the most unsettling is the sexual type. To non-Gethenian eyes, an inhabitant of Gethen at first keeps slipping undecidably from one sexual category to another. Meanwhile, to a Gethenian, other humans are themselves different; King Argaven exclaims in disgust: "'I don't see why human beings here on earth [i.e., Gethen] should want or tolerate any dealings with creatures so monstrously different'" (36).

Although the difference between Gethen and the Ekumen begins with these divergent sexualities, it goes still further. Gethen is a single planet, a place, an entity, while the Ekumen is a government of multiple planets, an idea, a relationship. The planet and the Ekumen thus differ in kind as well as degree. The entire book runs along this fault line, the border where Gethen and the Ekumen meet, grind together, stick, slip without warning. Each side—and, in microcosm, each protagonist—is alien to the other, and that alienness generates much of the plot's narrative energy. The text spins a web of various kinds of otherness, each functioning as a metaphor for the rest. For example, when the Ekumenical Investigator reports on Gethenian sexuality, she notes that Gethen lacks patriarchal privileging of man over woman, and she links that absence to freedom from other ways of privileging self over other: "There is no division of humanity into strong and weak halves, protective/protected, dominant/submissive, owner/chattel, active/passive. . . . [T]he whole tendency to dualism [in my terms, pseudo-duality and other types of centrality] that pervades human thinking may be found to be lessened, or changed" (94). Her comment raises the possibility that to challenge patriarchy on Earth is not only to advance feminist goals but also more generally to transform the very structures of Terran power and thought.

Science fiction provides especially fertile ground for representing other and self, because "the alien"—the unknown other—can take the form of "an alien"—a being from another planet.[12] Le Guin herself connects the two meanings of "alien" in "American SF and the Other," and critics have described the striving toward de-alienation in her works (Bittner, 33; Suvin, "Parables"). *Left Hand* traces the ramifications of otherness by employing a classic science-fiction form, the alien encounter story, which, as Robert Scholes and Eric S. Rabkin say, "has been subtly altered by Le Guin until it becomes the obvious metaphor for relations between the human sexes" (229).[13]

In *Left Hand* this metaphor functions in several ways. To begin with, an individual Gethenian is a split subject, since he goes between somer and kemmer and between female and male. In order to accept even himself, a Gethenian must accept internal alienation more than people on Earth need to. And to accept Gethenians, Terrans (in Genly's time and our own) must learn to open themselves to otherness more than usual. Furthermore, the alien-encounter metaphor deconstructs what it means to have a relationship with someone of the "same" sex or of a "different" sex. Because when only two people are present a kemmering pair always includes female and male, Gethenian society is more heterosexual than any on Earth; yet, since Gethenians in a sense all belong to one sex, their society is also more homosexual than any here. And, because everyone from Gethen sometimes has a female sexual partner and sometimes a male one, the society is more bisexual than any on our planet.

As Gethenians demonstrate, people can differ from each other in noteworthy ways even without differences of sex and gender. Even in somer Gethenians vary in intelligence, ambition, attractiveness, and any number of other features. This point addresses concerns of those implied readers who may fear excessive sameness in a couple here on Earth if its members are of the same sex or are of different sexes but are not polarized by conventional gender difference. Genly expresses worry about sameness among Gethenians, remarking to Estraven on how biologically different his people are from the planet's other species:

"You're isolated, and undivided. Perhaps you are as obsessed with wholeness as we are with dualism."

"We are dualists too. Duality is an essential, isn't it? So long as there is *myself* and *the other*."

"I and Thou," [Genly] said. "Yes, it does, after all, go even wider than sex." (234)

Estraven is noting that people need not cling to sexual difference in order to find difference; eliminating sexual difference can in fact make other, more profound differences stand out.

Ironically, it is sometimes a lessening of distance that accentuates how much distance still remains between other and self.[14] Only Gethenians unfamiliar with Genly, for instance, dismiss the Ekumen as a hoax and think its alleged Envoy merely one of themselves, albeit a pervert: "One must know him to know him alien" (154). Thus, although urging openness to otherness, the novel avoids the platitude that such receptiveness will necessarily eliminate the gap between other and self. Furthermore, *Left Hand* emphasizes that reaching out to the other can require wrenching sacrifice. Genly first finds the process of adjusting to Estraven very painful but then finds it still more painful to adjust to the death of the man he has come to love. Like the Fisher King, Estraven is sacrificed for others (Scholes and Rabkin, 165): he dies because of his open-mindedness toward Orgoreyn, the Ekumen, and Genly.

In spite of revealing the recalcitrant distance between other and self and the difficulty of crossing that distance, *Left Hand* still manages, through belief-bridging, to make the effort seem worthwhile. The very sacrifices made by admirable characters such as Genly and Estraven convey the great value of the goal for which they make the sacrifices. And, although increased closeness can bring awareness of remaining distance, the novel indicates that awareness of distance can also bring a kind of closeness, for *Left Hand* suggests not that one ignore otherness but that one accept it. Genly describes the night he is first able to accept Estraven for what he is: "[I]t was from the difference between us, not from the affinities and likenesses, but from the difference, that [our] love came: and it was itself the bridge, the only bridge, across what divided us" (248–49). In these ways Gethenian physiology functions literally and metaphorically as otherness that the text both describes and evaluates—a factor in persuading implied readers toward pragmatic questioning of dominant male focus.

Mappings: Patterns of Focus

Each major setting on the planet, while vividly realized in its own right, also acts as a metaphor that contributes to the book's feminist persuasion. After constructing a binary opposition between one figuratively female country and one figuratively male one, the novel then opens the

metaphors to a series of protean transformations intended to inspire readers to change what they believe about the sexes and about relations
between them.[15] The metaphors go through four stages: by the time
Genly has made four trips—to female Karhide, to male Orgoreyn, to the
Gobrin Ice-Sheet, and back to Karhide—his beliefs have changed profoundly, for he has reluctantly transformed his focus. By the end of the
novel, the Karhide/Orgoreyn opposition has been deconstructed and,
along with it, the female/male opposition.

Meanwhile, belief-bridging invites readers toward the particular
descriptions and evaluations at each stage. Moving from stage to stage
draws implied readers into a process of pragmatic feminism, energizing
the narrative. In fact, as I tell the story of how Genly's focus changes, I
shall be describing how the text, too, switches focus from patriarchal
Stage One, with its male singularity and male centrality—to feminist
Stage Four—with its extreme multiplicity. The gradual, pragmatic sea
change in Genly's beliefs provides a model for implied readers to follow,
even during the reading process.[16]

Stage One: Putting Sex on the Map

Stage One consists of Genly's stay in Karhide and sets that country up as
the female half of the binary opposition. The Envoy initially reacts to
Karhide suspiciously, much as he would to a woman. Although he starts
to value it a bit, his focus remains mostly patriarchal, and since the
implied author anticipates that most implied readers will already hold
patriarchal beliefs, little belief-bridging is needed in this stage to make its
patterns attractive.

Karhide's female connotations stem from its values and way of life,
which resemble those that Western societies conventionally associate with
women, through both stereotypes and female-associated gender. Women
do not necessarily possess all these characteristics; indeed, we can read
Karhide as a mockery of essentialism—a "female" land with no biological
women.

These traits are epitomized in the area farthest from male Orgoreyn,
Karhide's Old Land, where flourishes the Handdara religion. Genly realizes that under Karhide's "politics and parades and passions runs an old
darkness, passive, anarchic, silent, the fecund darkness of the Handdara.
And out of that silence inexplicably rises the Foreteller's voice" (60). The
religion has an affinity for negatives; members of the cult revere darkness
as ignorance, as might be expected in Karhide, a land of dimly lit rooms

and gloomy, labyrinthine streets. The Weaver of the Foretelling group explains that the Handdarata try to avoid answers and have perfected Foretelling in order to "'exhibit the perfect uselessness of knowing the answer to the wrong question'" (70). Genly sums up life in the Handdarata Fastness: "It was an introverted life, self-sufficient, stagnant, steeped in that singular 'ignorance' prized by the Handdarata and obedient to their rule of inactivity or non-interference" (60). The Envoy may be exaggerating the stagnation, but his comment can help us understand how the Handdarata way resembles the nation's anarchic political life and how both strongly evoke female-associated gender traits and stereotypical femininity.

Although Genly does not travel to Karhide's rival country until Stage Two, it will be helpful to introduce Orgoreyn at this point, since Karhide is defined in opposition to its metaphorically male neighbor. As a bureaucracy like the former Soviet Union, it has abolished the titles and hereditary privilege that are retained in Karhide. No wealth can be inherited, but some citizens are more equal than others (117). Orgoreyn pleases the Envoy when he arrives there from Karhide: "The Orgota seemed not an unfriendly people, but incurious; they were colorless, steady, subdued. I liked them. I had had two years of color, choler, and passion in Karhide" (114). The buildings of the capital form "simple stately blocks all built to a pattern. . . . There was no clutter and contortion, no sense of always being under the shadow of something high and gloomy, as in [Karhide's capital]; everything was simple, grandly conceived, and orderly. I felt as if I had come out of a dark age" (115). Mention of leaving a dark age refers not only to Orgoreyn's respect for light and enlightenment but also to its aura of modernity.

Its Yomesh religion, which sprang from Karhide's Handdara, values specular mastery. The religion began when the Lord of Shorth forced a group of Foretellers to answer the question, "What is the meaning of life?" After six days and nights most members of the group were catatonic or dead, and one had killed the Lord of Shorth. But the Weaver Meshe, for the rest of his life—not just for the usual single moment—was able to see the past and future: "In the Sight of Meshe there is no darkness" (164). The difference between the Yomesh and Handdarata cults epitomizes the differences that divide the two nations, with Orgoreyn bringing to mind the conventions of masculinity and male-associated gender: order and reason, light and straightforwardness.

Commenting on *Left Hand* in "Is Gender Necessary? Redux," Le Guin makes the geography/sex metaphor explicit when she describes the grow-ing dominance of the male nation's power: "*[. . . The domain allotted to women [on Earth]—'the family,' for example—is the area of order without coercion, rule by custom not by force. . . . [M]en make the wars and peaces, men make, enforce, and break the laws. On Gethen, the two polarities we per-ceive through our cultural conditioning as male and female are neither, and are in balance. . . . But . . . at the moment of the novel, it is wobbling per-ilously]*" ("Redux," 11–12, original italics).

Because Karhide is figuratively female, Genly's reactions to the country play a large role in Stage One of the novel's feminist argument. When the story begins, he is suffering from the cold, feeling confused, frustrated, betrayed—and his feelings seem well justified, for his mission is making almost no headway. Alienated from the female land, his focus swings between male singularity and male centrality: sometimes he doesn't even notice the otherness that surrounds him, as when he fails to realize that it is politeness that prevents Gethenians from giving him advice; at other times he observes but denigrates otherness, as when, for instance, it is exhibited in the intricacies of shifgrethor, the custom of face-saving. Metaphorically, all such reactions to Karhide are reactions to femaleness, but sometimes the sexual dimension actually becomes explicit. In this sense he normally evinces male singularity, for he usually sees the Karhiders as male, as similar to himself. Every once in a while, though, their femaleness becomes visible to him, as when he feels resentment at taking advice from a shorter person who is built somewhat like a woman (218); at such times, his focus is male centrality. By the end of Stage One, however, readers are encouraged to become a little more receptive to femaleness as Genly begins to find Karhide, and thus femaleness, a bit more visible and valuable. This process occurs as he travels deeper into the old, more Karhidish part of Karhide, where he starts to appreciate its profound otherness.

Stage Two: A Remapping

Stage Two, setting up the male half of the binary opposition, consists of Genly's stay in Orgoreyn, to which he travels when exasperated with being ignored in the female country. Despite having softened his attitude toward Karhiders near the end of his stay with them, Genly still remem-bers them as basically alienating. The Orgota begin by treating him well, giving him the first warm room he has had on frigid Gethen, so that the Envoy gets a sense of being at home, in a place familiar and understand-able (117). His focus is male singularity at the times when he immerses himself so deeply in Orgoreyn that he practically forgets its female rival (122). More often, though, his initial focus is male centrality: he compares female Karhide with male Orgoreyn and greatly prefers the latter.

The longer he stays there, though, the more the male land sinks in his estimation and the female land rises.[17] Genly learns that beneath Orgoreyn's order and fairness lie stupidity and cruelty: the government eventually sends him to a prison camp, where he is drugged, tortured, and interrogated. Significantly, it is a Karhider—Estraven—who rescues the helpless Envoy from the prison camp. By the end of Stage Two Genly values the two countries equally and in some ways even prefers the female one: his focus shifts to duality and even female centrality.

To encourage readers to emulate Genly's shift of focus, more complex belief-bridging is required than what we encountered in Stage One. Most obviously, his mistreatment in the prison camp and his rescue by Karhidish Estraven turn implied readers away from Orgoreyn and toward Karhide. Violence, cowardice, and hypocrisy are increasingly associated with the male land. And, as we shall find, belief-bridging takes subtler forms as well.

How Narrative Belief-Bridging Supports Duality

The major form of belief-bridging by which the novel recommends duality is self-reflexively literary—the dramatic use of dual imagery, black and white.[18] Western society tends to belittle both darkness and femaleness, but *Left Hand*'s implied readers learn to value Karhide's darkness as much as Orgoreyn's light, to esteem femaleness as much as maleness. From the title onward, *The Left Hand of Darkness* is flooded with chiaroscuro, and such imagery becomes particularly salient in Stage Two, the phase that emphasizes duality, teaching implied readers how to interpret the black and white images in this stage and elsewhere in the text. Ever since Le Guin published the book, critics such as David J. Lake have been struggling to figure out exactly what darkness and light stand for. We have already examined how the novel paints Karhide with darkness and Orgoreyn with light.[19] While the two do function individually, the effort to interpret each in isolation has distracted critics: we need to go beyond asking what dark and light mean and ask what their relationship reveals.[20]

Neither image possesses a sense consistent through the entire book. Sometimes the prevailing sense is reversed, as when black evokes maleness or white snow evokes ignorance (12, 225), and sometimes one color hints at so many meanings that it seems to have none. By loosening the ties between darkness and femaleness, between light and maleness, this shake-up of meaning saves the novel from essentialism. At times, and most remarkably, dark and light images seem to function not at all as individual metaphors but only in contrast to each other, as when the protagonists play *go* with black and white stones (223). Occasional passages mention only black or only white, but, from the opening scene, in which clouds conceal and reveal the sun, every few pages of the book present the two colors together, usually in explicit contrast—duality in a pattern that is sometimes complementarity, sometimes incomparability. Aside from presenting a setting, often the two mean nothing but difference itself.

What matters is the contrast between darkness and light—and their interdependence. The novel itself provides a gloss when Estraven quotes a traditional lay:

> Light is the left hand of darkness
> and darkness the right hand of light.
> Two are one, life and death, lying
> together like lovers in kemmer,
> like hands joined together,
> like the end and the way. (233–34)

The book's title, *The Left Hand of Darkness,* seems to mention only darkness, but the lay I have just quoted discloses that each term, like a snake biting its tail, evokes its opposite as well. Indeed, even the nation linked with one depends on having a bit of the other, which hints at the pattern I have called similar duality.

Belief-bridging through chiaroscuro is literary, because *Left Hand* itself signifies through black ink on white paper; this self-reflexive novel explicitly links black/white difference to semiotic difference. Estraven and Genly can read difference spelled out in black and white in the very landscape, as when, on the way to a hazardous glacier, the two fugitives go through an active volcanic range, with "ridges to [the] right and left, basalt and snow, piebald and patchwork of black and white brilliant under the sudden sun in a dazzling sky" (219). The men ski toward the glacier, "into that silent vastness of fire and ice that said in enormous letters of black and white DEATH, DEATH, written right across a continent. The sledge pulled like a feather, and [the men] laughed with joy" (220). Semiotic difference matters because it is contrast, otherness, that gives birth to information: a totally blank page is meaningless, as is a page totally covered with black ink.

Similarly, in information theory, the utterly redundant is utterly predictable, meaningless (Lyons, 89). Entropic uniformity signifies nothing,
whereas in the heat of contrast grows signification. Associating black/white
imagery with print and with communication in general can make duality
attractive to readers of novels, of communication in print.

Left Hand explicitly urges readers to value semiotic difference: both
black and white are needed for information. For instance, Genly meets
with white weather on the Ice, and, although he has daylight to see by, the
"unshadow" makes crevasses almost invisible. After inching along for
hours, he becomes paralyzed with fear, and Estraven decides they should
stop. When the Envoy laments his loss of courage, his companion says,
"'Fear's very useful. Like darkness; like shadows. . . . It's queer that daylight's not enough. We need the shadows, in order to walk'" (267).

Although pervasive, the black/white imagery functions to reinforce
dualistic focus in Stage Two in particular. *Left Hand* reveals admirable
consequences, such as detecting crevasses, that stem from the appreciation
of duality. Since it is the heroes who especially acknowledge the need for
chiaroscuro, their assessment carries special weight for implied readers.

How Belief-Bridging Supports Female Centrality
In a variety of ways the novel fosters female centrality as well. Ordinarily
centrality would clash with advocating openness to otherness, but, since
Left Hand's implied reader is male, female centrality does elevate the
other. Gethen is in a sense matrilineal, since the whole planet reckons
descent through "the parent in the flesh" (92). On Earth, matriliny signals
a rare degree of respect for females, and so Gethen's matriliny metaphorically evokes female centrality. Additionally, Gethen has more females
than males since, after the period of sexual activity in kemmer, only people who are pregnant or lactating—some of the females and none of the
males—retain the physical form they have taken on.

The text's most noteworthy source of female centrality, though, is the
privileging of Karhide over Orgoreyn[21]—from the very cover of the book,
"the left hand of darkness" refers explicitly to darkness, an attribute of
Karhide. *Left Hand* allots good and bad characteristics to each country
but waters down the good traits it has granted to Orgoreyn. At first, for
example, the male land's greater physical comforts delight Genly, but he
comes to see them as catering to the material at the expense of the non-
material. Finally, the horrors of the prison camp expose the brutality that
is luxury's dark underside.

A major means by which belief-bridging directs admiration to the female nation is the heroic figure of Estraven, for in many ways he embodies Karhide. He is a "fallible paragon," to use Sheldon Sacks's term in an extended sense. To avoid provoking implied readers' disbelief or hostility, the novel employs underdetermination, alloying Estraven's virtues with faults: as Barbara Bucknall notes, he commits all the crimes most despised by his fellows (*Ursula K. Le Guin,* 71). Yet Estraven retains his heroic stature, partly because most of his misdeeds occur offstage and in the service of a good cause. Furthermore, he faces such daunting challenges that it seems anyone else would make the same mistakes. Implied readers' regard for him culminates when Karhide joins the Ekumen, thus fulfilling a desire instilled in them by belief-bridging throughout the book. Estraven was the only Gethenian who had truly worked from the start toward joining the Ekumen. And, though it is only grudgingly that Karhide becomes part of the interplanetary union, his country is nonetheless the first Gethenian nation to do so, and thus surpasses Orgoreyn. Estraven also arouses admiration by the esteem he eventually calls forth in Genly, the character with whom implied readers can most easily identify. Objectionable characters live in both countries, but only Karhide produces an Estraven.

Estraven's prominence functions not just on the thematic level of heroism but also on the formal level of narrative structure. Only he comes near to matching Genly in degree of involvement as a protagonist of the novel's action or as a teller of its narrative. In the same way, his country looms large in the narrative structure; for example, its texts are interpolated more frequently and earlier in the book than texts from its rival. Whether favorably or unfavorably, the female country serves as the standard against which the male one is measured, a reversal of patriarchy's male centrality.

Most importantly, the narrative begins and ends in the female land, establishing a pattern that defines Karhide as "home" and Orgoreyn as "away." Although not homey to Genly, Karhide is in a sense home to readers, the place where they get their first foothold in the story. The sonata-like home/away/home pattern, so basic to romance, carries special force for Le Guin, who has compared narrative structure to a snake biting its tail or its tale ("It Was a Dark and Stormy Night"). Such rounded works leave implied readers with a satisfying sense of closure, a sense that privileges the return home—in this case, the return to Karhide. It is in Stage Two that *Left Hand*'s romance pattern starts to manifest itself, for it is in Orgoreyn that Karhide's value starts to emerge, as does the need to return there. The pattern is completed when Genly and Estraven return to Karhide, when the country is finally ready to join the Ekumen. Most romance journeys transform the traveler, the home, or both: indeed, Genly's trip has both changed him into a person who can appreciate Karhide and changed Karhide into a country that can appreciate him and his mission.

Female centrality is also supported by the narrative type of belief-bridging, involving language. First of all, naming practices elevate Karhide above its male neighbor. The Orgota value labels over names, as Estraven mentions in criticizing citizens of the rival country (83). And the names that the Orgota do use lack the resonance of Karhidish ones, which recall other words that occupy a central position in the book: Estraven-estrus, Harth-Hearth, Gethenen-Gethen, Handdara-hand. As for language in general, Karhide, the land of discomfort, not surprisingly has a language that at first sounds to Genly "like rocks rattled in a can," while Orgoreyn, the land of superficial comfort, has a superficially pleasing language (112, 132), suitable for lies (287) and for euphemisms such as "Voluntary Farm." Instead of lying, people in Karhide substitute "an agreed, understood silence—an omission of questions, yet not an omission of answers" (287). The Karhidish Handdara religion encourages speechlessness, whereas a profusion of language characterizes Orgoreyn: in the car that takes Genly to the Orgota capital, the radio is on whenever the engine is. Overall, Karhide's emphasis on names and on a discreet, speaking silence has more appeal than Orgoreyn's inclination toward labels, lies, and, at times, a concealing or passive silence.

The type of narrative belief-bridging that most strongly reinforces female centrality is black and white imagery—evoking print on a page—which we have already encountered as support for duality. One might expect the novel to represent the superiority of Karhide over Orgoreyn through the superiority of darkness over light, but something more complex happens. We find that Karhide's attitude toward *both* darkness and light proves superior to Orgoreyn's attitude: both darkness and light exist in both countries, but dark-loving Karhide integrates the two, while its light-loving neighbor separates them and denies darkness and shadows. Although when Genly arrives in Orgoreyn its illumination provides welcome relief from Karhidish obscurity, he begins to notice that "well-lit streets" alone cannot guarantee good vision: "There was something fluid, insubstantial, in the very heaviness of this city built of monoliths. . . . There were vivid personalities among [the Orgota] . . . and yet each of them lacked some quality, some dimension of being; and they failed to convince. They were not quite solid. . . . It was, [Genly] thought, as if they did not cast shadows" (146–47). Orgoreyn officially boasts only of light, but when the Envoy is "locked in the dark with uncomplaining, unhopeful people of Orgoreyn" during the harrowing truck ride to the prison camp, he comes to understand that the nation has a hidden, totally dark, but equally shadowless side (167). In "The Child and the Shadow," Le Guin refers to Carl Gustav Jung's theories and speaks of the shadow as an irrational part of the self that people must acknowledge before they can become mature and whole. Karhiders are not more moral than Orgota, but their evil is rarely linked to the shadow, because neither is hidden.

The Orgota attitude toward the dark/light opposition extends to oppositions of all sorts. Estraven comments:

> "The Yomeshta would say that man's singularity is his divinity."
> [Genly replies,] ". . . Other cults on other worlds have come to the same conclusion. They tend to be the cults of dynamic, aggressive, ecology-breaking cultures. Orgoreyn is in the pattern, in its way; at least they seem bent on pushing things around." (233)

The Orgota praise oneness, not in the sense of integrated complexity, but in the sense of singularity. Karhiders cannot wholly accept otherness either, but at least they absorb rather than reject it.

Orgoreyn's repressive splitting is condemned by the belief-bridging discussed in the section on duality, bridging that stresses the need for darkness as well as light, and in particular the need for the relationship between the two. Figuratively, the novel is criticizing patriarchal societies that deny and repress what is female or female-associated. Orgoreyn's neglect of otherness gives its citizens a focus of male singularity, or at best male centrality, whereas Karhide's recognition of otherness moves its focus toward duality, which the implied author and eventually Genly regard as preferable.

How Binary Oppositions Start to Wobble

Even while retaining their binary nature, some of the oppositions we have been examining start to deconstruct themselves, anticipating their greater breakdown in later stages.[22] Sometimes two poles switch sides, as when male Genly is rescued by relatively female Estraven. At other times two elements prove not to have been complete opposites anyway:[23] Orgoreyn's bureaucracy, for instance, differs from but does not complement Karhide's monarchy. What is more, even an opposition that remains stable in isolation can, in relation to other oppositions, reveal its fragility. Sweating under an unusually hot sun, Genly rejoices when King Argaven seems to have finished mortaring the keystone that joins two halves of an arch. The uncomfortable Envoy is dismayed to find that the king is now starting in "on the other side of the keystone, which after all has two sides" (6). A single duality is not enough in a three-dimensional world. And, just as one duality can build on another, so one duality can fragment into another. The most memorable example is the teeth of one slickly insinuating character: "He smiled . . . , and every tooth seemed to have a meaning, double, multiple, thirty-two different meanings" (9).[24]

As fundamentally dualistic structures start to deconstruct themselves in these ways, they feed the novel's feminist persuasiveness. For instance, just as the governments of Karhide and Orgoreyn turn out not to complement each other, so women differ from but are not the opposite of men. And, as dualities multiply, they edge toward becoming multiplicities. A feminism of multiple focus then blossoms in the next stage.

Stage Three: Another Remapping

Stage Three represents Genly's time on the Gobrin Ice-Sheet, which lies in northern Orgoreyn, above its inhabited region and adjacent to northern Karhide. He and Estraven escape Orgoreyn by traveling to the unforgiving ice sheet and, miraculously, crossing it. During part of the journey, Estraven goes through kemmer, taking on female traits. It is on this forbidding ice sheet that the two fall in love and Genly finally understands and accepts Estraven.

The Envoy's focus shifts to mild multiplicity, the sort consisting of three terms, as this stage deconstructs the earlier female/male binary opposition by inserting a third term into the protean metaphor: if Karhide were the thesis and Orgoreyn the antithesis, then the ice sheet would be the synthesis. In the wobbling binary oppositions mentioned above, duality was already starting to approach multiplicity; now the two poles cease to remain completely separate, and sometimes light and darkness even blend along a continuous spectrum—a third term—as in the many scenes set at dusk or dawn (e.g., 280–81).

The implied author takes *Left Hand* onward to other kinds of mild multiplicity, as well as to the strong sort, but interestingly the real author's extratextual statements stop here, with the mildest type. Le Guin frequently rejects either/or choices, praising what I call duality and the kind of mild multiplicity that integrates two poles. She does so, for instance, in an essay criticizing our society: "Instead of a search for balance and integration, there is a struggle for dominance. . . . The dualism of value that destroys us [what I would term pseudo-duality], the dualism of superior/inferior, ruler/ruled, owner/owned, user/used, might give way to what seems to me, from here, a much healthier, sounder, more promising modality of integration and integrity" ("Redux," 16). The wholeness she advocates never slips into singularity but nonetheless hampers multiplicity. While not rigidly dichotomizing, Le Guin's statements outside the novel—like the commentary by those who write about her—barely go beyond a fundamental binarism.[25]

Yet *Left Hand* itself goes further,[26] for the Gobrin Ice truly introduces a third term, instead of merely integrating Karhide with Orgoreyn.[27] The former country threatens Estraven's life, the latter threatens Genly's, and the glacier, although deadly, offers the only refuge. After the protagonists flee there, they are literally in a place of both darkness and light, having left the countries where only one or the other dominates. High above sea level and high on the map, the ice sheet provides a way to rise above, to transcend, the international rivalry. Alternatively, that opposition has a different third term, the Ekumen—for Estraven also hopes that the two countries can transcend their rivalry by joining the interplanetary union (87–88). Located out among the stars, it, too, rises above international conflict. In these ways the Gobrin Ice and the Ekumen, each serving as a third term to complicate the opposition between Karhide and Orgoreyn, invite readers to challenge simple female/male dualities.

A third term also sprouts in another duality, that between Gethen as a whole and the Ekumen. The Gobrin Ice adds a third element, for it provides the two travelers with the isolation and adversity they need to help them accept each other's interplanetary differences. By enabling love to develop as a third entity between individuals, Estraven and Genly, the Gobrin Ice becomes the foundation for the agreement that will later be created as a third entity between the larger entities Gethen and the Ekumen.

How Mediation, a Type of Narrative Belief-Bridging, Supports Mild Multiplicity
The chief form of mediation in *Left Hand* is communication, a theme that indeed suffuses all of Le Guin's writing, enriching its self-reflexiveness. Genly, for example, tells the Gethenians that his real job is to find out if

they are "'willing to communicate with the rest of mankind'" (138). Communication, like all other forms of mediation, can be thought of as mild multiplicity, for when two entities communicate they are linked by a third term, the medium. Even as the medium enables people to reach across the gap separating other from self, the very need for a medium makes that gap all the more visible; while advocating communication as a way to open oneself to otherness, *Left Hand* reminds the implied readers of this poignant irony.

In the worlds created by tough-minded Le Guin, characters learn that they must always pay a price for what they want. So, with regard to communication, some methods require less mediation than others, but every method requires some. Communication and its dependence on mediation are epitomized in telepathy, or "mindspeech," introduced in Stage Three. One might expect mindspeech to be unmediated (after all, it permits no lying), but it still has concrete properties: Estraven still mispronounces Genly's name when mindspeaking (254). The Envoy writes that the "intimacy of mind established between us [by mindspeech] was a bond, indeed, but an obscure and austere one, not so much admitting further light (as I had expected it to) as showing the extent of the darkness" (255).

More generally, communicating with a foreigner brings out the irreducible otherness of the foreign culture. *Left Hand* is not the type of science fiction to recuperate otherness by providing some sort of universal "magic decoder" to translate from any language into a known one: Le Guin's novel explains how the Ekumen's secret investigating team learned Gethenian languages, so that the Envoy came prepared to speak them (38). Genly mentions the difficulty of translating (109), and in a sense his report, the entire book, is a translation, an effort to mediate between two cultures.[28] By such means the novel, especially in Stage Three, presents mild multiplicity positively by linking it to communication. Communication in turn is represented approvingly, in spite of its limitations; actually, those limitations render more precious the communication that does succeed.

How Gethenian Sexuality Supports Multiplicity

A key component in the novel's tendency toward multiplicity is Gethenian sexuality. Although its strangeness ripples through all the stages, it comes to the fore in Stage Three, when kemmer overtakes Estraven. Along with Genly, readers must confront discomfiting alterity: ironically, the more closely Estraven resembles a woman, the more deeply Genly understands that a Gethenian constitutes a third entity, "a woman as well as a man" (248)—or neither. Less explicit but equally overwhelming in the Terran's confused feelings is the related question of whether his bond with Estraven is homosexual or heterosexual. Actually the relation between the two protagonists is of a third sort. Furthermore, although we have observed that the bond between two Gethenians is partly homosexual and partly heterosexual, it is neither purely; it is of a third sort as well, but different from that which links Genly and Estraven. These are some of the ways Gethenian sexuality deconstructs the homosexual/heterosexual opposition as well as the female/male one.

The bittersweet ambiguities that Estraven and Genly encounter on the ice sheet evoke the multiplicity of ways one can think about Gethenian sexuality even when no off-worlders are involved. Its shifting quality permits analogies with each kind of focus:

> *singularity:* Everyone on the planet has the same kind of sexuality. In somer everyone's body is the same.
>
> *centrality:* Somer prevails over kemmer, since people are usually in somer. Or, in another sense, kemmer prevails over somer, since, during the brief time people *are* in kemmer, it rules their lives, and society accepts that.
>
> *duality:* Two states exist—somer and kemmer. Kemmer itself has two states—female and male.
>
> *mild multiplicity:* Three states exist—somer, female kemmer, and male kemmer. The first of these undermines the binary opposition of the other two. The female/male split prevents kemmer from standing in neat binary opposition to somer.

The dynamic instability of Gethenian difference means that Genly and the implied readers must make continual efforts to reclassify it—efforts that help catalyze the novel's feminist pragmatism. The presence of more than three models itself constitutes a kind of strong multiplicity, the sort that will typify the next stage.

Stage Four: A Different Remapping

Stage Four begins when Estraven and Genly, exhausted by the Gobrin Ice, at last manage to cross into Karhide. Because the order of exile still hangs over Estraven, his countrymen greet him ambivalently; one finally betrays him, and Karhidish border guards kill him as he skis back toward Orgoreyn. His death unleashes complex political maneuverings: Genly's ship lands as Karhide makes overtures to the Ekumen, which the whole planet will eventually join. In the end Genly, still almost annihilated by Estraven's death, goes to his friend's domain, where the Envoy meets the dead man's father and son.

Although a time of overwhelming loss for Genly, this final stage of the protean metaphor also brings richness. Its strong multiplicity goes further beyond duality than mild multiplicity did, more energetically decon-structing the female/male opposition. Possibilities for the future branch out, stimulated and symbolized by the landing of the Ekumenical ship. Now there are multiple members of the Ekumen on Gethen, including several women—one of whom was the first person off the ship and the first to speak (296). Genly's shipmates travel to other countries, beyond the two he has visited. Meanwhile the Ekumen itself has finally become real to the Gethenians, with its multiple worlds and its "philosophy . . . couched more in terms of multiples than dualities" (Hayles, 104). Apparently still more worlds lie unknown outside its boundaries, to be discovered in the future.

How Narrative Structure, a Type of Narrative Belief-Bridging, Supports Strong Multiplicity
Le Guin's novel begins:

> *From the Archives of Hain. Transcript of Ansible Document 01-01101-934-2-Gethen: To the Stabile on Ollul: Report from Genly Ai, First Mobile on Gethen/Winter, Hainish Cycle 93, Ekumenical Year 1490–97.*

> I'll make my report as if I told a story, for I was taught as a child on my homeworld that Truth is a matter of the imagination. The soundest fact may fail or prevail in the style of its telling . (1)

Left Hand is very self-reflexive, and a major reason for its self-reflexive-ness is that it is a narrative about narratives. In addition to offering obser-vations such as the one above, the book is about people full of multiple narratives—most Gethenians are "well stuffed" with myths and tales (181)—and the novel itself consists of multiple narratives, employing a multitude of techniques.

The opening passage, quoted above, heralds the narrative multiplicity that pervades the book. The content of Genly's comment is the multiplic-ity of truth, and the form of the comment is also multiple, for its shift from bureaucratese to storytelling signals the numerous genres that are to follow.[29] Multiple answers are possible to the question he soon raises: ". . . I am not sure whose story it is; you can judge better" (1–2). "Whose story it is" may simply mean who the protagonist is—Genly, Estraven, or both. Or perhaps the story belongs to Estraven because he has brought about many of its events and has paid for the story with his life. "Whose story it is" could also mean its narratees, those who hear or read it within the novel or in reality.

Or "whose story it is" could mean its multiple narrators. Half the chapters are narrated by Genly, one by a woman from the earlier, secret Ekumenical expedition, and the rest by an assortment of Gethenians. Of those Gethenian chapters, almost half consist of excerpts from Estraven's journal. Genly and Estraven appear as major characters in their own chapters and in each other's, but the other narrators do not appear in the chapters they narrate. The variety of narrators makes for a variety of styles. For instance, the tales and the myth sound like oral storytelling: "He . . . would not come out for friend or foe, for seedtime or harvest, for kemmer or foray, all that month and the next and the next, and six months went by and ten months went by, and he still kept like a prisoner to his room, waiting" (44). Meanwhile the Yomesh chapter captures the rhythms of religious writing, while the report on Gethenian sexuality, stiltedly describing "the individual" whose "genitals engorge," serves as a gentle parody of scientific prose (90).

In addition to the profusion of truths, genres, protagonists, narratees, narrators, and styles, multiplicity is also furthered on the level of point of view. As Eric S. Rabkin says, "Le Guin's remarkable achievement is that she can manipulate our habitual point of view so that we come to see things from a new point of view, that for which point of view itself is central" ("Determinism," 5–6). When applied to *Left Hand,* "focus" in the sense of narrative technique suggests "focus" in the sense in which I have been using it, relating to visibility and value.

Actually, movement toward multiple narration starts with duality. If we ask Gérard Genette's questions, "Who speaks?" and "Who sees?," for Genly's, Estraven's, and the Ekumenical Investigator's chapters the literal answer to both questions is "the person who records the chapter." But one of Genly's chapters almost has a second narrator, Estraven: by the first page of the last Ice chapter, the two men have grown so close that Genly discloses his identity as narrator only at the bottom of the page (263).[30] "Who speaks" oscillates again later in that chapter, when the two see other people for the first time after crossing the Ice (Bittner, 284–85):

"Will you look to my friend?"
    I thought I had said it, but Estraven had. (272)

Later Genly's point of view, while still literally his alone, seems to move
from duality to mild multiplicity. In Genly's chapters, he is in fact the one
who perceives, yet when he begins to perceive things as Gethenians would,
in a sense his point of view becomes multiple: by the end of the book the
off-worlder sees the women and men who have just stepped off his ship as
"great, strange animals, of two different species[,] . . . all of them in rut, in
kemmer," while his Gethenian physician's face, "not a man's face and not a
woman's, a human face," seems familiar and right (296). Genly's altered
perceptions affect his language as well, so that near the end of his report he
uses a shadow metaphor as a Karhider would (288).

Among the interpolated chapters, in the three tales and the myth, "who
speaks" is a narrator outside the story being told, but "who sees" differs as
narrative practices develop from singularity to duality.[31] All four chapters
tell of kemmering pairs. The two older stories focus on just one of the two
kemmerings: the other person appears only when the two are together. In
contrast, the narrator of each of the more recently narrated tales sees
through the eyes of each of the two kemmerings in alternation, so that the
newer stories are opening to otherness.

The multiplicity of narration also takes another form: Left Hand invites
readers to speculate about possible ways to rewrite it and thus adapts the
notion of the "writerly" text for science fiction.[32] For example, the book
has been criticized for using words such as "king" and "he," but what
those complaints actually indicate is that the novel has at least aroused the
critics' imaginations, calling forth a kind of rewriting. Since no single set
of terms can translate Gethenian sexuality perfectly, only multiple rewritings, imagined together, can approximate a faithful translation. And, as a
"thought-experiment," the text can inspire readers to imagine other experiments: what would Gethen be like if the Envoy were a woman, or if
somer did not exist, or if female/male variation did not exist, and so on?
Le Guin acknowledges that real readers' comments can function as a form
of rewriting, for she says she "can only be very grateful to those readers,
men and women, whose willingness to participate in the experiment led
them to fill in [an] omission with the work of their own imagination"
("Redux," 15). Perhaps they will become rewriters of the world around
them as well, striving to change society.[33]

Le Guin herself has in a sense rewritten *Left Hand*. Despite her initial opposition to invented pronouns, in response to a critic she has rewritten two passages from the novel using such words "for those who want to try the effect, and also as a means of testing the alleged masculinity of Estraven" ("Reply to Lem," 91).[34] Another kind of rewriting appears in her short story "Winter's King," which takes place on Gethen after the planet has joined the Ekumen. She wrote the story before the novel and originally made Gethenian sexuality no different from that on Earth. After writing *Left Hand*, she revised "Winter's King," retaining male nouns such as "king" but substituting female pronouns such as "she."[35] The device's mind-boggling effect on implied readers deserves a study of its own, but in relation to *Left Hand* the story holds interest as a model for one of many possible rewritings invited by the longer work.

The invitation to rewrite becomes most explicit in Stage Four. At the end of the main plot, Estraven's son—perhaps speaking for young male implied readers—asks Genly, "'Will you tell us how he died?—Will you tell us about the other worlds out among the stars—the other kinds of men, the other lives?'" (301). If the son asked only the first question, it and his grandfather's request for the tale of the Gobrin Ice-Sheet would make *Left Hand* into another snake biting the end of its tail, for the answer to the questions would lie in the book that preceded them. But this snake bites its tail just before the tip: the son's questions move from death to life. At the death of the narrative that readers have read (the tale of Estraven's death) his son asks for the birth of a narrative that they have not read (the tale of other lives). The book has been inviting rewritings; now it invites the writing of what Norman N. Holland calls "another, untold novel" (135). Because the boy inquires about the otherness of the Ekumen, the ending tempers sadness with hope, the multiplicity so strong as to suggest indefinite, even infinite, extension.

Mappings: Patterns of Power

Equal Power

Left Hand represents two patterns of power, mostly celebrating equality and criticizing inequality. A certain kind of equality is created by Gethenians' biology, making the entire planet a feminist utopia, since, as we have observed, the lack of gender ensures there is no division into dominating men and subordinated women. This striking lack of sexism accounts for the novel's international reputation as a feminist text. My description of Gethenian sexuality sketched out how the novel's belief-bridging urges readers to admire that sexuality and the utopian equality of power associated with it.

Lest that static utopian perfection sap narrative interest, *Left Hand* answers the threat of stagnation in a variety of ways. To begin with, from the Gethenians' standpoint the lack of gender and the resulting lack of sexism would seem not utopian (or dystopian) but meaningless. In encouraging readers to question their initial paradigm, in inviting them to try thinking as a Gethenian would, *Left Hand* is not condemning the utopian aspects of Gethen but suggesting a pragmatic way of pondering them. The novel avoids stasis by other means as well. The inhabitants may not have to confront sexism, but they face a host of other problems: betrayals, suicides, assassinations, and raiding parties. Gethenians struggle with the question of whether they should believe in the Ekumen, much less trust it. The planet may even be heading toward its first war. And the climate is merciless. Gethen is both an embattled utopia facing external conflicts and a partial utopia facing internal ones, but this less-than-Eden does have the advantage of providing a fecund source of narrative complexity, creating sites for reader involvement and, through underdetermination, preventing the utopia from seeming saccharine. The existence of so many problems on Gethen also cautions readers that static utopian feminism does not by itself suffice; and feminism alone is not perfectly utopian. By such constructions the text manages to present equal power positively but not statically.

Unequal Power: Dominant Male Power

The potential stasis of utopia is also disturbed by inequality in its patriarchal form—dominant male power, which the text generally criticizes, by associating it with war. Of course, literally speaking, Gethenians are neither male nor sexually unequal; the pattern occurs, rather, on the figurative level, where male Orgoreyn has more power than female Karhide. Orgoreyn, having recently become much more centralized than Karhide, is itching to invade its neighbor and start the planet's first war. *Left Hand* largely attributes this danger to the male country's dominant power and finds fault with both war and the power inequality that makes it possible.

Responding to Orgoreyn's superior strength, Karhide can keep its traditions, remaining vulnerable, or it can work to ward off Orgoreyn, in the process becoming more and more like its rival—taking on male-associated traits, thereby regaining equal power but losing something precious (85). A comparable double bind is faced by many women in patriarchal institutions, who must choose between forgoing power or adopting the ways of male-associated gender, even to resist the institutions. As Estraven says in another context, "[I]f you turn your back on Mishnory [the capital of Orgoreyn] and walk away from it, you are still on the Mishnory road" (153).

Belief-bridging teaches implied readers not only how to understand dominant male power, but also how to evaluate it. Having associated the male country's dominant power with impending war, *Left Hand* in turn links war with values that are likely to repel the implied readers. The belief-bridging involving war deserves a detailed examination because the process typifies how Le Guin's novel manages to convey beliefs through a combination of over- and underdetermination. To begin with, war is defamiliarized, presented as a constructed phenomenon, in a comment by one of the Ekumenical explorers who visited Gethen secretly before Genly arrived: "I am a woman of peaceful Chiffewar, and no expert on the attractions of violence or the nature of war. . . . But I really don't see how anyone could put much stock in victory or glory after he had spent a winter on Winter, and seen the face of the Ice" (96–97).

Fundamental to the belief-bridging concerning war is the novel's juxtaposition of two very different characters. Karhide and Orgoreyn are engaged in a territorial dispute that Estraven, when still Prime Minister of Karhide, tries to obviate—an action that seems unpatriotic to the king, accounting in part for Estraven's fall from his position. He is replaced by Tibe, who in contrast uses the dispute as a way to unify Karhide through jingoism. The traits of bellicose Tibe—with his long, yellow teeth and hypocritical smile—make war and chauvinism unappealing. "He talked much about pride of country and love of the parentland, but little about shifgrethor [a kind of face-saving or oneupmanship], personal pride or prestige. . . . His themes were not pride and love at all, though he used the words perpetually; as he used them they meant self-praise and hate" (102). In contrast, the spokesman for peace is one of the book's heroes, Estraven. When he condemns "patriotism," he sounds reasonable because he defines his terms carefully, avoiding dogmatism: "'I don't mean love [of one's homeland], when I say patriotism. I mean fear. *The fear of the other.* And its expressions are political, not poetical: hate, rivalry, aggression'" (19, emphasis added). Estraven's discourse is itself what he has called "poetical"—an instance of literary belief-bridging. Such techniques create the belief-bridging intended to turn implied readers against war and so against dominant Orgota power and the dominant male power it represents.

Karhide's double bind is deconstructed when the off-worlders arrive, but a new opposition is set up—this time between the whole planet and the Ekumen. On the literal level the distinction between the Ekumen and Gethen seemingly has little to do with the distinction between men and women, for the interplanetary union consists of both sexes and the planet consists of neither. On the figurative level, though, each has a sex. Men apparently dominate the Ekumenical worlds (235), and their Envoy is a man, while in comparison Gethen is female since it lacks male domination. Because war and technology are traditionally male-associated on Earth, the absence of war and the slow pace of technology also give Gethen a female air. The female/male division continues on the individual level, that of the protagonists' relationship: Genly is a man who, like a man confronting a woman, finds Estraven alien because of sexual difference, specifically the presence of female and female-associated traits. In this sense Gethenian Estraven functions as a female to Ekumenical Genly's male, a role that becomes literalized when the Gethenian enters kemmer. His name even sounds like the name of the female hormone "estrogen."

Just as between female Karhide and male Orgoreyn, the relation between female Gethen and the male Ekumen is one of dominant male power. The inhabitants of the more technologically advanced, male union of planets far outnumber those of female Gethen, and Genly's presence on the planet proves that it is possible, if not easy, for outsiders to get there. Gethen as a whole is in a double bind similar to that of Karhide: the planet can escape its position of inferior power only by joining the federation—a gesture that in itself is a form of surrender.

Surprisingly, though, the novel represents the Ekumen's dominant male power much less critically than Orgoreyn's. Heroic Estraven and Genly want Gethen to join the Ekumen, and concern about the power gap is voiced only by characters such as King Argaven, whose jagged paranoia makes his fears seem petty (34). Lest implied readers worry about Ekumenical high-handedness, they are reassured that the interplanetary union has no laws or police; it seeks communication and cooperation, not economic or military conquest. Yet nothing guarantees that the nonintrusive benevolence will persist. The relation of the Ekumen to Gethen resembles that of a man to a woman under chivalry: her safety relies not on her own strength but on his goodwill, so that his very restraint accentuates her relative lack of power.

The Ekumen's dominant male power neither shrinks (like Genly's dominant male focus) nor is criticized by the implied author (like Orgoreyn's dominant male power). Instead the federation's superior strength is oddly glossed over, thus bearing a telling resemblance to the power of Lessing's Providers in *Marriages.* In both cases beings hover, usually unseen, somewhere above the planets, exercising superior power remarkably similar to that of the authors. Lessing's Providers and Le Guin's Ekumenical representatives, like novelists, know more than the characters on the planets do and can in large part control the fate of those characters. Both novels thus have their blind spots, no doubt inevitably, given the intractability of questions involving free will and determinism. Perhaps such beings are needed as a plot device. Or, in the case of *Left Hand,* the Ekumen's dominant male power may simply be part of the text's overall male orientation, which will be explored in the next section.

Male Orientation

Left Hand is widely regarded as a feminist book, but a snag remains: its male orientation, a trait castigated by a number of critics.[36] *Left Hand* does indeed have a male orientation, but I claim that it actually enhances the novel's feminist persuasiveness. In order to unpack this seeming paradox, we first need to review how the book gives such an impression of maleness.

The simplest reason is that women (as opposed to Gethenians in female kemmer) are absent from the main story and most of the interpolated chapters: from the time Genly lands until his shipmates join him just before the end, not a single woman appears on the planet. Furthermore, it would be significant that the voice of a man dominates *Left Hand* as both narrator and character, even if feminism pervaded his words and deeds. In fact, patriarchal beliefs color much of what Genly says and does, thus becoming another source of the novel's male orientation. Just as the Envoy is male and patriarchal, so, as noted, the Ekumen is figuratively male and literally patriarchal (235). Its male orientation matters, both because the voice of its Envoy dominates the novel and because the book's readers, living on Earth as they do, have reason to identify with the federation that represents their planet in the future and is composed of people who resemble them physically. Since *Left Hand* generally gives a positive slant to both the interplanetary union and its representative, the novel might seem to be endorsing their patriarchal beliefs.

Strangely enough, the novel's male undercurrent is so strong that it even seeps into metaphorically female areas: a surprising source of male orientation is that, as real readers have complained, the planet's inhabitants usually seem male, as exemplified in Estraven, the most salient Gethenian character. Even though we have found ways in which he is female in comparison to Genly, in comparison to other Gethenians he has the strongest (metaphorically) male focus: Estraven is the only Gethenian who truly values the male Ekumen, and he stands out from other Karhiders in his efforts to work with their comparatively male rival, Orgoreyn—traits that the novel presents as noble. His figuratively male norms also make it easier for him to earn the Envoy's eventual trust, though if Estraven literally were completely male, heterosexual Genly probably would not fall in love with him. Estraven's male focus, familiar to Genly, may make it easier for the Envoy to observe, "'With you I share one sex, anyhow . . .'" (235). In short, the text fuels its male orientation by casting one and a half of its two heroes as male. Estraven is the extreme case, but other Gethenians often seem male as well, despite Le Guin's intention, their alien physiology, and the types of metaphorical femaleness I have sketched out.[37]

Until Genly at last comes to accept Estraven on the Gobrin Ice-Sheet, the Envoy tends to see the planet's inhabitants as belonging to one sex or the other—usually as male, and so they often seem male to readers. As a patriarchal man, he considers people to be men until they are proven guilty of being women. Only someone such as Genly's "landlady," whom he does not respect and with whom he does not want to identify, rates consistent description as female (48). When Genly occasionally does see Gethenians as female, he is inclined to speak of them, not as such, but with words such as "effeminate" (8), which suggest a defective man.[38] The notion that the generic *is* male also affects which Gethenian activities he chooses to recount in his own chapters and which accounts by other people he selects as other chapters for his report. As Joanna Russ, for instance, has noted, the book gives little information on female-gendered topics such as family structure and childrearing ("The Image of Women," 90).[39]

Nevertheless, in response to one critic who says the Gethenians appear male, Le Guin has written, "Will he, or anyone else, please point out one passage or speech in which Estraven does or says something that *only a man* could or would do or say?" ("Reply to Lem," 91). Representing Gethenians in male-gendered activities can have a feminist influence by showing that non-men can do what our society classifies in the male gender. The book's focus remains male, however, since female-gendered experiences stay in the background.

It is in Genly's choice of words that his perception of Gethenians as male has the strongest impact, for he refers to them consistently with male pronouns and usually with male nouns. Indeed, no perfect alternative exists in English. Among nouns, for instance, mixed terms like "king-bee" (5) provide no general solution, and neutral terms can sound odd—Le Guin cannot substitute "Monarch Argaven XV" for "King Argaven XV." Pronouns are even less tractable than nouns. After ceasing to call Estraven a "person" and starting to call him a "man," Genly comments, "*man* I must say, having said *he* and *his*" (5). Genly's remark testifies to the awareness that "he" and related pronouns call up an image of men, but Le Guin chose male words as the least of a variety of evils ("Reply to Lem," 91). Later regretting the decision, she has proposed other possibilities ("Redux," 15), but in my view the male vocabulary was the best choice, being consistent both with how the Envoy would perceive Gethen and with how he would express what he perceived to his readers in the patriarchal Ekumen. The real author's later regrets show less wisdom than the implied author's decision.

Having surveyed what makes this text seem so male, we can go back to the tougher question of how that orientation serves as one tactic in a larger feminist strategy. The answer lies in belief-bridging: the book needs a male orientation in order to build a bridge to the patriarchal beliefs of its main readers. This orientation gives those readers a comfortable nook in which to feel at home, so that the book's feminist forces do not seem too threatening. As Craig Barrow and Diana Barrow say, in the novelist's audience "lies the key both to her own feminism and the feminist misunderstanding of her contribution to the cause" (84). In 1969, when the book was published, the readers of U.S. science fiction consisted largely of adolescent boys and young men (Pamela Sargent, xiv)—a group that held mostly patriarchal beliefs. Significantly, Le Guin has said: "Since the larger percentage of science fiction readers are male . . . I though [*sic*] it would be easier for them if they had a man—and a rather stupid and slightly bigoted man actually—to work in with and sort of be changed with" (Brookmire, 1155).[40] The real author evinces the same intention here as the implied author does by coupling the book's male orientation with the gradual introduction of pragmatic utopian feminism. The meticulous calibration for patriarchal implied readers means that the novel grates on many feminists, as evidenced by the real readers' complaints mentioned above.[41] *Left Hand* does not ignore feminist readers, and it may reinforce their existing beliefs, but they remain in the background, for the male orientation means that the novel rarely caters to such readers directly. It has a much more specific implied reader than *Marriages* and *Les Guérillères*.

The feminist impulses and the male orientation do not cancel each other out but combine in a compromise that directs the text toward the particular implied readers who stand to benefit from the feminist impulses. In primarily addressing such readers, *Left Hand* is trying to inspire them to take an initial dip into feminism. The implied author does not intend to make feminists swim out farther than they have already. If the novel tried the latter task—or tried to plunge the patriarchal readers in too deeply—it would risk putting off the readers most suspicious of feminism.

How Genre Supports Pragmatic Utopian Feminism: Science Fiction

Unlike *Marriages, Left Hand* fits comfortably into the genre of science fiction. The prominent science-fiction critic Darko Suvin defines science fiction by "*estrangement and cognition*" (*Metamorphoses*, 7–8); both *Marriages* and *Left Hand* offer estrangement (in the sense of distance from ordinary reality), but only Le Guin's book achieves cognition (in terms of a basis in science). To refer to Samuel Delany's terminology, in effect *Marriages* says, "This could not have happened," while *Left Hand* takes the stance typical of science fiction, saying, "This has not happened" ("About Five Thousand Seven Hundred and Fifty Words," 43–44). Another helpful definition is provided by Robert Scholes, who concentrates not on "science fiction" in general but on "structural fabulation": science fiction written by an author capable of measuring up to the genre's "cognitive responsibility to imagine what is not yet apparent or existent, and to examine this in some systematic way" (*Structural Fabulation*, 102). Scholes examines *Left Hand* as one of the chief examples of structural fabulation.

Le Guin's own idea of science fiction as a thought experiment similarly entwines imagination with cognition (Introduction, *Left Hand*, n.p.). "At this point, realism is perhaps the least adequate means of understand-

ing or portraying the incredible realities of our existence. . . . The fanta-
sist [in the broad sense], whether he uses the ancient archetypes of myth
and legend or the younger ones of science and technology, may be talking
as seriously as any sociologist—and a good deal more directly—about
human life as it is lived, and as it might be lived, and as it ought to be
lived" ("National Book Award Acceptance Speech," 58). Le Guin's remark
suggests that, contrary to what some might think, the imaginative nature
of the genre can act against escapism rather than abetting it.

Her science fiction encourages critical, pragmatic thinking in implied
readers.[42] She says: "One of the essential functions of science fiction, I
think, is precisely this kind of question-asking [thought experiments]:
reversals of an habitual way of thinking, metaphors for what our language
has no words for as yet, experiments in imagination" ("Redux," 9). The
pragmatic questioning in *Left Hand* enables it to change implied readers'
beliefs without making bald prescriptions. Significantly, it is this book
whose introduction notes that after reading a novel "we may find—if it's
a good novel—that we're a bit different from what we were before we read
it" (n.p.).

Regardless of the near impossibility of emulating Gethenian physiology,
the book can still inspire readers to question and perhaps change present
reality. It is vital to understand that, while Gethenian society illustrates the
benefits of certain feminist goals, the novel does not suggest that the only
way to reach them is to have Gethenian bodies.[43] Readers who find a goal
appealing may work by other means to achieve it in their own societies.
The improbability of Gethenian physiology actually protects the book
from being read as a blueprint instead of as stimulation to thought.

In case readers doubt that *Left Hand*'s feminism could be achieved by
any means other than biological ones, we should note that Le Guin writes
in the introduction: "The purpose of the thought-experiment, as the term
was used by Schrödinger and other physicists, is not to predict the future
. . . but to describe reality." She applies her idea of science fiction as
descriptive to *Left Hand*: "Yes, indeed the people in it are androgynous,
but that doesn't mean that I'm predicting that in a millennium or so we
will all be androgynous, or announcing that I think we damned well
ought to be androgynous. I'm merely observing, in the peculiar, devious,
and thought-experimental manner proper to science fiction, that if you
look at us at certain odd times of day in certain weathers, we already are"
(Introduction, n.p.). Although I do not consider "androgynous" the best
term to describe Gethenians, the passage does suggest the fundamental

insight that we need not wait for our bodies to morph before we can hope for feminism; in Le Guin's sense we are already ready. *Left Hand*'s thought experiment can nurture change, not by providing a specific goal and instructions on how to reach it, but by opening readers' imaginations to possibility.

Tuned for a young male implied reader with patriarchal beliefs, the novel brings to life the third element of feminism, by asking him and the Envoy to recognize the patriarchal strand in their own beliefs. *Left Hand* then leads them both on a protean journey toward more feminist beliefs, especially multiplicity of focus and equality of power. Various sorts of belief-bridging, including the narrative kind, are deployed to foster openness to otherness, especially to the strangeness of an alien sexuality. The text presents the static utopian feminism of a place, Gethen, but also the pragmatic utopian feminism of travel between places. Le Guin's thought experiment thus welcomes readers to rewrite it.

CHAPTER 8

Monique Wittig's *Les Guérillères*

ALL ACTION IS OVERTHROW
—Monique Wittig (*Les Guérillères*, 5)[1]

Introduction

Set in no place at no time with no protagonist but a band of women with no names (or too many names), and addressed to ambiguously implied readers, Monique Wittig's *Les Guérillères* (1969, translated 1971) is the most challenging of the novels I am discussing. In some ways this tale of Amazonian lesbians does resemble the two more conventional texts: it, too, presents a female society and a male one, then complicates them. Like the other novels, this one introduces four stages of protean metaphor corresponding to various sorts of focus and power. And belief-bridging, especially the narrative kind, is employed to incline readers toward feminism, especially in its pragmatic form.

Yet in other ways Wittig's queer book diverges from the others. First of all, the experimental technique of this well-known *nouveau roman* makes it seductively difficult to grasp. Of particular interest here is the way the novel challenges itself, the way it risks undermining some of the major techniques that *Politics, Persuasion, and Pragmatism* has introduced.[2] At times, for instance, belief-bridging seems to gnaw at itself, demolishing the very values it has been setting up. Meanwhile, protean metaphor crumbles as well: while sometimes reveling in the technique of metaphor, trusted characters at other times censure it sharply, apparently with the implied author's blessing. *Les Guérillères* also problematizes protean development—of metaphors or anything else—because the text's experimental structure dissolves chronological development. As a result of that dissolution and other pressures, narrative energy and pragmatism are deeply threatened. But finally, in many ways paradoxically, these techniques metamorphose into new forms and prove to be necessary even for such a formidable book; in fact they turn out to be especially necessary for such a book. Wittig's novel comes to parallel the others in the force of its feminist persuasion.

Thus this chapter both sums up and opens up the argument I have been making. The novel's elliptical nature means that the chapter is briefer and more speculative than those on the preceding two books. After reviewing the author's feminism and the text's plot and experimental genre, I explain how belief-bridging supports the novel's feminist utopia. The rest of the chapter then explores how *Les Guérillères* puts its feminist persuasion at risk and yet manages to rescue it.

Wittig's Feminism

Monique Wittig is a radical lesbian feminist who was born in France and moved to the United States. In addition to drama, essays, and experimental fiction, she writes texts that defy ordinary genre classification.[3] *The Lesbian Body* mixes the lyrical with the anatomical, and *Lesbian Peoples: Material for a Dictionary* is what Ambrose Bierce might have written if he were a modern-day lesbian. Often her texts transpose male-centered myths, epics, and fairy tales into a female key.

Lesbian feminism undergirds all of Wittig's writings, even her first novel, *The Opoponax*, though initial reviews of it concentrated more on the avant-garde style and the representation of childhood. Her most famous statement, "Lesbians are not women" ("The Straight Mind," 32), does not mean that lesbians lack ovaries or breasts, but that they are not women as our culture defines them, for "women are a class, which is to say that the category 'woman' as well as the category 'man' are political and economic categories not eternal ones. Our fight aims to suppress men as a class, not through a genocidal, but a political struggle. Once the class 'men' disappears, 'women' as a class will disappear as well, for there are no slaves without masters. . . . Lesbian is the only concept I know of which is beyond the categories of sex (woman and man), because the designated subject (lesbian) is *not* a woman. . . . For what makes a woman is a specific social relation to a man" ("One Is Not Born a Woman," 15, 20).

An opponent of *écriture féminine*, Wittig differentiates herself from other French feminists such as Hélène Cixous and Luce Irigaray by emphasizing materialist lesbian analysis and political action. The feminist women in *Les Guérillères*, for instance, say, "[L]et those who call for a new language first learn violence" (85). Yet Wittig cares as fervently as Cixous and Irigaray about language and representation, and her desire to revolutionize language accounts for much of the difficulty of her work ("The Trojan Horse"). In *Les Guérillères*, women living under patriarchy are told: "[T]he language you speak is made up of words that are killing you . . .

[and] of signs that rightly speaking designate what men have appropriat-
ed" (114). Wittig's feminism can be problematic because her materialist
concerns at times clash with her linguistic ones.

The Plot of the Novel

Les Guérillères presents four groups of people: feminist and nonfeminist
women, and patriarchal and nonpatriarchal men.[4] The novel does not say
exactly where they live, much less whether each group has its own country with its own language—or how reproduction occurs. Most of the story
is set among the feminist women, in their all-female utopia.[5] Its women
warriors lead a pastoral life of sensuality and creativity, a life in which
work is integrated with laughter, eroticism with religion. In this lesbian
society, loving oneself and other women calls forth celebration.[6]

Outside the utopia live the nonfeminist women, of unspecified sexuality, whom the utopian women passionately exhort to free themselves.
Another society consists of patriarchal, heterosexual men, with whom the
feminist women are at war and over whom they triumph on the last page
of the book. By the end, the fourth group—the young, formerly patriarchal men, whose sexuality is not mentioned—have joined and been welcomed by the feminist women, who at last celebrate victory and mourn
the dead. Along with this general plot, there are the embedded plots of
the many brief stories that various characters tell.

The utopia's lesbian sexuality is fundamental to the book. This society
is not only all-female, not only a place where women identify with and
focus on women, but also a place where women love, desire, and have sex
with women. The contrast with patriarchal practices and values could
hardly be greater. In addition to practices and values that, by their very
existence, deflate patriarchy, lesbians have unusual potential to understand and critique it.[7] As renée c. hoogland argues, in Western culture the
lesbian occupies neither the female nor the male heterosexual subject
position nor that of the homosexual, conventionally perceived as male:
"Occupying a site of discursive absence, the lesbian subject in Western
culture is invisible, indeed 'unnameable' within the terms of the law.
Concrete, material lesbians nevertheless do raise their voice to speak out
from their impossible positions and thus insist on breaking through the
closed system of patriarchal epistemology. . . . [They] not only call into
question the binary system of a 'natural' heterosexual difference, they also
de-naturalize the very categories of sex, of 'man' and 'woman'" (26).
Furthermore, hoogland observes that the "'queer' perspective" can give

impetus to what I have called pragmatism: "In disrupting the tract of Oedipal desire in which both masculinist and hetero-feminist discourses are deeply, if differently embedded, the lesbian subject of theory may . . . open up possibilities for posing new questions, pursuing new lines of thought, and eventually generate new modes of knowledge" (26). Thus in a variety of ways the lesbianism of Wittig's utopia makes it revolutionary.

Genre and Narrative Structure

Wittig sounds a bit like a science-fiction writer when she tosses in the occasional death-ray weapon (107–8), but she never attempts to give such elements a convincingly scientific aura. In like manner, she toys with the genre of fantasy when she imagines women who sport wings, like those of "giant bats" (132), but such moments seem to grow out of her overall playfulness rather than from the desire to write a full-scale fantasy novel. Death rays, bat wings, and all, *Les Guérillères* seems to fit best in a more experimental genre. The novel's avant-garde nature is hinted at, for example, by the brevity and generality of the plot summary I have given. This experimental form may well be inspired by the book's lesbian themes; lesbian discourse can of course take a variety of forms, but recent theorists have criticized traditional narrative conventions for being heteronormative.[8]

The particular form taken by much of Wittig's experimentalism is based on the French *nouveau roman* (new novel), a genre associated with Alain Robbe-Grillet and Nathalie Sarraute, among others (Wittig, "Quelques Remarques," 117). The *nouveau roman* usually has no conventional plot, characters, or setting. The characters who do appear generally lack rounded identities and are represented with little psychological interiority, often not even a name. Nor does the reader learn details of time or place, history or geography. Instead of characters or context, the genre concentrates on physical objects and on the fact of its own writing.

Les Guérillères has all the *nouveau roman* traits I have touched on, characteristics crucial to understanding Wittig's book. For example, it mostly consists of vignettes less than a page long, separated by gaps of white space, no vignette bearing a clear relation to the one that precedes or follows it. After every few pages, readers encounter a page that is blank except for a list of women's names. The names vary greatly, for they seem to come from France, China, ancient Greece, and a number of other cultures; yet they have a uniform format—each list is entirely in uppercase letters and always occupies the middle of the page.[9] In the same format as the names, two lyric passages are also inserted (5, 143), and the text is further fragmented by the intrusion of three large circles, each on a page by itself (8, 51, 96).

Indeed, circularity in multiple senses is central to the text, which Wittig in "Quelques Remarques" calls an epic "cycle" (119). The letter *O* begins many of the words that the author playfully makes up; the "ospah," for instance, is the "most formidable weapon" of the "Ophidian women the Odonates the Oögones" and so on (103–4). As a traditional female symbol, the circle suits this female society well: the book refers frequently to round shapes, all of which the characters associate early on with the vulval ring (14). Western culture links women more often with the moon than the sun, but this novel reclaims the solar metaphor, at times through non-Western sun goddesses such as the Japanese Amaterasu (26–27).

The circles also suit the nonhierarchical nature of the utopia and the text that represents it: just as King Arthur gave his knights equal status by seating them at a round table, so these circles serve as abstract illustrations of the communal nature of the feminist women's society. Susan Sniader Lanser interprets the book as recounting the development of community, even on the level of narrative voice: although most of the novel is technically in the third person, "this is not the conventional authorial voice that looks down upon and interprets a community. The text avoids the markers that suggest hierarchies of voice" and, in the final vignette, actually shifts to the communal first-person "we" (Lanser, *Fictions of Authority,* 270, 274).[10] Appropriately, not only is there no individual protagonist but rarely is a character even referred to in more than one vignette. The subject of many sentences is female, plural, and unnamed: it is the pronoun *elles,* which is translated as "they" or "the women." This fluidity of the subject—of both grammar and agency—foreshadows the postmodern lesbian described by Cathy Griggers, drawing on the theories of Walter Benjamin, Gilles Deleuze, and Félix Guattari.

Circularity appears in the plot as well as in the characters, prompting Elizabeth A. Meese to say the text "simultaneously attacks the linearity of male sexuality and narration" (128). Except for the last vignette, which is told in *passé simple,* the past tense normally used in French narrative literature, the story is largely recounted in the present tense, which evokes a timeless, unchanging moment—more lyric than narrative. Moreover, actions within a vignette are commonly recounted as if they were habitual or cyclical, as in: the "women visit the market to obtain provisions" (11). The lack of explicit connection between vignettes suggests that they are not necessarily arranged chronologically or in any other progression.

If the plot events are rarely situated in relation to each other, even less often are they located in a specific historical moment, fictional or extrafictional. Because the feminist women build a huge bonfire of objects such as typewriters, ironing boards, and vacuum cleaners (73), one can assume that at least this vignette is set in the twentieth century or later, but the time never gets more precise. Nor does the novel usually locate its happenings geographically. The feminist women and patriarchal men seem to live in separate societies, but nothing is said about the extent of their territory. What *Les Guérillères* does describe, in loving detail, is objects, especially rounded, natural ones: "There are melons water-melons paw-paws avocados green almonds medlars" (11). The other point to which the novel, as a typical *nouveau roman,* devotes itself is self-reflexivity, which we shall explore later in some detail.

How Belief-Bridging Supports the Feminist Utopia

Like *Marriages* and *Left Hand, Les Guérillères* creates a female society and makes it attractive through belief-bridging; unlike the other two, Wittig's novel never significantly undercuts that evaluation. Her text goes beyond the utopia not to uncover its flaws but to situate it, to help define it by what it is not. Perhaps the positive belief-bridging must be directed toward the utopia unflinchingly, despite the risk of stasis, because that society is the most radically unfamiliar of the four in *Les Guérillères.* In any case, its beauty and appeal play a major role in the novel's feminist persuasion.

Ordinary Belief-Bridging

Much of the utopia's attraction comes simply from being a site of pleasure. Awash in colors, scents, sounds, and tastes, the inhabitants spend much of their time singing, dancing, swimming, telling stories, and playing games. The women as much as the girls enjoy a childlike lack of inhibition about their bodies; in fact, in the first vignette the sound of rain causes one woman to urinate, and "some of them form a circle around her to watch the labia expel the urine" (9). Although the novel says surprisingly little about actual sexual activity, the female genitals are frequently both analyzed and extolled: "The women say that in the feminary the glans of the clitoris and the body of the clitoris are described as hooded. It is stated that the prepuce at the base of the glans can travel the length of the organ exciting a keen sensation of pleasure. . . . They compare [the entire genital] to mercury also called quicksilver because of its readiness to expand, to spread, to change shape" (22–23). For real readers who find such pleasures appealing, these details make the utopia seem more attractive.

These delights are carefully underdetermined, for this is no dull, cotton-candy utopia. The women feel grief as well as joy; they get drunk, take drugs (19–20), and confront pain and death in a variety of forms aside from war. While swimming, for instance, "they collide with the floating decaying carcase of an ass, at times the swell of the sea reveals sticky shapeless gleaming lumps of indescribable colour. They say that they shouted with all their might, shedding many tears, complaining that no sea-breeze got up to drive away the smell, supporting under the arms and groins [*sic*] one of them who has fainted, while the vomit accumulates around them on the surface of the water" (10–11).

Belief-bridging goes beyond the characters' pleasure and pain to the very structure of the novel, which privileges the feminist women over the other groups. Their society becomes the standard against which the others are compared, for it is the first that readers encounter and the one to which by far the most pages are devoted. Not until two-thirds of the way through does another group of characters definitively appear; even then, the other groups are always seen through the point of view of the feminist women.

They are the only group referred to by the title, which presents in microcosm some of the novel's main values. Although the term *les guérillères* is very roughly equivalent to "the women warriors," it is finally untranslatable—which is probably why even the English edition bears the French title.[11] Wittig invented the word *guérillère,* basing it on an existing word that sounds the same: *guerrière* (warrior [feminine] or Amazon). But, because her word has only one *r,* it also mirrors *guérisseuse* (healer [feminine]), so that a *guérillère* is a woman associated with curing as well as warring (Lanser, *Fictions of Authority,* 268). Moreover, Wittig's use of a single *r* and her addition of a double *l* recall the French word *guérillero* (guerrilla fighter [masculine only]), an apt term given the feminist women's military operations "without orders" (102).

The double *l* in *guérillère* has a subtler connotation as well, for in French grammar it often marks feminine gender. For example, if the masculine form of an adjective or noun ends in *-l* (e.g., *cruel*), the feminine form ends in *-lle* (*cruelle*). The third-person pronouns follow a similar pattern: *il* (he) contrasts with *elle* (she), and *ils* (they [masculine]) with *elles* (they [feminine]).[12] So the phallic singularity of one *l* contrasts with the female or feminist duality of the double *l*—a pattern also conjured up in

"When Our Lips Speak Together," where Irigaray contrasts the singular phallus with dual lips, oral and genital.

In fact, those who read the French version find that the word *elles* pervades the entire book, a practice Wittig explains in "The Mark of Gender" as an effort "not to feminize the world but to make the categories of sex obsolete in language" (85).[13] As mentioned, the protagonist is *elles*—not a proper noun, not even a common noun, but a pronoun, and a plural one at that. Almost every vignette about the feminist women is phrased in terms of what *elles* are doing. Since English has no gendered form of "they," no perfect translation is possible. Usually David Le Vay, who translated *Les Guérillères* into English, renders *elles* as "the women," a solution that preserves the plural and female meanings but loses some of the pronoun's *nouveau roman* generality and undermines the author's attempt to give it the universality ordinarily enjoyed by *ils*.[14] Wittig says he instead should have used "they," which "is not only a collective pronoun but . . . also immediately develops a degree of universality which is not immediate with *elles*" ("Mark," 86). Oddly, she ignores the fact that Le Vay sometimes does employ "they," solving one problem but introducing a new one, since it is not always clear if "they" refers to women or men. In the French original, however, the presence of the plural form and the double *l*, both in the title and in the ubiquitous *elles*, reinforce the novel's privileging of the feminist women.

While belief-bridging works in all these ways to make the feminist women seem impressive, it makes the other three groups seem less so. As the enemies of the feminist women, the patriarchal men are by definition accorded less value, a status that falls still lower when the women criticize them, as for their "ineffectual" strategy and tactics (94). If the "glenuri" (pets with "long filiform bodies") are metaphors for patriarchal men and their phalluses, then such men also receive a subtler, more satirical critique: the glenuri "constantly endeavour to move away to some place other than where they are. . . . [T]hey systematically insinuate themselves into any interstice that affords passage to their bodies, for example, the gates of public gardens, the grills of drains. They enter these backwards, . . . they find themselves trapped, they begin to utter frightful shrieks. Then they have to be freed" (22). The other two groups, while not mocked, are not ideal either. The nonfeminist women are often called slaves by the utopian women and are occasionally accused of complicity in their own degradation (115–16). The nonpatriarchal men receive praise, but only for joining the feminist women. And so the utopia retains its superior value.

Narrative Belief-Bridging

One of the assumptions behind narrative belief-bridging is that, without evidence to the contrary, the implied reader tends to consider the author worthy of some trust or admiration. In *Les Guérillères* one way the feminist women appeal to the implied reader is through their resemblance to authors, especially the implied author of this particular novel. Just as the writer of this *nouveau roman* is an aesthetic revolutionary, so they are political revolutionaries. And, absorbed with twining together memory and invention, they are storytellers like her. Just as she is transforming the epic genre, so they are transforming myths and fairy tales: the "golden fleece," for instance, here refers explicitly to pubic hair (44).

What is more, the feminist women actually write books, printing "feminaries" of feminist wisdom that include blank pages on which the women sometimes write (14–15). A feminary looks much like *Les Guérillères* itself: "Essentially, it consists of pages with words printed in a varying number of capital letters. There may be only one or the pages may be full of them. Usually they are isolated at the centre of the page, well spaced black on a white background or else white on a black background" (15).[15] In addition, the women write in and read from the "great register," which also is akin to *Les Guérillères*: "[I]t is useless to open it at the first page and search for any sequence. One may take it at random and find something one is interested in" (53)—hypertext *avant la lettre*. The notion of readers as writers also extends outside the novel: since some of the women who read the great register and the feminaries also write in them, and since those texts resemble *Les Guérillères,* the novel's implied author is intimating that its implied readers in turn can continue unbroken the cycle of readers as writers, writing in the text's many blank spaces, writing about it, or writing more texts like it.[16]

Being verbal artists like the implied author, the feminist women not only rely heavily on metaphorical discourse but also discuss the technique: "They say that vulvas have been compared to apricots pomegranates figs roses pinks peonies marguerites. They say these comparisons may be recited like a litany" (32). Finally, it is also as feminist rhetoricians that the women have a good deal in common with the implied author: their attempt to influence the nonfeminist women parallels her attempt to sway implied readers. Because the utopian women's persuasion is addressed to "you" and because the nonfeminist characters are not particularized, the persuasion reaches out from the text as if to embrace the implied readers along with the characters being addressed.

In fact, though we cannot definitely pin down whom the text is addressing, this parallel gives a clue that nonfeminist women may be among Wittig's implied readers. Nonfeminist women readers would be best placed to benefit from the critique of patriarchy and to be stirred by the feminist utopia's attractions. Men are less likely than women to read this book; indeed, patriarchal men are probably what I have called negatively implied readers, although those who had never before seriously thought about women's subordination might be inspired by *Les Guérillères* to consider changing their ways. The text may be attempting to persuade men who have the potential to be, or are, nonpatriarchal, but they play a smaller role than nonfeminist women, both as characters and implied readers: the novel includes no persuasion directly addressed to them, and it expresses a good deal of hostility toward men, animosity that would be hard for a man to ignore even if he felt it were addressed only to men different from himself. Finally, the implied readers may include feminist women, women who—despite the lack of a utopia like Wittig's—nonetheless manage to share at least some of the beliefs of her utopian women. For such readers the book would have the effect of confirming or refining or radicalizing existent beliefs rather than arguing for new ones. These varied possibilities for implied readers may all be in play, since, as explained earlier, a text can have multiple ones, each of whom is addressed in a different manner.

Ultimately, though, whether implied readers are female or not, or feminist or not, the most crucial trait demanded of them by this novel may be tolerance, perhaps enthusiasm, for the rigors of the *nouveau roman*. When I have taught *Les Guérillères,* my students have proved remarkably open to its formal challenges, but that may be because the course was about narrative theory, which tends to attract that sort of real reader. In contrast, *Left Hand,* with its less difficult but still complex structure, has drawn complaints from students in a science-fiction course, presumably because such a course does not particularly attract readers with a taste for daunting narrative form.

How Feminist Persuasion Is Put at Risk

Endangering Belief-Bridging

In spite of the positive belief-bridging that links the feminist women to pleasure and the implied author and gives their utopia prominence in the narrative structure, at times they are linked to values that would find fewer matches among those of real readers. For instance, the feminist women are occasionally cruel to animals (34), a trait that presumably would attract a few real readers but would repel many more. In more complex examples, the novel associates the utopian women with rage and violence against the patriarchal men.

Some other texts make antiwar sentiment a fundamental value of their utopia, with the result that battling to defend it would entail a double bind such as that faced by Karhide in *Left Hand,* but such a sentiment does not really characterize the utopia in *Les Guérillères*. Although the feminist women's violence will repel readers who believe wars are always wrong, it will not turn away readers who believe wars like this one are just. Even the latter group may nevertheless be appalled when the feminist women break the rules of war, as when they "slaughter" men who have made "signs of surrender" (103). Sometimes male prisoners are mocked: "When they have a prisoner they strip him and make him run through the streets crying, it is your rod/cane/staff/wand/peg skewer/staff of lead" (106). In the most extreme vignette, some men are tortured, and their skins are exhibited "with labels that record the name of their former proprietors or that recall their most striking catch-phrases. It forms a subject of unending humour among them" (110). While some real readers will find the rage, even the violence, exhilarating, others will find them repugnant.

One could argue that the rage and violence are only unfortunate means to a laudable end and are rejected once that end is achieved; after all, near the close of the book the feminist women say to the nonpatriarchal men, "[L]et us repeat as our slogan that all trace of violence must disappear from this earth" (127). Yet, as I shall argue in a moment, the novel's chronology is so tangled that we cannot be sure that the war really has ended and therefore that violence is definitively renounced. The issue is further complicated by the fact that the specific group at war consists of women, rather than some other traditionally subordinated group. Since many patriarchal societies have forbidden women in particular not only violence but even anger, the very presence of violence and anger in the novel can serve as a feminist move, as it does in much of Joanna Russ's work. On the other hand, many feminists, such as those in peace movements, consider most violence a male norm from which feminism can free people, not something that feminism should claim for women. It is not my purpose here to go through the complex feminist debates on this subject; I simply want to indicate that, by introducing violence and anger, the novel is risking its belief-bridging, not only for real readers who are non-feminist or male but also for those who are feminist or female.

Sometimes it is narrative belief-bridging that is undone. For example, despite the exuberant inventiveness with which the feminist women have multiplied metaphors for the parts of their bodies, at several points the women reject such figurative language. It may seem that they are eschewing only those that are conventional: "They do not say that the vulva is the primal form which as such describes the world in all its extent, in all its movement. They do not in their discourses create conventional figures derived from these symbols" (61). Or perhaps they are simply rejecting comparisons invented by other people: "I shall not rest my tired body before this earth to which I was so often compared" (126). Or they may just be dismissing metaphors based on binary oppositions: "The women say that they have been given as equivalents the earth the sea tears that which is humid that which is black that which does not burn that which is negative those who surrender without a struggle. They say this is a concept which . . . deploys a series of terms which are systematically related to opposite terms. Its theses are so crass that the thought of them makes the women start laughing violently" (78, 80).

Yet the utopian women also renounce their own metaphors: "The women say that they perceive their bodies in their entirety. They say that they do not favour any of its parts on the grounds that it was formerly a forbidden object. . . . They do not say that the vulvas are like black suns in the shining night" (57–58). It does make sense to decry these metaphors for fragmenting and objectifying female bodies, but the critique—especially in the beauty of its "black suns," a metaphor under erasure—risks causing a pang in the implied readers, who may well be sorry to lose such verbal artistry. The revolution is turning against its own symbols, a move that can put off even the most revolutionary reader. Similarly, when the utopian women propose burning patriarchal books because "everything has to be remade" (134), that plan threatens to alienate those who, as readers, find book-burning repugnant, whether or not they like patriarchal writings. Even more disturbingly, at another point the feminist women say "that it may be that the feminaries have fulfilled their function" and should be burned (49). It is especially shocking to propose burning books that so closely resemble the one that readers hold in their hands.[17]

One could hypothesize that these instances of undoing belief-bridging simply represent underdetermination, an attempt to prevent the utopia from seeming annoyingly perfect. But that explanation falters. Sometimes, as with the cruelty to animals, the implied author fails to acknowledge that the women are doing anything questionable, and thus perfection is not effectively undercut. At other times it is too effectively undercut: when the women reject metaphors and feminaries, they themselves acknowledge that they are overthrowing previous practice, but in doing so they are attacking some of the strongest narrative belief-bridging on which the utopia's appeal was built. Perhaps when *Les Guérillères* unravels its belief-bridging, it is merely taking a step in a pragmatic development, the tearing down of one model in order to replace it with another. Yet, because of the ambiguous chronology, the novel seems less to develop than to oscillate: between exalting something like metaphor or violence as a means and repudiating it as an end. The nagging contradiction is reminiscent of those we found earlier, when Lessing's Providers and Le Guin's Ekumen functioned as anti-authoritarian authorities.

Endangering Protean Metaphor

Although, as explained below, the novel employs protean metaphor, the technique is threatened—first from the metaphorical side, by the rejection just mentioned. The device is threatened even more strongly from the protean side. In *Marriages* and *Left Hand,* we observed protean metaphors undergoing transformations that become steps in an argument as the plot travels from one stage to another. In *Les Guérillères* something different happens: because the plot does not follow a clear chronology, it has no distinct stages, and so the metaphor's protean changes and the stages of the argument are indistinct. Perhaps because the final vignette shows the women in triumph, critics tend to write as if the text contained at least one complete narrative action—a war won by the feminist women.[18] In a later essay Wittig herself writes of the war as singular, but with a twist: in order to establish *elles* as the "sovereign subject," "two-thirds of the text had to be totally inhabited, haunted, by *elles*," and that portion had to come first, with the circular result that "the chronological beginning of the narrative—that is, the total war—found itself in the third part of the book, and the textual beginning was in fact the end of the narrative" ("Mark," 85). Whether a single war follows the utopian period, as most critics imply, or whether the utopian period follows a single war, as the real author says in describing the war as a flashback, both interpretations are tempting. Closer examination reveals, however, that the implied author is doing something more radical: vignettes before the final one have also announced victory, only to be followed by others describing continued fighting (e.g., 128).

Implied readers are faced with three unsatisfying choices in interpreting the chronology. According to the first, only one war, with only one conclusion, has been fought, and many of the vignettes concerning the war simply appear in the wrong order. This interpretation is satisfying insofar as it involves a single, well-defined narrative event, but a problem arises: if readers point to the final segment as evidence of a conclusive outcome, then they are inconsistently exempting that vignette from suspicion, as if it occupied its proper place while all the others were scrambled. Because it is written in the literary past tense rather than the present, it does differ from the rest, but the very nature of that difference implies that perhaps it should come before, not after, the rest.

Another, more consistent interpretation is possible: the order of the vignettes may correspond to the order of events, in which case every previous victory has been followed by the outbreak of a new war. Thus, the triumph at the end of the book is final only in the sense that narration stops there. Presumably, wars will surge forth again, phoenix-like. Thirdly, readers may decide that *all* the segments are jumbled. Here it is impossible to decide whether one war or many have been fought; since readers are assuming that it is arbitrary to represent victory in the last vignette, they are letting go of the sole piece of evidence that only one war has taken place. The triumph on the last page now seems like a parody of closure. Because the book presents an undecidable chronology, it presents no plot stages on which to build stages of a persuasive argument.

How Feminist Persuasion Is Reborn: Mappings of Protean Metaphor

Yet an argument does emerge. As in the other novels I examine, readers go through four stages of feminist persuasion, in which a binary opposition between the sexes is set up and then deconstructed.[19] In this novel, however, the argument is based not on the characters' actions, the order of which we do not know, but on the order in which readers come upon descriptions of those actions. In the other novels, each stage corresponds to a place or to a relationship between places; here, each stage corresponds to a society with no definite place. Readers of Lessing's and Le Guin's texts usually follow a traveler who is a major character, such as Al·Ith or Genly, as that person travels from place to place; in Wittig's novel, since there are no major characters and no clear places, that traveler is the reader, who is in effect going from society to society. A new stage begins when the reader comes upon a new society, so that the sequence corresponds to a reader's time rather than a character's time and space. In *Marriages* and *Left Hand,* each stage is discrete, bounded; in *Les Guérillères,* while vignettes from a given stage do tend to cluster together, those from one stage are sometimes interspersed with those from another. And no stage has a clear endpoint.

Stage One: Putting Sex on the Map

The book opens in the feminist women's fanciful utopia, which metaphorically represents women, not only because it is all-female but also because it possesses feminist values—evident from the start in its strong, self-confident inhabitants and most fully articulated later, in speeches to rouse the nonfeminist women. Power relations within the utopia are egalitarian; we read nothing of a government or other potential hierarchy. Occasionally a particular woman stands out by writing in a feminary or telling a story, but then another follows her, as if in a circular rotation of power.

The utopia's feminist focus takes several forms, beginning with multiplicity. The sexes are not literally multiple, but almost everything else is, and copiously so: the circles, the metaphors for the vulva, the lists of names, the storytellers and their stories, the epic catalogs of objects. The sense of multiplicity is enriched because the items in the various lists are rarely separated by commas. Even the phoenix, of which there is by definition only one, becomes multiple—and twice over: "THE PHOENIX-ES THE PHOENIXES" (5). In another sense the focus during Stage One is female singularity, for no men are mentioned and traditionally female-associated norms, particularly the female body, are visible and valued. When patriarchal men do appear, in the next stage, the focus becomes female centrality, for at that point men are the enemy, and things male may be visible but not valued. The feminist women at times evince a focus of duality later in the book, after the nonpatriarchal men have joined them.

Stage Two: A Remapping

After getting to know the feminist women well, readers are introduced to the next group, the patriarchal men. The two groups truly form a binary opposition: they differ in sex, they possess diametrically opposed beliefs, and they are literally at war. Stage Two comes to the fore about two-thirds of the way through the book, which only then makes explicit that the women are battling men (97), but innumerable hints appear long before.

Granted, each could conceivably have another explanation: a male army may represent allies instead of enemies (94), and so on. But the frequency of such hints keeps increasing, until the following passage explosively removes any doubts (and reveals that these men, even when threatened, just don't get it): "The women say that they could not eat hare veal or fowl, they say that they could not eat animals, but man, yes, they may. He says to them throwing his head back with pride, poor wretches of women, if you eat him who will go to work in the fields, who will produce food consumer goods, who will make the aeroplanes, who will pilot them, who will provide the spermatozoa, who will write the books, who in fact will govern? Then the women laugh, baring their teeth to the fullest extent" (97).

Since the entire book is apparently written from the point of view of the feminist women, we never learn what the patriarchal men say or think among themselves, but passages such as this one indicate these men have a focus of male singularity that, challenged by the feminist women, is grudgingly shifting to male centrality. As for patterns of power, the glimpses we get indicate that inequality prevails among the men themselves: their armies, for instance, "are not formidable, their effectives being conscript, participation not being voluntary" (94). Over the women in their society, the men of course exercise dominant male power; in relation to the utopian women, the patterns of power are more ambiguous. Several vignettes mock the patriarchal men's way of fighting (e.g., 94), and, if one believes that the feminist women actually win the war, then such clues point to dominant female power. But other vignettes reveal the terrible losses the utopian women suffer, and, as we have found, they may not win the war anyway. The two groups diverge so drastically that perhaps their power relation should be characterized as difference rather than inequality.

Stage Two injects otherness and narrative energy into the novel, since the patriarchal men and the feminist women differ profoundly, a difference made vivid in their bloody war. This otherness gives an edge to the utopia, both in the sense of providing a conceptual, if not geographical, borderline—showing that the utopia does not exist everywhere—and in the sense of permitting the utopia to prove that it has a tough side and is not saccharine or solipsistic. Although this *nouveau roman* never truly acknowledges history, Stage Two brings in a taste of it. Perhaps the utopia did not always exist, and this war echoes one in the past that was needed to bring the feminist society into existence. Or perhaps the war points to a possible future, indicating that without vigilance the utopia could be annihilated.

Stage Three: Another Remapping

The remaining two stages deconstruct the binary opposition set up in the preceding, lengthier stages. Complicating the earlier female/male opposition, Stages Three and Four encourage anti-essentialist, pragmatic rethinking of earlier categories, and, by introducing female and male categories beyond the original two, evoke multiplicity. Stage Three, which begins about three-fifths of the way through the book (88–89), brings in the nonfeminist women.[20] By introducing women quite unlike those in Stage One, this stage makes plain that differently situated women hold different beliefs.[21]

Feminist persuasion permeates all the novels on which this study concentrates, but Stage Three of *Les Guérillères* is the most extended section in any of them in which such persuasion is addressed by some characters to others. While doing so, the feminists give a devastating description of patriarchy (and thus add to readers' information on the patriarchal men introduced in the previous stage). While Stage One made a strong, lyrical, indirect appeal *for* feminism, this stage makes an equally strong, enraged, direct attack *against* patriarchy: "He has stolen your wisdom from you, he has closed your memory to what you were, he has made of you that which is not which does not speak which does not possess which does not write, he has made of you a vile and fallen creature, he has gagged abused betrayed you" (110–11).

The feminist women criticize patriarchal essentialism: "The women say, the men have kept you at a distance, . . . constructed with an essential difference. They say, men in their way have adored you like a goddess or else burned you at their stakes or else relegated you to their service in their back-yards. . . . They say, they have described you as they described the races they called inferior" (100–102). The feminists also excoriate patriarchal language: "The women say, unhappy one, men have expelled you from the world of symbols and yet they have given you names. . . . They write, of their authority to accord names, that it goes back so far that the origin of language itself may be considered an act of authority emanating from those who dominate" (112–14).

In spite of such disturbingly graphic descriptions, the power and focus of the nonfeminist society are difficult to discern, for these women's own words almost never appear. Most of the time their beliefs can just be inferred through the utopian women's speeches, since presumably the feminists try to persuade the nonfeminists only of beliefs that the latter currently lack. Of course, living under patriarchy means that they live under dominant male power and focus, but the nonfeminist women do not necessarily approve of their situation. The feminists do sometimes condemn the nonfeminists for accepting their condition: "They say, you strut about, you have no other care than to enjoy the good things your masters hand out, solicitous for your well-being so long as they stand to gain" (135). At such moments it seems that the nonfeminists share their oppressors' patriarchal beliefs about power and focus and are being reproached for it. Like the long passages just quoted, however, most vignettes in this stage imply that these women simply lack what I have called the third feminist element, the ability to recognize a patriarchal society. Such passages suggest the listeners hold beliefs antipatriarchal enough that, once they recognize their condition as patriarchal, they will condemn it.

At still other moments, it appears that they lack just the fourth feminist element, the belief that action can successfully resist patriarchy. To attain that belief, they must first be able to imagine themselves existing without patriarchy, a vision created in the very first address to nonfeminist women: "Elsa Brauer says something like, There was a time when you were not a slave, remember that. You walked alone, full of laughter, you bathed bare-bellied" (89). Conjuring up a utopian past could fill the nonfeminists with yearning for a different life and could give them hope, by indicating that such a life has been and can be possible, even for women like themselves. The vignette ends, "Make an effort to remember. Or, failing that, invent" (89). Imagination, too, can inspire resistance.

The feminists also mention specific resources for resistance: "Whatever [men] have not laid hands on . . . does not appear in the language you speak, . . . [in] the intervals that your masters have not been able to fill with their words of proprietors and possessors, . . . the gaps, in all that which is not a continuation of their discourse, in the zero, the O, the perfect circle that you invent to imprison them and to overthrow them" (114). Instead of referring to a past—remembered or invented—this speech calls attention to forms of power the nonfeminists already have in the present, techniques that can help them in the future. In particular, the speech epitomizes the sort of revaluation that runs through the entire novel, pointing out that what patriarchal eyes see as nothingness can in fact be strength. Like "The Blank Page" of Isak Dinesen, the blanks that overrun the pages of this volume have something to say. And its circles, even when read as the digit meaning nothing, recall the power the Arabic placeholder brought to Western mathematics and the indispensable role played by zero in the binary code of computers, which ultimately rely on the contrast between the upright one and the rounded zero.

Despite the poignant, fierce persuasion addressed to the nonfeminist women, the novel does not actually show any of them joining the utopia. In a few vignettes, however, the persuasion seems to be at least sparking revolt: "They say . . . that although laughter is the prerogative of man, they want to learn how to laugh. . . . They say they are leaving the museums the show-cases the pedestals where they have been installed" (124–26). Significantly, in recounting this step toward feminism, the passage uses the same phrase for these women that is used so often for the feminists: "they say" (*elles disent*). The pronoun associated with the nonfeminists has gone from singular and genderless (*tu*) to plural and feminine (*elles*); and, like the utopian women, they are "saying"—they are brandishing language. Thus, one group of women starts to resemble the other both in their feminism and in the discourse that refers to them. Such moments bring in a whiff of temporality, as if the nonfeminist women might join the utopia in the future, or equivalent persuasion in the past might have convinced women to create the utopia in the first place.

Oddly enough, at times the deployment of "*elles disent*" brings up the possibility not just that the nonfeminists are starting to resemble the feminists but that the two groups are really one. In one vignette, for instance, the first "*elles disent*" apparently refers to the feminists, the second to the nonfeminists: "They say, we must disregard all the stories relating to those of them who have been betrayed. . . . They say, we must disregard the statements we have been compelled to deliver contrary to our opinion" (134). If Stage Three is to represent one group literally speaking to the other, they cannot actually be identical, but the blurring of the boundary between them does serve to create other effects, such as breaking down the opposition between the groups, revealing the possibility of shared traits and even solidarity between them. Indeed, as we have observed, possibly the nonfeminist women were once feminists or the feminists were once nonfeminists. Or the blurring may represent the struggle between feminist and nonfeminist thoughts within a single individual who ostensibly belongs only to one group or the other. Finally, if the abrasive degree of vehemence with which the feminist women address the nonfeminists has been annoying some real readers, placing them in a negatively implied relationship with implied readers, then recognizing the fuzzy boundary between the novel's two groups of women may lessen that annoyance and move those real readers closer to matching the implied ones.

Stage Four: A Different Remapping

In the last stage readers meet the nonpatriarchal men, the young men who willingly join the feminist women. Although this stage appears only briefly, and four-fifths of the way through the book (122), it plays a compelling role in the feminist argument. Like the previous stage, this one works against essentialism. Before opening a book about battles between women and men, one might expect it to polarize the two, but *Les Guérillères* presents differences between old and young men, between feminist and nonfeminist women, and even among feminist women. So while sexual difference is accorded its due, it is nonetheless regarded pragmatically, and different kinds of difference are also introduced. Stage Four goes still further than Stage Three, reminding us that people can act out of motives other than narrow self-interest, that men can turn to feminism. In fact, this stage even implies that feminism is in men's broader self-interest, for the utopian women tell the young men, "we have been fighting as much for you as for ourselves" (127).

Although the young men are not described in enough detail to reveal their precise beliefs about power and focus, those beliefs are represented as feminist ones. The men certainly object to dominant male power—consider a statement one of them apparently wrote earlier: "When the world changes and one day women are capable of seizing power and devoting themselves to the exercise of arms and letters . . . , I am certain they will pay us out a hundredfold. . . . We shall richly deserve it" (135). After the young men have come to the utopia, power relations there follow feminist patterns—at certain times unequal, with women dominating, and at other times equal: for example, sometimes the women teach the men, whereas at other times the "women choose names with the men for the things round about them" (137).

As for focus, the nonpatriarchal men are not afraid to act according to norms conventionally associated with women, almost reversing roles: "The women cry out and run towards the young men arms laden with flowers which they offer them. . . . Some of the women pulling quantities of heads off the flowers . . . throw them in their faces. The men shake their hair and laugh, moving away from the women and coming nearer again. Some run away and let themselves fall down limply, eyes closed, hands outstretched. Others are completely hidden by the heaps of flowers the women have thrown over them" (122–23). Female centrality again appears when the men are described as having traits such as long hair and smooth, round faces, which our society commonly considers female (142, 138). Meanwhile, the focus I have called similar duality is invoked at the moments when, for example, the two groups dress alike (124).

While we are told these men used to be enemies of the female utopia (131), we never learn exactly how or when they acquired their nonpatri-archal beliefs, nor whether they will live from now on in the utopia. We do find out that they will join the feminist women in their struggle "to transform the world" (128), but it is not specified whether the struggle will be a continuation of the fighting against the patriarchal men or another sort of effort still needed after that one, such as erasing it "from human memory" (127). Especially since the chronology of the wars or war tends to flicker, it seems that the young men are joining the feminists in some cases during the conflict (141), in other cases after the feminists have won (142), and in still other cases after a war has ended in an unspecified way (127–28).

Whatever the nature of the future struggle, it will be a struggle, for, despite the utopian imagery of flowers and embraces (142), this will not be a static future. The very act of selecting names "for the things round about them," of redoing Adam's work, will transmute their world. The novel's most sustained representation of people who have changed their minds, this stage especially encourages hope for transformation. While brief, Stage Four occupies a strategic location near the end of the novel, connoting hope for the readers' future, for the time that begins at the moment they close the book. As the four mappings have established, while protean metaphor is put at risk, *Les Guérillères* ultimately does man-age to employ the technique in its own way, accomplishing a pragmatic deconstruction of the female/male opposition that it originally construct-ed.

How Feminist Persuasion Is Reborn: Narrative Energy and Pragmatism

The back cover of an early U.S. edition (1973) hails *Les Guérillères* as "a beautiful, wildly exciting story," but actually the novel often risks being anything but "wildly exciting." Nancy Gray refers to the "near-stasis of much of the first half of the text" (167), and indeed a large percentage of the book describes a utopia homogeneous in sex, sexuality, and feminist belief—a utopia seemingly unrippled by deep problems and never seriously criticized by the text. The narrative also threatens to stumble to a halt because of its *nouveau roman* traits, such as the catalogs of objects and vulval metaphors, the large quantities of white space, and the intrusion of pages containing nothing but a circle, a list of women's names, or a lyric passage in upper-case letters. Such items arrest the movement of implied readers' attention; any momentum that has grown within or between vignettes comes to a halt. Even the plot events that are recounted are broken into separate vignettes in indeterminate order. Stories told by characters last only the duration of a vignette, not time enough to build up force. The lack of an ordinary protagonist and of a distinct setting in time or place leaves readers with little to cling to.

Yet in certain ways the novel does generate energy (see Tucker, chap. 7). Strangely enough, the utopia itself produces some: it may be internally homogeneous in the ways just described, but it veers sharply from conventional homogeneity, being not male, patriarchal, and heterosexual, but female, feminist, and lesbian. Furthermore, as we have observed, within the utopia can be found the unusual multiplicity of *elles,* plural. Nor does uniformity reign among *elles;* narrative tension results when occasional disagreements arise among them (e.g., 76) and when they pragmatically question their metaphors and feminaries. Of course, much of the book also concerns confrontations between the utopia's inhabitants and others: the war against the patriarchal men and the efforts to persuade the non-feminist women. Conflict also enters through fleeting references to pre-utopian feminist struggles (39). Thus, in a range of ways, despite its unconventional form, the novel manages to spark narrative energy through the conventional means of conflict.

In addition, the very circle that drains narrative energy can also feed it. A circle need not represent static, enclosed space: "The system is closed. . . . At the same time it is without limit, the juxtaposition of the increasingly widening circles configures every possible revolution. It is virtually that infinite sphere whose centre is everywhere, circumference nowhere" (69). Even when interpreted as a zero, the circle becomes a sign not of lack but of total revolution: "They say that they are starting from zero. They say that a new world is beginning" (85). Although one picture of a circle appears near the beginning of the book, none symmetrically appears near the end to signify closure. Nor need a circle per se mean closure: instead of presenting the circle as the border of a limited, contained space, this novel turns the figure inside out, reminding us that every circle also borders the unlimited space outside it. The novel associates the circle with the vulval ring, not with the womb: with a place of repeated erotic excitement, not with a place of repose that one leaves in a single unrepeatable act.[22] Furthermore, every circle encloses an infinite number of points and in fact consists of infinite points itself, as if the endless number of female characters joined hands.

A circle need not stand still; after joining hands, those characters can move in a dance (93). Like the cycle of seasons or the life cycle of a phoenix, a circle can rotate, from peace to war—or from a vignette of peace to a vignette of war—and around again. The French original actually calls the dancers' movement "*révolution*" (133), a term with political connotations as well, since "THE WOMEN AFFIRM IN TRIUMPH THAT ALL ACTION IS OVERTHROW" (5). Furthermore, like a hoop spinning through the air (60), the rotation can travel, so that each rotation is different, each vignette differing from the others. The story is set in motion—even by circularity, which proves to be not only a static hindrance to the narrative but also a pragmatic energy source for it.[23]

The final, most crucial source of narrative energy lies not in the text but in its interaction with implied readers, for the same experimental techniques that hobble the plot serve to create a plot of another sort, the drama of those readers' attempts to figure out the puzzles presented by *Les Guérillères*.[24] Implied readers, as noted above, can never know how many wars the utopian society has fought, but narrative interest is galvanized by the very attempt to come up with alternative models that might solve the riddle. By teasing readers, by denying them definitive closure on the last page, the text encourages them to continue pragmatic thinking after closing the book.

This critical process occurs not just in response to relatively simple questions such as the number of wars, but also regarding more complex issues such as the novel's contradictory belief-bridging. The difficulty of the process is part of the lesson: the rigors of revolutions should not be underestimated. Thus, *Les Guérillères* draws narrative energy from a variety of sources, ironically including some of the very elements, such as circularity, that threatened to drain it. The experimental techniques call forth a critically pragmatic attitude about storytelling itself as well as about the events of this particular story. Implied readers are taught a pragmatic process of thinking, both specifically, during the four stages that deconstruct the female/male opposition, and more generally, during confrontations with the novel's disquieting unconventionality (see Zerilli, 17).

Is this novel more dynamic and challenging than Lessing's and Le Guin's? While precise quantification is of course impossible, we can make some general comparisons. In terms of pragmatic feminism, all three narratives deny readers a comfortable ending: the novels imply that the characters will continue their pragmatic questioning long after the time represented in the book. In terms of narrative technique, however, *Les Guérillères* is certainly more experimental than the other two, because it attacks not only patriarchy but also conventional discourse, including ordinary narrative technique. It may seem, then, that Wittig's book succeeds better than the others in carrying the energy of its feminist pragmatism to the narrative level. We should remember, though, that *Les Guérillères* also has more stasis to compensate for—more homogeneity, fragmentation, and lyricism. The bolder experimentation dissipates much of the energy that would animate a normal novel, and so the extreme stasis and extreme dynamism may balance each other out. Compared to *Marriages* and *Left Hand,* Wittig's novel does evince greater pragmatism about narrative technique in general, but its narrative energy and pragmatic feminism roughly equal theirs.

Conclusion

If telling was the skill of the maz, listening was the skill of the yoz. As they all liked to remark, neither one was any use without the other.
—Ursula K. Le Guin (*The Telling* 123)

Having examined *Marriages, Left Hand,* and *Les Guérillères* during a journey on which we have met with the enigmatic Providers, a pregnant king, and warrior women with bat wings, we can now draw together some of these disparate elements by turning back to the central question I posed early in this study: how does persuasion work in feminist utopias? *Politics, Persuasion, and Pragmatism* has attempted to answer the question by delving into the specific details of how such persuasion, often taken for granted, actually functions.

After defining utopias, in both their static and their pragmatic modes, and after defining the varied facets of feminism, including power and focus, I have described how feminist utopian narratives strive to persuade readers by changing their beliefs. Implied authors build bridges from their beliefs to those of implied readers, and, to the extent that those implied readers are in turn matched by real readers, real beliefs can change. Such theories contribute to understanding how texts make a belief appealing by, for example, building a bridge to feminism from implied readers' passion for narrative.

We have also observed how some novels—such as *Marriages, Left Hand,* and *Les Guérillères*—also employ protean metaphor to guide readers step by step through a feminist argument. Thus, protean metaphor is one of the pragmatic ways these novels cope with the threat of stasis and boredom, not by retreating from utopia but by going to a more lively and achievable form of it. In particular, readers are invited to find their own means to the feminist ends presented in the texts. Although I have provided definitions of terms, I have tried to offer various possibilities within some of those definitions. I have steered away from imposing some grand scheme on the novels and instead have striven to account for their narrative energy, their metamorphoses, their specificity: hence my emphasis on stages and the protean—in short, on pragmatism.

Overall, this volume has attempted to present devices that are important in subtle literary persuasion, as exemplified in these feminist utopian narratives that go beyond stasis to pragmatism. The conclusion will now briefly touch on three issues: certain unexpected generalizations that we can make in retrospect about the novels, extensions of the theories to a more recent novel, and speculations on directions for future work.

Looking back over Lessing's, Le Guin's, and Wittig's novels, we can now observe that some of their ostensible weaknesses have turned out to be strengths. The three texts may initially have seemed unpromising as examples of feminist utopian persuasion. All three are touched by contradictions, and each is problematic in its own fashion: *Marriages* critiques a feminist utopia, *Left Hand* has no major female characters, and *Les Guérillères* is structured as a stutter. Moreover, each book gambles with genre. Lessing's mixes genres in a way that might put off some readers: it employs allegory and fantasy to clarify its argument and employs realism to make it plausible. In contrast, Le Guin's novel calls on a single genre, science fiction, to do both—the fiction clarifying the argument and the science making it plausible. But this choice of genre, given the time at which Le Guin was writing, means that her book also addresses a very specific implied reader, the young male science-fiction reader of the late 1960s, and so risks alienating other readers. Wittig's *nouveau roman* takes a different sort of chance, tying its implied readers to a cable of experimental technique. The very rope that swings them out over an abyss, however, manages to be the one that pulls them back in.

How does persuasion work in these contradictory and problematic books, each of whose genre choices threatens to turn away a number of implied readers? One could answer that the texts compensate for these difficulties through the skillful use of devices like belief-bridging and protean metaphor. Indeed, for certain readers such compensation does occur, but I'd like to go further and suggest that for other readers the difficulties themselves enhance persuasion.

They function on two levels, thematic and formal. Difficulties work on the thematic level in narratives such as the three just studied, for all three advocate pragmatism by presenting admirable characters, like Al·Ith, who accept the need to struggle with difficulties in order to improve conditions in their worlds. In turn, readers are to emulate such hard work and even self-sacrifice in their own lives. Each novel leads implied readers through a pragmatic process as they read the text, preparing them to enact pragmatic feminism later, and, as part of those pragmatic processes, each novel roughens the road that implied readers travel while reading, so they will be ready for rough roads later. The three authors are united in the certainty that there is no such thing as a free lunch.

Secondly, in these three novels (and in some others, where difficulty is not a theme) the difficulty works on a formal level.[1] Obstacles can make persuasion subtle, the opposite of simplistic propaganda that would either bully or spoon-feed its readers. Instead this rhetoric taunts, teases, or puzzles, so as ultimately to attract. It is these very hindrances that have made the three novels intriguing, challenging us to embrace them more fully, and when real readers meet this challenge, they are all the more engaged by the feminist argument. For such readers persuasion succeeds because of, not in spite of, the obstacles. What seemed problematic or off-putting in the novels, then, ends up making surprising sense when subjected to a detailed inquiry into persuasive technique.

Given that *Marriages, Left Hand,* and *Les Guérillères* exemplify the persuasive devices I have introduced, how might an understanding of these techniques prove useful when extended to analyses of other texts? Part I of this study has already given examples of the theories as applied individually to different texts; I'd like now to spend some time showing multiple theories working in concert for a single text, as in part II. For this I have chosen Ursula K. Le Guin's novel *The Telling* (2000), because it offers a striking example of how theories of utopia, belief-bridging, and matching can work together.

I have also chosen *The Telling* because—through its differences from *Marriages, Left Hand,* and *Les Guérillères*—it typifies how the literary niche occupied by feminist utopian fiction has changed since the earlier books were written. That change was sparked by the shift from Second- to Third-Wave feminism, discussed below. The niche, which can be characterized as containing feminist narratives that lie outside conventional realism, was dominated by feminist utopian fiction at one time, including the period when the novels in part II were published (1969–80). Recent writing in that literary domain is exemplified in *The Telling.*

One of the strongest catalysts for change in the niche of feminist non-realist narratives has been the evolution from Second- to Third-Wave feminism.[2] Both Second- and Third-Wave beliefs are defined by the four elements of power, focus, recognition of patriarchy, and resistance to patriarchy, but the beliefs differ in how they emphasize other points. The

Second Wave tended to value unity, while the more postmodern Third Wave tends to value diversity, especially in terms of race, ethnicity, and class. The stress on diversity, in privileging such politics, has given relatively less attention to sexual politics, a lessening that ironically also stems from the successes of the Second Wave: since some advance has been made toward feminist goals, they no longer occupy such an urgent place on the agenda. Queer sexuality is similarly taken more for granted than in the Second Wave, when it often used to be celebrated in the form of lesbian separatism or else met with condescension or obliviousness.

Before considering how Third-Wave feminism has imbued *The Telling*, it is worth noting that comparing it with the part II novels will resemble a controlled experiment, since *Left Hand* in particular shares not only its author but also a number of other traits with the more recent book. To begin with, both are utopian and have feminist implied authors. In both, more specifically, a Terran Envoy of the Ekumen attempts to comprehend the inhabitants of another planet, only to encounter lonely frustration. Eventually, an arduous trip through a snow-covered wilderness leads the Envoy to a better understanding of self and other, and in the end another character's suicidal self-sacrifice advances Ekumenical goals. Of course, the two novels also differ in a number of points. In *The Telling* the Envoy is a woman named Sutty, and the planet she visits is named Aka. The people there are physiologically like Terrans and engage in a similar range of sexual practices rather than confront her with the disconcerting bodies and sexuality of Gethen. In *The Telling* Earth is controlled by antiscience religious fanatics, and Aka is controlled by antireligion scientific fanatics. Out in the countryside of Aka, Sutty eventually finds the remnants of an older culture, suppressed within the last century and imbued with a nonhierarchical cross between religion and philosophy, reminiscent of Buddhism or Taoism (102). If Aka has a utopia, it is this counterculture.[3]

As might be expected, some of the key ways in which the two Le Guin novels differ stem from the fact that *Left Hand* grew out of the Second Wave of feminism and *The Telling* out of the Third Wave. In the later book, for instance, race and ethnicity are somewhat more salient, diverse, and hybrid: Sutty was born in India and spent her youth in Vancouver, her lover was Sino-Canadian, and Sutty, apparently like most people on the planet she visits, is dark-skinned. In *The Telling* a Third-Wave position is also occupied by queerness, which is neither denigrated nor exalted. The heroine is a lesbian, but her queerness is low-key; in the Third Wave it need not play a large role in the plot. Similarly, the implied author takes queerness enough for granted to use it as a means to an end: she employs it in the belief-bridging that encourages readers to prefer the counterculture, with its tolerant sexuality, over the dominant Akan regime, which is homophobic.

In an analogous manner, sex and gender no longer receive the attention they did in *Left Hand.* The protagonist of the later narrative is female, as are several other major characters, but the very progress that makes that possible means feminist issues do not occupy a particularly prominent place in the book, for the implied reader is someone who neither needs nor wants to be vehemently persuaded toward feminist beliefs. An implied reader who needed to be shouted at about feminism would find few matches among real readers apt to pick up this book. The implied author's feminist, antipatriarchal beliefs are clear (for example, the Unist religious zealots on Earth are violent as well as patriarchal), but feminism is only one among several values advocated. This text's feminism is definitely Third Wave—a bass beat in the background, not the main melody.

Since *The Telling* is feminist, and since Aka's counterculture is utopian, does that make the novel a "feminist utopian narrative"? I would insert a conjunction and argue that at most the novel is a "feminist and utopian narrative" because the utopian qualities privileged by the implied author are not primarily its feminist ones. In this *The Telling* typifies current tendencies: even if a feminist implied author creates a utopian society, it is rarely a specifically feminist utopia, just a society that is utopian by feminist standards *among others.* Similar Third-Wave trends also characterize texts that basically lack utopias but that, like *The Telling,* have recently come to occupy the niche of nonrealist feminist narratives. Consider novels such as Octavia Butler's *Parable of the Sower,* whose society is dystopian by feminist standards among others, or cyberpunk fiction such as Melissa Scott's *Trouble and Her Friends,* whose society is not strongly utopian or dystopian by feminist or other standards.[4] The feminism in such narratives is low-key, diverse, and often queer.

If feminism does not lie at the heart of *The Telling,* what does? The highest value is "telling," a kind of narration that occurs in the utopia. Perhaps Le Guin has turned to this theme because, like William Shakespeare in *The Tempest,* she is an aging artist reflecting on a lifetime of art. And perhaps she has been influenced by the late-twentieth-century tradition Tom Moylan has called "critical utopias," which tend toward self-reflexivity (*Demand the Impossible,* 46).

"Telling" conveys "a way of thinking and living developed and elaborated over thousands of years by the vast majority of human beings on [Aka], an enormous interlocking system of symbols, metaphors, correspondences, theories, cosmology, cooking, calisthenics, physics, metaphysics, metallurgy, medicine, physiology, psychology, alchemy, chemistry, calligraphy, numerology, herbalism, diet, legend, parable, poetry, history, and story" (98). Note that the profuse multiplicity of focus characterizing the utopia does not relate necessarily to sex or gender and so is not specifically feminist, but refers more often to the infinite branchings of telling in general. Even race and ethnicity, while more prominent than in *Left Hand,* are subordinated to the emphasis on telling.

The issues privileged in *The Telling* thus differ a good deal from those in *Left Hand,* but the persuasive devices used to privilege them do not. How the novel urges readers to appreciate the phenomenon of telling can best be understood through the theory of belief-bridging. The device repeatedly builds a bridge to telling from trustworthy characters who perform or praise the phenomenon. For instance, the most respected people in the utopia are the maz, the professional tellers, who don a red or blue mantle and then pass on some part of the body of lore: "[T]he essential work of the maz, what gave them honor among the people, was telling: reading aloud, reciting, telling stories, and talking about the stories" (115). Given the nonhierarchical bent of the society, however, after a telling even a maz returns to ordinary status upon removing the mantle, and listeners are valued too: "If telling was the skill of the maz, listening was the skill of the yoz [fellow person]. As they all liked to remark, neither one was any use without the other" (123). The people reverence not only spoken but written telling and are fighting to preserve texts written in their ancient ideograms, which the dominant regime has banned, in fact discouraging writing of any kind. Issues of telling shape the plot, which culminates in the remote caves where, in reaction to the recent oppression, people from the utopian culture have painstakingly hidden thousands of texts.

Not only does belief-bridging employ the utopia's values to endorse telling, but, since the device can work both ways, telling in turn endorses other values associated with it, in particular the utopia itself. Because telling is a form of narrating, this is an instance of the specialized technique I have called narrative belief-bridging. Narrative, words, speaking, listening, writing, and reading are revered in the old culture, and so implied readers, admiring language, will be inclined to admire the culture. Most real readers will likely match the implied readers in their respect for these linguistic matters if nothing else and so to some extent be impressed by the utopia. Conversely, narrative belief-bridging invites readers to disapprove of the fanatical cultures on Earth and Aka because both of them destroy libraries and ban certain types of speech. Thus, the technique has unusual force in the novel's persuasion, which flows strongly, perhaps too strongly, in favor of the utopian counterculture.

Such a self-referential narrative prompts the question of how telling on Aka relates to how the novel itself is told. Strangely enough, the two are at odds, for I find Le Guin's book to be a single-minded tract in favor of multiplicity, a heavy-handed tract in favor of subtlety. David Kipen comments:

> In interviews and elsewhere . . . Le Guin has encouraged readers to view "The Telling" as a recapitulation of Chairman Mao's heinous scourging of Taoism and its adherents.
>
> This sorry chapter in the annals of modern religious intolerance would make for a fascinating, cautionary historical novel, but transmuted into science fiction, it remains inert. The subjugated believers a re too pure, the Akan oppressors too robotic, the dialectic between them too chilly. . . .
>
> Le Guin may have sensed the problem when she has Sutty deride Akan social-realist writing as so deeply and "flatly political. Of course every art is political. But when it's all didactic, all in the service of a belief system, I resent, I mean, I resist it."
>
> So do we. (C1)

The persuasion is so overdetermined that the implied reader is mismatched in degree with me, as a real reader. It is also important to remember that the text's self-referentiality includes listening as well as telling: listeners in the utopia respond to a telling with "*Ah, ah,*" not with the judgments and analyses proffered by a literary critic such as I (168). If those listeners represent the implied reader, perhaps *The Telling* is addressing itself to someone unlike me, an implied reader with whom I am mismatched in kind. The notion of matching, while incapable of blocking out the disappointment evoked by some elements of the novel, can at least help me understand my reaction.

The preceding brief discussion has been intended not only to describe the current status of the niche once filled by feminist utopian narratives but also to suggest the broader relevance of theories developed in this study. I would now like to say a few words, speculatively rather than exhaustively, about paths for future work. As suggested by the diagram in the Introduction and by the many brief examples in part I, the theories developed in those pages could prove helpful in current fields of scholarship and even activism, beyond the particulars of the feminist utopian narratives of part II—and beyond other feminist nonrealist narratives such as *The Telling*.

Politics, Persuasion, and Pragmatism especially opens horizons concerning the larger question of persuasion in fiction. To give a sampling of such possibilities, I will mention a few lines of inquiry that could be enhanced by the notion of belief-bridging, the broadest of the concepts introduced by this study. Thinking about belief-bridging can prove useful beyond the realm of feminist utopian narratives, including understanding patriarchal narratives. In fact, for feminist critiques of patriarchal texts, the analysis of belief-bridging not only can contribute to future efforts but is a common if rarely theorized method in existing efforts.

Take, for example, Ernest Hemingway's "A Very Short Story," the tale of a wounded American soldier in Europe who gets engaged to his nurse but is jilted by her and then contracts gonorrhea from another woman. Robert Scholes has skillfully analyzed how the story "presents a male character [and men] favorably and a female [and women] unfavorably. . . . The good, loyal, reticent male character is supported by the discourse. . . . The bad, treacherous, talkative female is cast out. . . . [T]he anger at the root of the story is transformed into what we may take as the cool, lapidary prose of the pure impersonal artist" (*Semiotics and Interpretation,* 120).

Scholes observes that the story's ostensibly objective third-person point of view is actually the subjectivity of the male character, to whose perspective the point of view is limited. Furthermore, the man clings to reticence ("He went under the anaesthetic holding tight on to himself so he would not blab about anything during the silly, talky time" [Hemingway, 65]), a value paralleled by the narrator's own reticence (Scholes, *Semiotics and Interpretation,* 117). The story thus favors the man "by mapping certain traits on to a value structure"—what I call belief-bridging—"through its covert first-person perspective and the complicity of its style with those values" (120)—what I call narrative belief-bridging. Although not recognized as such, similar detection of patriarchal belief-bridging unifies a number of otherwise disparate feminist analyses.

Another area in which belief-bridging can spark future work is that of realist narratives. To understand how the technique might apply here, we need to review the nature of beliefs. Although this book, with its concentration on feminist utopian narratives, has stressed beliefs about values, beliefs can also concern states of affairs. Persuasion, in literature and elsewhere, always involves an evaluative and a descriptive strand, but utopian literature tends to stress the evaluative one whereas realism may well stress the descriptive one.[5]

I suspect this is because, to create a persuasive illusion of reality, realism needs to build bridges to its fictional world from what the readers believe about the state of their own world, or at least about its conventional representation.[6] While reading Christina Stead's *The Man Who Loved Children,* we can taste every cup of tea and can locate the family's house on a map of Georgetown but may have trouble deciding who is right and who is wrong in the family battles. In contrast, when a text such as *Marriages* creates a fictional world where four adjacent zones each correspond conveniently to a different relation between the sexes, then it is unlikely that the narrative will be able to build a bridge to readers' beliefs about geography. In *Marriages* that inability matters little, though, because it does not interfere with the utopian text's more important goal—to advocate particular value judgments about relations between the sexes.

The distinction I am drawing between realism and nonrealist genres resembles that drawn by Northrop Frye between realism and romance (35–52). Frye says that realism features otherness and reality whereas romance features a shaping spirit and imagination. In my terms, realism is devoted to description—of otherness, of some sort of reality external to the text—while nonrealist genres give themselves more to evaluation, part of the spirit that shapes them.

Reality itself calls forth widely different evaluations from different people, and so, if realist texts succeed in creating an illusion of reality, in all its messiness and ambiguity, that very success will probably work against their ability to convey particular beliefs about values. For instance, Georg Lukács observed that although Honoré de Balzac deplored the fall of the aristocracy, he described it so well that his fiction appeals to Marxists, who applaud the aristocrats' downfall (21); the French realist's descriptive persuasion outweighs his evaluative persuasion. Or take the example of belief-bridging in *The Awakening* (1899), a realist narrative by Kate Chopin. The text powerfully spins its descriptive strand, employing everything from dialect that evokes local color to silences that evoke the tensions of married life. In contrast, while the novella's evaluative strand certainly endorses feminism, it is surprisingly tricky to say exactly how. Readers in Chopin's day read Edna as a villain, while Second-Wave feminists read her as a heroine; actually, the text does not evaluate her definitively as bad or good—and therein lies some of the realism. The text suggests much more sympathy for Edna's problems than it does for her responses to those problems; a thorough analysis of both strands of belief-bridging might enable us to trace how that is achieved. These examples suggest that it would be rewarding to compare the descriptive and evaluative strands of belief-bridging in a range of realist narratives.

Regardless of whether a narrative is feminist or patriarchal, utopian or realist, other tempting projects are opened up by the self-referential technique I have called narrative belief-bridging. Texts that use it vary a good deal in which narrative traits are associated with the beliefs being advocated: *The Telling* associates a wide variety of traits with the utopia—speaking, listening, writing, and reading, among others—but some texts are more selective. It would be interesting to observe which traits are evoked by various texts' narrative belief-bridging and then to ask how that affects the texts' persuasion. Moreover, does the effect vary, depending on how precisely the technique refers to narrative traits? For instance, in Virginia Woolf's *To the Lighthouse* Lily Briscoe is a painter; would the values linked to her function differently if she were specifically a novelist instead? While this book has concentrated on Second-Wave feminist utopias, other narrative periods and genres could yield dissimilar patterns; one might be able to trace a history of narrative belief-bridging. Perhaps, say, the technique appears with special frequency or intensity in the writings of movements that revel in the self-referential; a seemingly solipsistic movement such as postmodernism might, through narrative belief-bridging, turn out to touch readers more than previously thought.

We have been considering the device in narrative literature but could branch out to non-narrative literature and nonliterary narrative. For instance, literary belief-bridging can occur in drama, as when Hamlet's appreciation of the traveling players encourages the implied audience to admire him. Similarly, as mentioned in an earlier chapter, Aurora Leigh's poetic vocation contributes to constructing her as the heroine of Elizabeth Barrett Browning's epic poem. Meanwhile, the author of a nonliterary narrative, such as history, can foster plausibility by attributing facts to other historians or can solicit trust for someone such as Winston Churchill by underscoring his role as a historian. In these realms, as in narrative literature, a variety of inquiries could be pursued; one could, for example, figure out a history of dramatic, poetic, or historical belief-bridging.

Having touched on a few possibilities for future work, I'd like to conclude by returning to where we started, by emphasizing the need to continue current efforts that meld the formal with the political more than has generally been done in literary scholarship. The formal helps explain how the political works, while the political helps explain why the formal matters. *Politics, Persuasion, and Pragmatism,* having explored formal concepts—such as persuasion, matching, belief-bridging, and protean metaphor—and political concepts—such as feminism and static and pragmatic utopias—has tied the two strands together when analyzing the novels on which I have focused. The knot that joins the two strands is the reader: the form of the text aids in conveying political beliefs through the implied reader to the real reader, who may then go on to act in the real world. This power of literature to stretch out to the real world is one of its most disturbing and most gratifying features, a major reason it continues to fascinate us.

Notes

Notes to Introduction

1. Utopias count as "speculative fiction," a category by which theorists expand the abbreviation "SF" to include not only "science fiction" but related forms as well. Marleen S. Barr, for example, uses the term "to include feminist utopias, science fiction, fantasy, and sword and sorcery" (*Alien to Femininity*, xxin1). We can also read the feminist utopias I discuss as "feminist fabulation," a term coined later by Barr (adapting Robert Scholes's "fabulation") in *Feminist Fabulation.*

2. See Scholes, *Protocols of Reading*, 105–8. Some other scholars trace connections between persuasion and literature, though in ways very different from mine—e.g., Mailloux in *Rhetorical Power* and Phelan in *Narrative as Rhetoric.*

3. Feminism is a political issue because it has to do with power, as, early in the Second Wave of feminism, Kate Millett explained it in *Sexual Politics* (23–24). Since I am concentrating on narrative, my dual approach falls into what David Herman calls "postclassical narratology," which is reinvigorating narrative theory by uniting text with context (9).

4. E.g., J. Hillis Miller, *The Ethics of Reading;* Booth, *The Company We Keep;* Scholes, *Protocols of Reading,* chap. 3; and Newton, *Narrative Ethics.*

5. My belief in the transformative power of utopias belongs to the tradition of Ernst Bloch in *The Principle of Hope.* See, e.g., Moylan, *Demand the Impossible;* Daniel and Moylan, *Not Yet;* and Parrinder, *Learning from Other Worlds.*

6. For example, Le Guin reviewed Lessing's *Marriages.*

7. The 1975 Avon reprint of Le Guin's *The Dispossessed* bears on its cover the subtitle "an ambiguous utopia."

8. As Susan Moller Okin has pointed out, a theory can apply to a group not mentioned in it; the burden of proof is on its critics to show applicability is lacking ("Feminist Interpretations of Political Thought").

9. E.g., Sacks, *Fiction and the Shape of Belief.* David H. Richter has a similar but more specialized emphasis in *Fable's End.*

10. Early examples of the study of feminist belief include Fetterley, *The Resisting Reader;* Deutelbaum, *Woman as Reader;* and Flynn and Schweickart, *Gender and Reading.*

11. E.g., Iser, *The Implied Reader* and *The Act of Reading.* Mary Louise Pratt criticizes the latent formalism of reader-response theorists.

12. Peter J. Rabinowitz discusses this in "Assertion and Assumption" (411, 414).

13. E.g., Davis, *Resisting Novels* and Suleiman, *Authoritarian Fictions.* Suleiman's taxonomy of devices in *romans à thèse,* where the persuasion stands out, has opened the way for finding some of the same devices, in a quieter tone, in subtler literature.

14. E.g., Booth, *The Rhetoric of Fiction* and *The Company We Keep;* Dowst, "The Rhetoric of Utopian Fiction"; Jameson, *The Political Unconscious;* Nussbaum, *Love's Knowledge* and *Poetic Justice;* Phelan, *Narrative as Rhetoric;* and Rabinowitz, *Before Reading.*

15. A major collection of feminist narratology is Kathy Mezei, *Ambiguous Discourse.* Also see Joanne S. Frye (chap. 7).

16. Judith Butler has made a valiant effort to get around this problem, proposing the notion of "contingent foundations," but she still ends up privileging the contingency over the foundations ("Contingent Foundations").

17. I am grateful to Miriam Solomon for suggesting this term for my work. My position is akin to the "post/poststructuralism" of Susan Stanford Friedman (chap. 7).

18. Edward Rothstein reports an upsurge in books and exhibitions on utopias (A13). Recently the New York Public Library and the Bibliothèque Nationale de France put on a major exhibition about utopia; the resulting publication provides a useful overview of the subject (Schaer, Claeys, and Sargent, *Utopia*).

Notes to Chapter 1

1. Sally Foldenauer was a childhood mentor of mine, as well as a riding teacher, barn-builder, and, on three occasions, a rescuer of people who were drowning.

2. Patai, 165. Also see Sargent, "An Ambiguous Legacy."

3. Feminism in the West, and particularly in the United States, is generally categorized as First Wave (from the mid-nineteenth to the early twentieth century). Second Wave (from after World War II through the 1980s), and Third Wave (from 1990 through the present).

4. For useful reviews of criticism on utopias, see Sargent, "Contemporary Scholarship on Utopianism" and Moylan, *Scraps of the Untainted Sky.* Large-scale feminist studies of utopias include Barr and Smith, *Women and Utopia;* Rohrlich and Baruch, *Women in Search of Utopia;* Barr and Murphy, *Feminism Faces the Fantastic;* Thürmer-Rohr, *Vagabonding;* Bartkowski, *Feminist Utopias;* Jones and Goodwin, *Feminism, Utopia, and Narrative;* Bammer, *Partial Visions;* Sargisson, *Contemporary Feminist Utopianism;* Burwell, *Notes on Nowhere;* and Barr, *Future Females, The Next Generation.*

5. I define "utopianism" as dreaming of such a society. In some cases utopianism also leads people to work toward such a society or produce a text about one.

6. For simplicity, my definitions build on common parlance. For finer distinctions and for critical bibliography, see Lyman Tower Sargent's excellent overview, "The Three Faces of Utopianism Revisited." Some of my definitions are adapted from his, though I believe he too quickly dismisses the perfectionist impulse in utopias.

7. The tendency to differentiate between "static" and "dynamic" utopias is exemplified in a number of essays in the collection *Feminism, Utopia, and Narrative* (Jones and Goodwin).

8. E.g., Burwell and Sargisson.

9. Elisabeth Hansot finds dynamic, modern utopias overambitious in their attempt to reconcile ideals with change (20); pragmatism offers an answer to this concern by envisioning change itself as an ideal.

10. E.g., Bammer 7; Fitting; and Finney.

11. E.g., Moylan, *Demand the Impossible,* 10, 40; Jones, "Gilman," 117–18; and Albinski.

12. E.g., Ruppert; Jacobs; and Freedman, 89–90.

13. I do, however, disagree with her utter pessimism about envisioning the future.

14. Among those who have commented on the stasis of *Herland* are Frances Bartkowski, who contrasts it with the dynamism of *Les Guérillères* (16, 44), and Libby Falk Jones. Jones feels, though, that dramatic tension can be found in readers' relation to the text ("Gilman," 117–18).

15. This principle has been expressed, in other terms, by writers ranging from Vladímir Propp (102) to Mieke Bal (26).

16. I am grateful to Anita Silvers for her comments on pragmatism.

17. I employ the term "pragmatism" to evoke only particular aspects of the philosophical movement. I disagree with some of these philosophers' tenets, they disagree with some of each others' tenets, and some of their tenets are irrelevant to my subject here. Some scholars have begun studying literature or rhetoric from an explicitly pragmatic stance, though without taking a feminist approach as I do—e.g., Mailloux in *Rhetorical Power* and he and others in the collection he has edited, *Rhetoric, Sophistry, Pragmatism.*

18. Pragmatists disagree on whether we can ever reach certainty: Peirce would hope we can, while Rorty would say we cannot. Ian Hacking compares these two pragmatist branches (62–63). Not finding uncertainty inevitable, I agree with James Phelan's critique of Stanley Fish for seeing the interpretation of narrative as "endlessly malleable—according to the needs, interests, and values of the interpreter" (*Narrative as Rhetoric,* 11).

19. Jean Pfaelzer, commenting on an earlier version of my theory, expresses concern that it might represent an inability to imagine utopia (193). I intend, on the contrary, to account for how we might imagine an ideal society in multiple ways.

20. In later chapters this study develops a multifaceted definition of feminism that offers a number of different choices to try out during the pragmatic journey away from patriarchy. Nevertheless, some of the varieties I will be explaining do seem more compatible with pragmatism than others do: among patterns of power—equality and especially difference; among patterns of focus—duality and especially multiplicity.

21. A pragmatic text bears some similarity to what Stanley Fish calls a "dialectical presentation" or a "self-consuming artifact," which provokes readers, forcing them to work to make new meanings from moment to moment.

22. The Riding Women series consists of *Walk to the End of the World, Motherlines,* and *The Furies.*

23. Susan Stanford Friedman also sees narrative energy resulting from the fluidity of space and travel but emphasizes narrative sequence less than I (149).

Notes to Chapter 2

1. My definition of persuasion includes retention as well as change because the mechanisms for the two processes are the same. The definition does not include what might be called "passive confirmation" of belief, which is encouraged by another type of literature, such as Tolstoyan realism, in which the implied author intends neither to oppose nor to

foster feminism; readers are in effect being told, "Your views, positive or negative, on feminism are fine; don't bother to think about them."

2. Scholars of rhetoric have examined feminist persuasion, if not specifically in literature. For a good overview, see *Feminist Rhetorical Theories* (Foss, Foss, and Griffin).

3. She calls principled advocacy "communication" rather than "persuasion."

4. Unlike Gearhart, I find this idea compatible with "the intention to change another" as long as that intention is not one's only goal.

5. It is a matter of opinion what constitutes a good purpose (or an ideal society). I would not, for instance, want to live in Thomas More's Utopia or in the Norse warrior's heaven, with its continual fighting, but my theories of persuasion and utopia should work for someone who does consider one of those societies ideal.

6. Of course, to study belief in literature is not to claim that as the only literary inquiry worth pursuing. See Graff, 171.

7. Walter R. Fisher says, "Aesthetic proofs are representations of reality that fall somewhere between analogies and examples" (162).

8. It is beyond the scope of this study to tackle philosophical and psychological questions such as how one can determine another's beliefs. A variety of answers is possible, and most are compatible with the concept of "belief" as I use it.

9. I say "feminist beliefs" rather than "feminist ideology" because the latter term usually refers only to large-scale worldviews and often has pejorative connotations.

10. Classic statements include those by I. A. Richards (*Practical Criticism,* 180, 255–74); Wayne C. Booth (*The Rhetoric of Fiction,* chap. 5); and T. S. Eliot ("Dante," 218–22, 229–31).

11. The authorial audience is similar to the implied reader I analyze below but is addressed by the real author, while, as we shall see, the implied reader is addressed by the implied author. Other references in this paragraph are also to *Before Reading.*

12. I suspect that the authorial audience might but need not share the belief in fairy godmothers.

13. "Truth in Fiction," 131; "Assertion and Assumption," 411–12.

14. In the first ambiguity, "the narrative audience itself is unaware of where, exactly, the truth lies." In the second, "we are faced with an ambiguity about which of several narrative audiences we are to accept—although each potential narrative audience may itself face no ambiguity" ("Truth in Fiction," 136).

15. Conversely, real readers today may be so ignorant of history that some could read Leo Tolstoy's *War and Peace* while taking Napoleon for just another fictional character, directed at the narrative audience but not the authorial one.

16. Admittedly, even when a text is clear, what members of the actual audience end up believing depends not only on that, but also on complex variables, such as their pre-existing beliefs about history, magic, or the likelihood of a Martian invasion. See Haraway, "Situated Knowledges."

17. I am indebted to Anita Silvers for her help in thinking through these issues. Ch. Perelman and L. Olbrechts-Tyteca, in their classic work, make a similar but less refined distinction (66).

18. I am grateful to Catharine R. Stimpson for her comments on real and implied readers.

19. See Booth, *The Rhetoric of Fiction,* 151. Seymour Chatman gives a good explana-

tion of the implied author (chap. 5). Much of what I say could be extended to what Susan Sniader Lanser calls "the extrafictional voice," a figure that includes, along with the implied author, "the text-as-object" (*The Narrative Act,* 123).

20. A pioneer in this area is Wolfgang Iser (*The Implied Reader*).

21. I am aware that authors and readers *implied* by the text are by definition also *inferred*—inferred by me. While I consider it important to acknowledge my imprisonment in the hermeneutic circle, there is no way out of it, and I therefore choose to go on interpreting, aware that from one point of view I am only constructing.

22. The best-known attack on intentionality is by W. K. Wimsatt and Monroe C. Beardsley.

23. Jeffrey L. Sammons, following Malte Dahrendorf, summarizes some of the problems (78).

24. I realize that theorists such as the later Stanley Fish would object, saying that we should not attribute to the text an objective existence, complete with implied author and reader, for the only readers are real ones, who feel they are discovering elements of the text but are in fact only creating them. I disagree with Fish because his theory cannot explain why real readers ever agree about an interpretation, since he cannot explain what they are *responding to.* Like James Phelan, I differ from Fish "by insisting that although facts are always mediated, always seen from within the confines of a given perspective, the perspective does not create the facts" (*Narrative as Rhetoric,* 18).

25. Peter J. Rabinowitz hints at a sort of matching and the possibility of mismatches (e.g., *Before Reading,* 36, 98, 215; "Assertion and Assumption," 411), as do Perelman and Olbrechts-Tyteca (19–23).

Although I concentrate on matching in literature, the concept applies to all sorts of persuasion. We could, for example, contemplate the role of rhetoric in the classroom, for one way to think about teaching is as persuasion about beliefs that concern values and states of affairs. To the degree that a real student matches the implied student, teaching succeeds, yet all too often mismatches occur. Distinguishing among types of mismatches could enable faculty to construct a range of implied students so as to address different sorts of persuasion to each.

26. I am adapting an example from Sacks (64–65).

27. Matching should be distinguished from belief-bridging, described in another chapter, which does involve both implied reader and implied author.

28. For simplicity this paragraph refers to the real reader as "the reader."

29. E.g., Schweickart, "Reading Ourselves," and the innovator Rosenblatt.

30. I am using "kind of persuasion" as shorthand for "kind of implied reader for whom the persuasion is intended." The phrase does not refer to the kind of belief being advocated.

31. This appropriateness is needed in both the first, descriptive strand of the process and the second, evaluative strand. Degree of persuasion resembles Susan Sniader Lanser's ideas of explicitness and reinforcement of ideology, though she focuses more on how a belief is expressed by a text than on how the belief is intended to affect a reader (*The Narrative Act,* 216, 220).

32. My extension of "overdetermination" to belief can be seen as an extension of Susan Rubin Suleiman's "excessive redundancy" as well (*Authoritarian Fictions,* 195).

33. In his examples from Fielding, the paradigmatic fallible paragons are not protagonists or women, but I extend the concept to include those figures as well.

34. Reader-response theorists tend to ignore mismatches, while more traditional theorists tend to deal with mismatches by blaming either the writer or the reader.

35. Except in the highly unlikely case where an implied reader manages to match every real one.

Notes to Chapter 3

1. The idea of belief-bridging reveals the unity underlying many of the specific devices identified by pioneering theorists of narrative persuasion such as Sheldon Sacks and Susan Rubin Suleiman (*Authoritarian Fictions*). Peter J. Rabinowitz refers to "a kind of innocence by association: we trust the friends of our friends and the enemies of our enemies"; this is an example of "metonymical rules of [moral] enchainment," which are a subset of what I call belief-bridging (*Before Reading*, 90, 89).

2. I am indebted to jo keroes for her help in creating the term *belief-bridging* as well as some other terminology in this chapter.

3. Belief-bridging should also be distinguished from other concepts with which it has affinities. When the beliefs concern values, belief-bridging may recall ordinary ideas of sympathizing or identifying with characters, but belief-bridging involves those notions only when they follow a precise sequence of events. On the other hand, belief-bridging is broader than sympathizing or identifying because it need not be linked to characters. The technique also resembles Kenneth Burke's notion of "identification" but refines it significantly, in effect explaining why identification matters (579–80). Susan Rubin Suleiman's notion of the "amalgam" is a special case of belief-bridging (*Authoritarian Fictions*, 188–93). Belief-bridging may also bring to mind the rhetorical device of "ethos"; unlike belief-bridging, though, this creation of a persona emphasizes speakers' character traits more than their beliefs. Finally, belief-bridging should not be misconstrued as guaranteeing good or true beliefs.

4. Indeed, belief-bridging can backfire if a strong enough new belief outweighs an old one, reversing the normal direction of travel over the bridge. In *The Fountainhead*, for instance, Ayn Rand employs the beauty of the heroine and hero to make their objectivist views appealing, but real readers repelled by objectivism might end up feeling suspicious of their old belief in beauty.

5. I am grateful to Beverly Voloshin for helping me think this idea through.

6. My "resisting reader" is a modification of Judith Fetterley's term; hers refers to a real reader while mine refers to the negatively implied counterpart of hers.

7. Hence the unsettling effect of unreliable narrators. This effect is epitomized in the Agatha Christie novel in which the narrator turns out to be the murderer (I won't give away the title).

8. See Kristeva, 5, 7; and Irigaray, "The Power of Discourse," 76–78.

9. My work overlaps somewhat with Susan Stanford Friedman's in *Mappings*.

10. I am indebted to Jill Rubenstein for suggesting the term. I am using "metaphor" in the broad sense, to include metonymy, symbol, and most other types of figurative language. Protean metaphor is a subset of what Susan Sniader Lanser calls "figural" ideology (*The Narrative Act*, 217).

11. One protean metaphor may differ from another in the nature of its stages, their number, or the order in which they appear.

12. My emphasis on the sequential nature of narrative is indebted to the work of Peter Brooks, as in *Reading for the Plot*.

13. E.g., Iser, *The Act of Reading*. Fish particularly stresses the temporality of reading in his early work, such as *Self-Consuming Artifacts*. He also goes on to connect temporality to the process by which literature persuades readers, though he makes a somewhat different connection than I do.

14. I agree with Peter J. Rabinowitz, however, who emphasizes that readers not only make sense of a text as they read but also, in a different way, retrospectively make sense of its totality (*Before Reading*).

15. Citing Michel Beaujour, Suleiman mentions the unapologetic paternalism of such texts (*Authoritarian Fictions,* 240).

16. Roland Barthes examines this castration in *S/Z*.

Notes to Chapter 4

1. This has been recognized by a few thinkers, such as Fredric Jameson ("*History and Class Consciousness* as an 'Unfinished Project,'" 60).

2. Karen Offen convincingly criticizes several feminists who have renounced definition ("Defining Feminism," 120–21). Teresa Ebert cites "Joan Scott, Denise Riley, Teresa de Lauretis, Gayatri Spivak, and Donna Haraway" as examples of feminists whose "rewriting of difference in terms of a local, specific plurality . . . excludes and occludes the critique of global or structural relations of power as 'ideological' and 'totalizing'" (898).

3. For example, although the definition created by Catharine R. Stimpson (drawing on Virginia Woolf and Simone de Beauvoir) overlaps somewhat with mine and contains multiple criteria, it is brief and so cannot address the question of how the criteria relate to each other (2).

4. I am indebted to Karen Offen for helping me think through these terms.

5. I usually mean "women" and "men" to include females and males of any age. I have also coined the term "natural ideals" to refer to traits that some people believe, in a muddled way, both to be innate in every female (or male) and to be lacking in some females (or males) and worth acquiring. These stereotypical, patriarchal notions can be the objects of male focus but will not be explored further here.

6. We can also imagine a culture that would consider traditional gender conditioning desirable but would not divide it along sex lines. In other words, half the people in the imaginary society would wear dresses, rear children, and keep house, while the other half would not, but the half to which one belonged would bear no relation to one's sex. It would be intriguing to observe whether one group would possess dominant power and focus. Although this society would not single out either sex for discrimination, many feminists would consider it far from utopian.

7. We could say sex varies cross-culturally in that an inherited condition such as 5-alpha reductase deficiency syndrome causes a few societies to have a higher percentage than average of intersexed people. See Herdt, "Mistaken Sex."

8. Thomas Laqueur stresses the differences among views held by various cultures and by a single culture over time, though in less-publicized moments even Laqueur acknowledges the existence of bodies and of facts, such as the discovery that conception can occur without female orgasm (16, 182). Some poststructuralist feminists such as Judith Butler

appear to have thrown up their hands and declared that the ordinary notion of sex is hopelessly compromised because it is "both marked and formed by discursive practices" (*Bodies That Matter,* 1). Careful examination reveals, though, that she does not seem to be denying the existence of sex, so perhaps she is just stressing what cannot be perceived, while I am stressing what can.

9. A variety of sex and gender systems in different times and places are presented in studies such as Gilbert Herdt's collection, *Third Sex, Third Gender: Beyond Sexual Dimorphism in Culture and History.*

10. I use the term "focus" rather than "ideology" partly because "ideology" usually has pejorative connotations of mystification, whereas I use "focus" neutrally (what I object to is its dominant male form). In addition, the metaphor of "focus," when extended, permits me to specify the objects that are focused upon—sex and gender.

11. See Eisenstein, *Contemporary Feminist Thought,* part 2: "Developing a Woman-Centered Analysis."

12. E.g., Delmar, 8; Tong, 1; and Morris, 1.

13. E.g., hooks, 194–95; and Offen, "Defining Feminism," 152. Also see Humm, 94–95. An exception is Dorothy Dinnerstein, who says that feminists must seek not only women's rights but also, more fundamentally, a transformation in everyone's attitudes toward peace and the environment (15).

14. Although it would lie beyond the scope of this work to define justice, my use of "just" and "unjust" should fit within most feminist definitions of the terms. Furthermore, though I am grounding Belief One in justice, I am leaving open various possibilities of what that concept of justice is itself grounded in.

15. The phrase "sex and gender," here and elsewhere, serves as shorthand for the more cumbersome "sex and the gender traits associated with that sex but not limited to it."

16. I am, however, avoiding the terms "androcentrism" and "phallocentrism" lest "-centrism" make it seem that only male centrality, not male singularity, is included in male focus.

17. MacKinnon asks, "Why should women have to be 'like' men to be treated as equal citizens?" (214). Deborah L. Rhode raises similar questions in "Definitions of Difference." Good examples of male focus in influential books are provided by Daphne Patai (160–62).

18. Simone de Beauvoir discusses women's alterity (xv–xxxiv). Of course it is possible to react to an other with recognition rather than objectification; see Moura, 283.

19. In "Simmering" Margaret Atwood also depicts the hardiness of male focus, although in this case recounting how men get involved in a formerly female-associated activity. She wittily imagines a society in which cooking has high status because it is considered men's work; the women, excluded from the kitchen, sit forlornly in the living room with their briefcases and business suits.

20. One difference between patriarchal power and focus is that, though both harm women much more than men, dominant male focus leads to intellectual impoverishment that harms both sexes equally.

21. Irigaray explicates the analogy in "Questions" (154–55).

22. Dale Spender was among the leaders in exploring the linguistic implications of the male norm.

23. See Freud, "Femininity." For detailed criticism of the essay, see Irigaray, *Speculum,* 11–129. The theories propounded in Freud's essay are especially clear and influential articulations of patriarchal views held by much of Western society, if not by Freud.

24. Sir William Blackstone, *Commentaries of the Laws of England, Book the First* (Oxford, 1765), 442, qtd. in Gilbert and Gubar, *Madwoman,* 155.

25. Thomas Laqueur's one-sex model lies somewhere between my male singularity and male centrality.

26. Caroline Whitbeck says, "[I]t is Aristotle who provides the first extensive enumeration and explanation of differences between the sexes structured by the *woman-as-partial-man* motif" (55).

27. See Whitbeck, 57–59, 62–68. Thomas Laqueur's two-sex model resembles my concept of pseudo-duality.

28. E.g., Irigaray, "Questions," 161–62; Cixous, from "Sorties," 90–91; Wittig, "Homo Sum," 49–52.

29. This question is explored in greater detail in Peel, "The Riddle of Doris Lessing's Feminism."

Notes to Chapter 5

1. This emphasis on difference is typified by Luce Irigaray in "Why Define Sexed Rights?" and "A Personal Note."

2. Deborah L. Rhode traces the history of this issue in U.S. law ("Definitions of Difference," 208–211).

3. Karen Offen discusses this in terms of "relational feminism," which I would call a subset of difference feminism ("Defining Feminism," 142–43).

4. Some of the feminists Okin mentions believe that for biological or cultural reasons only women can possess female focus, whereas I believe it is possible, though not probable, for men to have it, too. I would add that some of these thinkers, such as Irigaray, at times endorse feminist duality as well as feminist centrality.

5. For a defense, see Heilbrun.

6. See Warren, 22. On the ways androgyny privileges men, see Farwell, "Toward a Definition of the Lesbian Literary Imagination," 68–70.

7. Thomas Laqueur says that, before the late eighteenth century, Western accounts of the sexes highlighted their similarities, but this model still presented males as superior and thus differed from what I am calling similar duality.

8. A related criticism is made by Susan Rubin Suleiman in "The Politics and Poetics of Female Eroticism."

9. The series consists of *Wizard, Titan,* and *Demon.*

10. Thomas Laqueur suggests the earlier, one-sex model at least sometimes consisted of various gradations of perfection, which I believe could be interpreted as a continuum of multiple sexes (52).

11. Also see Baker, 81–82.

12. When the definition of sex is expanded beyond mine, other types of multiplicity are added. For someone who defines sex as merely anatomical, not necessarily inborn, transsexuals could fall somewhere along the intersex continuum. And in societies that define the sexes to include such factors as behavior or sexual orientation, homosexuals sometimes count as a third sex. In some cultures what I call "sex" and what I call "gender" are combined to create still more categories, as for the *hijras* of India. See Herdt, *Third Sex, Third Gender.*

13. Grémaux, however, suggests that, because of their virginity, these women may carry out the role of a third gender (280–81).

14. The series consists of *Watchtower, The Dancers of Arun,* and *The Northern Girl.*

15. Duality is more integral to feminist theory than to most other political theories, however, because of the basic duality of the sexes. Not only are there basically two sexes, but the groups contain almost equal numbers, and for millennia reproduction has required both. Thus a theory of relations between sexes relies more on two-ness than theories of relations between, say, classes or races.

Notes to Part II, Introduction

1. I discuss the texts in different terms in "Utopian Feminism, Skeptical Feminism, and Narrative Energy."

2. Other texts that deconstruct the female/male opposition include Virginia Woolf's *Orlando* and Honoré de Balzac's "Sarrasine."

Notes to Chapter 6

1. Lessing has expressed support for women's liberation (Introduction, *The Golden Notebook,* viii; Saxton). Sometimes her attitude has been mixed (e.g., Howe). See Peel, "The Riddle of Doris Lessing's Feminism."

2. A similar conclusion can be reached about a number of other Lessing texts, based on the patterns skillfully observed by Agate Nesaule Krouse.

3. Gayle Greene describes the enormous influence of Lessing in general and *The Golden Notebook* in particular (*Changing the Story,* 51–52, 57).

4. The series is called *Canopus in Argos: Archives.* The other books are: *Re: Colonised Planet 5 Shikasta: Personal, Psychological, Historical Documents Relating to Visit by JOHOR (George Sherban), EMISSARY (Grade 9) 87th of the Period of the Last Days; The Sirian Experiments: The Report by Ambien II, of the Five; The Making of the Representative for Planet 8;* and *Documents Relating to the Sentimental Agents in the Volyen Empire.*

5. Many critics have commented on Lessing's use of enclosed spaces, especially rooms. One of the earliest to do so was Dorothy Brewster (89). The subject is treated with particular care by Roberta Rubenstein (*Novelistic Vision,* 247 and passim). Critics have increasingly observed Lessing's relation to space as linked to nation and exile; see, e.g., Sage.

6. Naomi Jacobs notes that, "with each twist of [Lessing's] fable, the pattern changes. . . . None of the interpretations suggested at various points in the book holds consistent throughout" (40). Robin Roberts observes that the Canopus series deconstructs binarisms and "resolves the conflict between masculine science and feminine magic" (117). Neither critic, however, comments on pragmatic development.

7. Although this movement introduces readers to the four countries and the relationships between them in four stages, the number of the former bears no neat correspondence to the number of the latter. Moreover, some stages deal with two zones at a time, others with only one.

8. On binary oppositions, see Sprague, "'Without Contraries Is no Progression.'"

9. Marleen S. Barr says: "Even though male feminists reside in Lessing's Zone Three,

since this zone excludes stereotypical masculine characteristics, I consider it to be separatist"—a locution that, in my opinion, unnecessarily blurs the distinction between females and female-associated norms (*Feminist Fabulation,* 153).

10. E.g., O'Brien, 152.

11. I am grateful to Elizabeth Sommers for observing how belief-bridging makes Zone Three's blurring of identities much more appealing than Zone Four's.

12. Zone Three has a good deal in common with feminist utopias as described by Carol Pearson, Joanna Russ ("Recent Feminist Utopias"), and Lee Cullen Khanna ("Women's Worlds"). Khanna gives *Marriages* as a feminist utopian example in "Frontiers of Imagination."

13. The concept of estrangement in a positive sense comes from the Russian formalists' *ostranenie* and Bertolt Brecht's *Verfremdung.* See Suvin, *Metamorphoses,* 6; Fishburn, *Unexpected Universe,* 11.

14. On Lessing's Derridean rejection of binaries, see Kaplan and Rose, "Lessing and Her Readers," 3–4. Claire Sprague explores how multiplicity, not only two-ness, exists throughout Lessing's work (*Rereading Doris Lessing: Narrative Patterns of Doubling and Repetition*).

15. On art in this novel, see Khanna, "Truth and Art"; Roberts, 129–30.

16. I analyze these issues in detail in "Communicating Differently."

17. On the relation of language, power, and knowledge in this novel, see Armitt, "Your Word Is My Command."

18. On Lusik's evolution, see Khanna, "Truth and Art." On how Lusik changes characters and readers, see Fishburn, *Unexpected Universe,* 96–103. For an interpretation of Lusik that, unlike mine, reads him as a masculine authority, see Tiger.

19. Interestingly, his gradual disillusionment with his community's ideas makes this one of the rare books that, to use Susan Sniader Lanser's terminology from *Fictions of Authority,* shifts narrative voice from "communal" to "personal."

20. To Genette's questions we could add the intermediate one of "Who perceives?": this would highlight issues such as what the narrator selects to mention, in this case often female-associated items such as clothing, even when looking through the eyes of a character from outside Zone Three.

21. By "allegory" I mean a narrative contrived to make sense on a literal level and at the same time to signify a second, correlated level. I adapt this from M. H. Abrams (*A Glossary of Literary Terms,* 4). Betsy Draine calls *Marriages* "an allegorical romance" (162). Modifying the work of Samuel Delany, I define "fantasy," including "space fiction," as what could not have happened, and "realism" as what could have happened, either of which genres might or might not be an allegory ("About Five Thousand Seven Hundred and Fifty Words," 43–44).

22. Nancy Shields Hardin notes that a number of Lessing's works have much in common with Sufi teaching tales ("The Sufi Teaching Story," 317).

23. Also see Draine, 144; and Roberts, 117–36.

24. According to Betsy Draine, "Lessing's unchanging subject is itself change—in the individual and the collective consciousness" (xiii). Roberta Rubenstein mentions exemplarity ("*Marriages,*" 201). Exemplarity overlaps with Rachel Blau DuPlessis's idea of the multiple individual (chap. 9).

25. Such accusations are made, e.g., by Michael L. Magie. But Judith Stitzel concludes

that Lessing rejects science only in its limited forms (502). C. J. Driver comes to a similar conclusion about Lessing's attitude toward politics (20).

26. The series as a whole has been criticized—e.g., by Nalini Iyer—for excusing Canopean imperialism, and benevolent imperialism in general.

27. Some critics have described this writer in ways suggestive of pragmatism: e.g., Rowe, 194; Greene, *Doris Lessing;* Fishburn, "Teaching Doris Lessing," 83; and Fishburn, *Unexpected Universe,* 59.

28. Dee Seligman summarizes the Sufi optimism about conscious evolution and the opposition to preconceived ideas (xii). See Hardin, "Doris Lessing and the Sufi Way."

29. Marleen S. Barr, who rightly emphasizes the importance of change in the novel, also notes the power of Ben Ata's example (*Feminist Fabulation,* 158).

30. Lessing criticizes "the pleasurable luxury of despair" ("The Small Personal Voice," 11).

31. I present this argument in detail in "Leaving the Self Behind in *Marriages.*"

32. Lessing believes that being reared outside of England gave her invaluable perspective (Brewster, 158–59). Martha Reid discusses the advantages and disadvantages of being an outsider and explores the nuances of "alien" and "exile."

33. Judith Stitzel comments on a similar process in reading other Lessing works (498–502).

Notes to Chapter 7

1. Naomi Jacobs discusses a similar use of narrative structure, but without the evolutionary quality of pragmatism, in Le Guin's *Always Coming Home* (41–43).

2. In fact, Mary Shelley's *Frankenstein* (written in 1816) was the first work of science fiction according to many people in the field, including Le Guin (*Nebula Award Stories 11,* 10).

3. Barr has written *Alien to Femininity,* including a bibliography of fiction and criticism (161–82), *Feminist Fabulation,* and *Lost in Space.* She has edited volumes, such as *Future Females: A Critical Anthology* and *Future Females, The Next Generation.* Other books include Rosinsky, *Feminist Futures;* Lefanu, *Feminism and Science Fiction;* Armitt, *Where No Man Has Gone Before;* Roberts, *A New Species;* Donawerth and Kolmerten, *Utopian and Science Fiction by Women;* Wolmark, *Aliens and Others;* and Donawerth, *Frankenstein's Daughters.*

4. On the politics of Le Guin's early fiction see Suvin, "Parables," and David L. Porter.

5. The two selves are described by John Fekete (91–92). James W. Bittner gives a comprehensive explanation of her relation to Taoism and provides "A Bibliographical Orientation to Taoism" (416–34).

6. I follow the chronology calculated by Ian Watson (68).

7. In "Is Gender Necessary? Redux," Le Guin retracts this: "*[. . . In any kemmerhouse* (i.e., among more than two people) *homosexual practice would, of course, be possible and acceptable and welcomed—but I never thought to explore this option; and the omission, alas, implies that sexuality is heterosexuality. I regret this very much]*" (14).

8. My explanation of sexuality refers only to normal Gethenians, since we, as "perverts" ourselves, are already familiar with the exceptions.

9. The absence of rape may stem not only from this biological fact but also from the

psychological results of female/male variation or from the absence of patriarchy and of "the masculinity that rapes and the femininity that is raped" (96).

10. As Barbara Bucknall says, without gender "we are still left with love and faith, disappointment and betrayal, face saving, incest, religion, politics, and the weather" ("Ursula K. Le Guin," 546).

11. Although Gethenians are definitely not androgynous in gender, one might stretch categories and consider them androgynous in sex. In somer everyone has vestigial organs of both kinds, and apparently in kemmer a female still has vestigial male organs and vice versa.

12. See Wolmark; Roberts; and Donawerth, chap. 2.

13. *Left Hand* plays with the echoes that resonate between "alien" and "alone" (18, 232).

14. Like certain characters, the implied readers go through this experience. They may initially think they know what words such as "king" mean, but, as they read farther, they learn they have been wrong to picture a male.

15. The female/male metaphor in its Gethen/Ekumen form (described below) does not, however, undergo protean transformation as the Karhide/Orgoreyn form does.

16. See Barrow and Barrow. In fact, this pragmatic process resembles the non-Euclidean type of utopian thought that Le Guin prefers ("A Non-Euclidean View of California").

17. The Orgota religion is static, whereas the Karhidish religion is pragmatic, valuing "Creation unfinished" (246). The novel's eventual privileging of Karhide thus supports pragmatism.

18. I discuss this in detail and from a different angle in "Reading Piebald Patterns." Other oppositions, such as left/right, resemble darkness/light in that they structure the novel and they both represent and are represented by the female/male opposition. I concentrate on darkness/light because it is the most richly embroidered of the oppositions. (For a good discussion of oppositions, see Lake.) In addition, the darkness/light pair could provide a springboard for a reading of *Left Hand* that would concentrate on race. Although such a reading lies beyond the scope of this chapter, it would prove rewarding, not only in the sense that any science fiction about aliens offers fertile metaphors for a meditation on race relations, but also because *Left Hand* in particular defies the science-fiction conventions of its day by mentioning, as if in passing, that its Terran hero is very dark-skinned, unlike most Gethenians (35).

19. Some of the meanings of "shadow" that I discuss are mentioned by Slusser (23–24).

20. Some critics mention the relationship in passing—e.g., Lake (159) and Rabkin ("Metalinguistics," 88–89).

21. Several of the instances of Karhidish superiority that I shall explain are mentioned by N. B. Hayles (102–4), David J. Lake, and Gary Willis (40).

22. The mediation of oppositions is discussed by Jeanne Murray Walker.

23. On Estraven's "rejection of simple dualities," see Barry and Prescott, 161.

24. Norman N. Holland refers to other senses in which this novel doubles doubleness.

25. Critics tend not to question or to go much beyond Le Guin's analysis in passages such as the one I have just quoted (e.g., Barbour). John Fekete perceptively but briefly criticizes the concepts of wholeness and balance (95).

26. Sometimes Le Guin's short stories also go beyond binarism to mild multiplicity.

"Schrödinger's Cat" is discovered to be neither dead nor alive, but gone. Similarly, "The Ones Who Walk Away from Omelas" do so to escape a double bind.

27. Although technically the ice sheet belongs to Orgoreyn, its uninhabitability and its role in the plot separate it from both nations.

28. Related to translation is a more kinetic form of mediation: travel between the female and male poles of a geographical opposition.

29. Fredric Jameson refers to "generic discontinuities" ("World Reduction," 221). The religious text, which is about timelessness, and the scientific report are not even narratives.

30. Eric S. Rabkin discusses the significance of the kemmer episode and of this page ("Determinism," 13–14).

31. In the Yomesh chapter, as in many other religious works, the question of which narrator sees or speaks can have no simple answer.

32. The writerly is defined by Roland Barthes (4).

33. I am grateful to Elizabeth Sommers for suggesting this point.

34. Sometimes when reading aloud from *Left Hand,* she substitutes female pronouns for male ones (Lecture).

35. Le Guin's revision makes the short story both younger and older than the novel, causing the story to resemble its eponymous protagonist, for traveling at near light speed makes Winter's king both younger and older than her child.

36. One of the first to do so was Alexei Panshin (51). A helpful overview of the issue is provided by Anna Valdine Clemens (435n2). Some critics nevertheless see the Gethenians as female: e.g., Holland (130) and Barr ("Charles Bronson," 141).

37. Le Guin hoped the Envoy's male qualities would make the Gethenians' female ones stand out in contrast ("Lagniappe," 280–81).

38. Susan Wood says he sees Gethenians "as males with certain negative traits he identifies as female" (167).

39. Although Russ mostly condemns *Left Hand*'s male orientation, in a note she admits that "one could make out a good case that the author is trying to criticize [Genly's] viewpoint" (94n29).

40. Given Gethenian society, Le Guin also felt a female protagonist would have damped narrative energy: "'I knew a woman would just love it. There wouldn't be any dramatic scenes; she would just settle right down'" (Gallagher, 26). (The use of an evolving male point of view to introduce a feminist perspective also appears in James Tiptree, Jr.'s "The Women Men Don't See.")

41. It is true that some feminists might be able to enjoy the male orientation as a parodic exaggeration of patriarchy. Anna Valdine Clemens indeed refers to "Le Guin's ironic intent in her presentation of a protagonist with an excessively masculine point of view" (423).

42. Natalie M. Rosinsky, although not discussing pragmatism, notes that *Left Hand* encourages reader activity within the text and outside it (29).

43. Granted, Le Guin says *Left Hand* "poses no *practicable* alternative to contemporary society since it is based on an imaginary, radical change in human anatomy. All it tries to do is open up an alternative viewpoint, to widen the imagination" ("Redux," 16). But I would argue that such an expansion of thought is itself powerful.

Notes to Chapter 8

1. I refer to the English translation, except where otherwise noted.

2. Other ways in which the text "subverts its own discourse" are examined by Owen Heathcote (81).

3. See Crowder's "Amazons and Mothers?" and, for a helpful bibliography and overview of Wittig's work and studies of it, see Crowder, "Monique Wittig."

4. Thus, while the feminist women do dominate the book, I disagree when Susan Rubin Suleiman says of the novel's "descriptive fragments" that "all of them [have] as their subject (both grammatically and in terms of content) . . . the *guérillères*" ("The Politics and Poetics of Female Eroticism," 131).

5. Wittig says the whole book may be utopian insofar as the pronoun *elles* situates the reader outside the categories of sex ("Quelques Remarques," 121). Joanna Russ discusses the text's utopian aspects ("Recent Feminist Utopias").

6. Since the setting is all-female, lesbianism has a different resonance than in most Western cultures, where heterosexuality is not only possible but, as Adrienne Rich says, "compulsory" ("Compulsory Heterosexuality and Lesbian Existence").

7. See Wittig, "Homo Sum," 46.

8. E.g., Farwell, *Heterosexual Plots and Lesbian Narratives*. But Judith Roof says that "Wittig's attempt, in the name of the more metaphorical lesbian," to challenge narrative works better than her representation of the literal lesbian (130–31).

9. Susan Sniader Lanser also points out that "French names and Western myths dominate" (*Fictions of Authority*, 270).

10. On collective protagonists, see DuPlessis, *Writing Beyond the Ending*, chaps. 10 and 11.

11. For further explanation of the word, see Wenzel, 276–77.

12. Dianne Chisholm mentions the title's connection to *guérrier* and *elles* ("Lesbianizing Love's Body," 198).

13. Also see Lanser, *Fictions of Authority*, 269.

14. Criticisms of Wittig as essentialist, made by Judith Butler and Diana Fuss, are reviewed and countered by Jennifer Burwell, who lauds Wittig for universalizing what is ordinarily marginalized (chap. 5).

15. The real author, however, refers to *Les Guérillères* as resembling only the great register and sees it as replacing the narcissistic feminaries ("Quelques Remarques," 121).

16. Susan Sniader Lanser makes similar points (*Fictions of Authority*, 271).

17. On the novel's "self-destructing" and "circular reasoning," see Homans, 190.

18. Even the most perceptive critics write of a single war (e.g., Laurence M. Porter). While Susan Rubin Suleiman does recognize that there is "no narrative line," she finds "something like an internal evolution among the fragments": "[A]t the end of the book, . . . 'elles' make peace with the surviving men" ("The Politics and Poetics of Female Eroticism," 132). Since the final fragment uses only feminine grammatical forms, some critics think it means men have been eliminated (Suleiman [133]) or assimilated (both Suleiman [133] and Lanser [275]), but perhaps this vignette is simply representing a scene from which men are absent.

19. Nancy Gray refers in another way to deconstruction in *Les Guérillères*, observing that the text deconstructs "the roles of dominator and dominated alike" (170).

20. Stage Three starts a bit before the page on which Stage Two becomes definite, but I still consider the patriarchal men's stage the earlier one, since so many clues precede that point.

21. Some of these differences resound more clearly in the French original. For example, "Elles disent, ils t'ont dans leurs discours possédée violée prise soumise humiliée tout leur saoul" (146) is translated as: "They say, in speaking they have possessed violated taken subdued humiliated you to their hearts' content" (100, 102). The translation loses the information that "you" refers to someone singular and female; the singular is appropriate, since the nonfeminist addressees lack the solidarity and multiplicity that characterize the feminists. Furthermore, in addition to rhyming more noticeably, the French original makes explicit what is clouded by the English version, the fact that "they" means women the first time and men the second.

22. Wenzel explores other implications of the emphasis on the vulva rather than the womb (281).

23. Lucy Sargisson says *Les Guérillères* "is a transgressive utopian text. It disrupts and negates binarisms, it rejects a dualistic conceptualization of 'Woman' and/or femininity. Moreover, it celebrates *process,* representing a dynamic and ever-changing society which conceives of itself in new ways that do not rest on old universalisms" (209).

24. Angelika Bammer discusses reader involvement, as well as a sort of pragmatism within the utopia (123–33). Margaret Homans has pointed out that "to the extent that we can read [Wittig's] book, we recognize the dependence of both writer and reader on the system of representation that her characters are represented as demolishing" (190). Similarly, see Jardine, 234–35. But the paradox has less dire consequences on the level of storytelling (as opposed, say, to syntax), where the conventional "system of representation" demands conflict and so contains the possibility of its own "demolishing."

Notes to Conclusion

1. This recalls the theory of Austin M. Wright, who argues that novels need not only forces of unification but also forces of disruption, which he calls recalcitrance (104–9). I am extending his idea to persuasion.

2. For commentary on recent developments in this niche, see Barr, *Future Females, The Next Generation.* I have also applied my theories to a First-Wave feminist utopian novel, *Corinne, or Italy* (1807), by Germaine de Staël: "He Reads, She Speaks: How Narrative Form Conveys Conflicting Values in *Corinne, or Italy*"; "Corinne's Shift to Patriarchal Mediation: Rebirth or Regression?"; and "Contradictions of Form and Feminism in *Corinne ou l'Italie.*"

3. Because the book concentrates on the counterculture, I refer to the text as a utopia, but Le Guin also pays attention to the two fanatical societies, which are dystopias.

4. *Parable* serves as a major example of "critical dystopia" both for Tom Moylan (*Scraps of the Untainted Sky*) and for Raffaella Baccolini, who explains that critical dystopias, like critical utopias, "negate static ideals," a process similar to my notion of pragmatism (17).

5. *Marriages* and *Left Hand* do draw on realism, but neither is conventionally realist.

6. Various definitions of realism differ in the degree to which they privilege reality or convention. Wallace Martin provides a good overview of the debate (chap. 3).

Bibliography

Abley, Mark. "Liberating Love in Outer Spaces." Rev. of *The Marriages Between Zones Three, Four, and Five,* by Doris Lessing. *Macleans,* 23 June 1980: 51–52.

Abrams, M. H. "Belief and the Suspension of Disbelief." In *Literature and Belief.* Ed. Abrams. New York: Columbia University Press, 1958. 1–30.

———. *A Glossary of Literary Terms.* 6th ed. Fort Worth, Tex.: Harcourt Brace, 1993.

Albinski, Nan Bowman. "'The Laws of Justice, of Nature, and of Right': Victorian Feminist Utopias." Jones and Goodwin, 50–68.

Armitt, Lucie. "Your Word Is My Command: The Structures of Language and Power in Women's Science Fiction." In *Where No Man Has Gone Before: Women and Science Fiction.* Ed. Armitt. London: Routledge, 1991. 123–38.

Arnold, June. *The Cook and the Carpenter.* Plainfield, Vt.: Daughters, Inc., 1973.

Atwood, Margaret. *The Handmaid's Tale.* 1985. New York: Fawcett-Crest, 1987.

———. "Simmering." *Murder in The Dark: Short Fictions and Prose Poems.* Toronto: Coach House Press, 1983. 31–33.

———. "Witches: The Strong Neck of a Favorite Ancestor." *The Radcliffe Quarterly,* Sept. 1980: 4–6.

Augustine, *On Christian Doctrine.* Trans. D. W. Robertson, Jr. New York: Bobbs-Merrill, 1958.

Austen, Jane. *Emma.* 1816. *The Complete Novels of Jane Austen.* New York: Modern Library, n.d. 761–1060.

Baccolini, Raffaella. "Gender and Genre in the Feminist Critical Dystopias of Katherine Burdekin, Margaret Atwood, and Octavia Butler." In Barr, *Future Females, The Next Generation,* 13–34.

Baker, Susan W. "Biological Influences on Human Sex and Gender: Review Essay." *Signs* 6 (1980): 80–96.

Bal, Mieke. *Narratology: Introduction to the Theory of Narrative.* Trans. Christine van Boheemen. Toronto: University of Toronto Press, 1985.

Balzac, Honoré de. *Père Goriot.* 1835. Garden City, N.Y.: Doubleday, 1951.

———. "Sarrasine." 1830. In Barthes, *S/Z: An Essay,* 221–54.

Bammer, Angelika. *Partial Visions: Feminism and Utopianism in the 1970s.* New York: Routledge, 1991.

Barbour, Douglas. "Wholeness and Balance in the Hainish Novels of Ursula K. Le Guin." *Science-Fiction Studies* 1 (1974): 164–73.

Barr, Marleen S. *Alien to Femininity: Speculative Fiction and Feminist Theory.* New York: Greenwood, 1987.

———. "Charles Bronson, Samurai, and Other Feminine Images: A Transactive Response to *The Left Hand of Darkness.*" In Barr, *Future Females: A Critical Anthology,* 138–54.

———. *Feminist Fabulation: Space/Postmodern Fiction.* Iowa City: University of Iowa Press, 1992.

———, ed. *Future Females: A Critical Anthology.* Bowling Green, Ohio: Bowling Green State University Popular Press, 1981.

———, ed. *Future Females, The Next Generation: New Voices and Velocities in Feminist Science Fiction Criticism.* Lanham, Md.: Rowman & Littlefield, 2000.

———. *Lost in Space: Probing Feminist Science Fiction and Beyond.* Chapel Hill, N.C.: University of North Carolina Press, 1993.

Barr, Marleen [S.], and Patrick D. Murphy, eds. *Feminism Faces the Fantastic.* Spec. issue of *Women's Studies* 14 (1987): 81–191.

Barr, Marleen [S.], and Nicholas D. Smith, eds. *Women and Utopia: Critical Interpretations.* Lanham, Md.: University Press of America, 1983.

Barrett, Michèle, and Anne Phillips, eds. *Destabilizing Theory: Contemporary Feminist Debates.* Stanford, Calif.: Stanford University Press, 1992.

Barrow, Craig, and Diana Barrow. "*The Left Hand of Darkness:* Feminism for Men." *Mosaic* 20.1 (1987): 83–96.

Barry, Nora, and Mary Prescott. "Beyond Words: The Impact of Rhythm as Narrative Technique in *The Left Hand of Darkness.*" *Extrapolation* 33 (1992): 154–65.

Barthes, Roland. *S/Z: An Essay.* 1970. Trans. Richard Miller. New York: Hill and Wang-Farrar, Straus and Giroux, 1974.

Bartkowski, Frances. *Feminist Utopias.* Lincoln: University of Nebraska Press, 1989.

Beauvoir, Simone de. *The Second Sex.* 1949. Trans. and ed. H. M. Parshley. New York: Vintage-Random House, 1974.

Bittner, James W. *Approaches to the Fiction of Ursula K. Le Guin.* Ph.D. diss. University of Wisconsin-Madison, 1979. Ann Arbor, Mich.: UMI Research Press, 1984.

Bloch, Ernst. *The Principle of Hope.* Trans. Neville Plaice, Stephen Plaice, and Paul Knight. 3 vols. Cambridge, Mass.: MIT Press, 1986.

Bolin, Anne. "Transcending and Transgendering: Male-to-Female Transsexuals, Dichotomy and Diversity." In Herdt, *Third Sex,* 447–85, 589–96.

Booth, Wayne C. *The Company We Keep: An Ethics of Fiction.* Berkeley: University of California Press, 1988.

———. *The Rhetoric of Fiction.* 1961. 2d ed. Chicago: University of Chicago Press, 1983.

Braudeau, M. "Out into the Stars." *World Press Review,* July 1981: 61.

Brewster, Dorothy. *Doris Lessing.* New York: Twayne, 1965.

Brontë, Charlotte. *Jane Eyre.* 1847. Harmondsworth, Eng.: Penguin, 1953.

Brooke-Rose, Christine. "The Readerhood of Man." In *The Reader in the Text: Essays on Audience and Interpretation.* Ed. Susan R. Suleiman and Inge Crosman. Princeton, N.J.: Princeton University Press, 1980. 120–48.

Brookmire, Paula. "She Writes about Aliens—Men Included." In *Biography News.* Detroit, Mich.: Gale Research, 1974. 1155.

Brooks, Peter. *Reading for the Plot: Design and Intention in Narrative.* 1984. New York: Vintage-Random House, 1985.

Brown, Barbara. "*The Left Hand of Darkness:* Androgyny, Future, Present, and Past." *Extrapolation* 21 (1980): 227–35.

Browning, Elizabeth Barrett. *Aurora Leigh: A Poem.* 1864. Chicago: Cassandra-Academy Chicago, 1979.

Bucknall, Barbara J. *Ursula K. Le Guin.* New York: Ungar, 1981.

———. "Ursula K. Le Guin." In *American Women Writers.* Ed. Lina Mainiero. Vol. 2. New York: Ungar, 1980. 546–47.

Bugliosi, Vincent, with Curt Gentry. *Helter Skelter: The True Story of the Manson Murders.* New York: Norton, 1974.

Bulkin, Elly. "An Interview with Adrienne Rich." In *Critical Essays on Doris Lessing.* Ed. Claire Sprague and Virginia Tiger. Boston: G. K. Hall, 1986. 181–82.

Burke, Kenneth. *A Rhetoric of Motives.* 1950. *A Grammar of Motives and A Rhetoric of Motives.* Cleveland: Meridian-World, 1962.

Burwell, Jennifer. *Notes on Nowhere: Feminism, Utopian Logic, and Social Transformation.* American Culture 13. Minneapolis, Minn.: University of Minnesota Press, 1997.

Butler, Judith. *Bodies That Matter: On the Discursive Limits of "Sex."* New York: Routledge, 1993.

———. "Contingent Foundations: Feminism and the Question of 'Postmodernism.'" In *Feminists Theorize the Political.* Ed. Judith Butler and Joan W. Scott. New York: Routledge, 1992. 3–21.

Butler, Octavia. *Parable of the Sower.* New York: Warner, 1993.

Carter, Angela. "The Company of Wolves." In *The Bloody Chamber.* 1979. New York: Harper Colophon, 1981. 142–53.

———. *The Passion of New Eve.* 1977. London: Virago, 1982.

Charnas, Suzy McKee. *The Furies.* New York: Tor-Tom Doherty Associates, 1994.

———. *Walk to the End of the World and Motherlines.* 1974, 1979. London: Women's Press, 1989.

Chatman, Seymour. *Coming to Terms: The Rhetoric of Narrative in Fiction and Film.* Ithaca, N.Y.: Cornell University Press, 1990.

Chisholm, Dianne. "Lesbianizing Love's Body: Interventionist Imag(in)ings of Monique

Wittig." In *ReImagining Women: Representations of Women in Culture.* Ed. Shirley Neuman and Glennis Stephenson. Toronto: University of Toronto Press, 1993. 196–216.

Chopin, Kate. *The Awakening.* 1899. New York: CommonPlace-Simon & Schuster, 1996.

Cixous, Hélène. "Castration or Decapitation?" 1976. Trans. Annette Kuhn. *Signs* 7 (1981): 41–55.

———. From "Sorties." 1975. Trans. Ann Liddle. In Marks and de Courtivron, *New French Feminisms,* 90–98.

———. "The Laugh of the Medusa." 1975. Trans. Keith Cohen and Paula Cohen. In Marks and de Courtivron, *New French Feminisms,* 245–64.

Clemens, Anna Valdine. "Art, Myth and Ritual in Le Guin's *The Left Hand of Darkness.*" *Canadian Review of American Studies* 17 (1986): 423–36.

Commager, Henry Steele. *The American Mind.* New Haven, Conn.: Yale University Press, 1950.

Conrad, Joseph. *Heart of Darkness.* 1902. Ed. Robert Kimbrough. 2d ed. New York: Norton, 1971.

Conway, Claire. *Stanford Medicine* 10.2 (1992): 10–14.

Cornillon, Susan Koppelman, ed. *Images of Women in Fiction.* Bowling Green, Ohio: Bowling Green University Popular Press, 1972.

Crowder, Diane Griffin. "Amazons and Mothers? Monique Wittig, Hélène Cixous and Theories of Women's Writing." *Contemporary Literature* 24 (1983): 117–44.

———. "Monique Wittig." In *French Women Writers: A Bio-Bibliographical Source Book.* Ed. Eva Martin Sartori and Dorothy Wynne Zimmerman. New York: Greenwood, 1991. 524–34.

Daly, Mary. *Gyn/Ecology.* Boston: Beacon, 1978.

Daniel, Jamie Owen, and Tom Moylan, eds. *Not Yet: Reconsidering Ernst Bloch.* London: Verso, 1997.

Davis, Elizabeth Gould. *The First Sex.* New York: G. P. Putnam's Sons, 1971.

Davis, Lennard J. *Resisting Novels: Ideology and Fiction.* New York: Methuen, 1987.

Delany, Samuel [R.]. "About Five Thousand Seven Hundred and Fifty Words." *The Jewel-Hinged Jaw: Notes on the Language of Science Fiction.* Elizabethtown, N.J.: Dragon, 1977. 33–49.

———. *Triton.* New York: Bantam, 1976.

Delmar, Rosalind. "What Is Feminism?" In *What Is Feminism?* Ed. Juliet Mitchell and Ann Oakley. New York: Pantheon, 1986. 8–33.

Derrida, Jacques. "Limited Inc abc . . ." Trans. Samuel Weber. In *Glyph 2.* Ed. Samuel Weber and Henry Sussman. Baltimore, Md.: Johns Hopkins University Press, 1977. 162–254.

———. "Signature, Event, Context." 1972. Trans. Samuel Weber and Jeffrey Mehlman. In *Glyph 1.* Ed. Samuel Weber and Henry Sussman. Baltimore, Md.: Johns Hopkins University Press, 1977. 172–97.

Deutelbaum, Wendy, ed. *Woman as Reader.* Spec. issue of *Reader: Essays in Reader-Oriented Theory, Criticism, and Pedagogy* 8 (1980): 1–39.

Dinesen, Isak. "The Blank Page." 1957. In Gilbert and Gubar, *The Norton Anthology of Literature by Women,* 1391–94.

Dinnerstein, Dorothy. "What Does Feminism Mean?" Harris and King, 13–23.

Donawerth, Jane [L.]. *Frankenstein's Daughters: Women Writing Science Fiction.* Syracuse, N.Y.: Syracuse University Press, 1997.

Donawerth, Jane L., and Carol A. Kolmerten, eds. *Utopian and Science Fiction by Women: Worlds of Difference.* Syracuse, N.Y.: Syracuse University Press, 1994.

Dowst, Kenneth Irving. "The Rhetoric of Utopian Fiction." Ph.D. diss. University of Pittsburgh, 1979.

Draine, Betsy. *Substance under Pressure: Artistic Coherence and Evolving Form in the Novels of Doris Lessing.* Madison, Wisc.: University of Wisconsin Press, 1983.

Driver, C. J. "Profile 8: Doris Lessing." *The New Review,* Nov. 1974: 17–23.

DuPlessis, Rachel Blau. *Writing Beyond the Ending: Narrative Strategies of Twentieth-Century Women Writers.* Bloomington, Ind.: Indiana University Press, 1985.

Eagleton, Terry. *Literary Theory: An Introduction.* Minneapolis, Minn.: University of Minnesota Press, 1983.

Ebert, Teresa. "The 'Difference' of Postmodern Feminism." *College English* 53 (1991): 886–904.

Edelstein, Marilyn. "Ethics and Contemporary American Literature: Revisiting the Controversy over John Gardner's *On Moral Fiction.*" *Pacific Coast Philology* 31 (1996): 40–53.

Eisenstein, Hester. *Contemporary Feminist Thought.* Boston: G. K. Hall, 1983.

Eliot, George. *Adam Bede.* 1859. Chicago: Maxwell, 1887.

Eliot, T. S. "Dante." 1929. In *Selected Essays.* New ed. New York: Harcourt, Brace and World, 1964. 199–237.

Farwell, Marilyn R. *Heterosexual Plots and Lesbian Narratives.* The Cutting Edge: Lesbian Life and Literature. New York: New York University Press, 1996.

———. "Toward a Definition of the Lesbian Literary Imagination." In *Sexual Practice/Textual Theory: Lesbian Cultural Criticism.* Ed. Susan J. Wolfe and Julia Penelope. Cambridge, Mass.: Blackwell, 1993. 66–84.

Fausto-Sterling, Anne. "The Five Sexes: Why Male and Female Are Not Enough." *The Sciences,* Mar.–Apr. 1993: 20–25.

Fekete, John. "Circumnavigating Ursula Le Guin." Rev. of *Ursula K. Le Guin: Voyager to Inner Lands and to Outer Space,* ed. Joe De Bolt. *Science-Fiction Studies* 8, pt. 1 (1981): 91–98.

Fetterley, Judith. *The Resisting Reader: A Feminist Approach to American Fiction.* Bloomington, Ind.: Indiana University Press, 1978.

Finney, Kathe Davis. "The Days of Future Past or Utopians Lessing and LeGuin [*sic*] Fight

Future Nostalgia." In *Patterns of the Fantastic.* Ed. Donald M. Hassler. Mercer Island, Wash.: Starmont House, 1983. 31–40.

Fish, Stanley. *Self-Consuming Artifacts: The Experience of Seventeenth-Century Literature.* Berkeley: University of California Press, 1972.

Fishburn, Katherine. "Teaching Doris Lessing as a Subversive Activity: A Response to the Preface to *The Golden Notebook.*" Kaplan and Rose, *Doris Lessing,* 81–92.

———. *The Unexpected Universe of Doris Lessing: A Study in Narrative Technique.* Contributions to the Study of Science Fiction and Fantasy 17. Westport, Conn.: Greenwood, 1985.

Fisher, Walter R. *Human Communication as Narration: Toward a Philosophy of Reason, Value, and Action.* Columbia, S.C.: University of South Carolina Press, 1987.

Fitting, Peter. "Positioning and Closure: On the 'Reading-Effect' of Contemporary Utopian Fiction." *Utopian Studies* 1 (1987): 23–36.

Flaubert, Gustave. *Madame Bovary: Patterns of Provincial Life.* 1856. Trans. Francis Steegmuller. 2d ed. New York: Modern Library, 1982.

Flynn, Elizabeth A., and Patrocinio P. Schweickart, eds. *Gender and Reading: Essays on Readers, Texts, and Contexts.* Baltimore, Md.: Johns Hopkins University Press, 1986.

Foss, Karen A., Sonja K. Foss, and Cindy L. Griffin. *Feminist Rhetorical Theories.* Thousand Oaks, Calif.: SAGE, 1999.

Freedman, Carl. "Science Fiction and Utopia: A Historico-Philosophical Overview." In Parrinder, 72–97.

Freud, Sigmund. "Femininity." In *The Standard Edition of the Complete Psychological Works of Sigmund Freud.* Trans. and ed. James Strachey. Vol. 22. London: Hogarth, 1964. 112–35.

Friedman, Susan Stanford. *Mappings: Feminism and the Cultural Geographies of Encounter.* Princeton, N.J.: Princeton University Press, 1998.

Frye, Joanne S. *Living Stories, Telling Lives: Women and the Novel in Contemporary Experience.* Ann Arbor, Mich.: University of Michigan Press, 1986.

Frye, Northrop. *The Secular Scripture: A Study of the Structure of Romance.* Cambridge, Mass.: Harvard University Press, 1976.

Gallagher, Nora. "Ursula Le Guin: In a World of Her Own." *Mother Jones,* Jan. 1984: 23+.

Gatens, Moira. "Power, Bodies and Difference." In Barrett and Phillips, *Destabilizing Theory,* 120–37.

Gearhart, Sally Miller. "The Womanization of Rhetoric." *Women's Studies International Quarterly* 2 (1979): 195–201.

Genette, Gérard. *Narrative Discourse: An Essay in Method.* 1972. Trans. Jane E. Lewin. Ithaca, N.Y.: Cornell University Press, 1980.

Gilbert, Sandra M., and Susan Gubar. *The Madwoman in the Attic: The Woman Writer and the Nineteenth-Century Literary Imagination.* New Haven, Conn.: Yale University Press, 1979.

———, eds. *The Norton Anthology of Literature by Women: The Traditions in English.* 2d ed. New York: Norton, 1996.

Gilligan, Carol. *In a Different Voice: Psychological Theory and Women's Development.* Cambridge, Mass.: Harvard University Press, 1982.

Gilman, Charlotte Perkins. *Herland.* 1915. New York: Pantheon, 1979.

———. "The Yellow Wallpaper." 1892. Gilbert and Gubar. In *The Norton Anthology of Literature by Women,* 1133–44.

Goethe, Johann Wolfgang von. *Goethe's Faust.* 1831. Trans. Walter Kaufmann. New York: Anchor-Doubleday, 1961.

Graff, Gerald. *Poetic Statement and Critical Dogma.* Evanston, Ill.: Northwestern University Press, 1970.

Gray, Nancy. *Language Unbound: On Experimental Writing by Women.* Urbana, Ill.: University of Illinois Press, 1992.

Greene, Gayle. *Changing the Story: Feminist Fiction and the Tradition.* Bloomington, Ind.: Indiana University Press, 1991.

———. *Doris Lessing: The Poetics of Change.* Ann Arbor, Mich.: University of Michigan Press, 1994.

Grémaux, René. "Woman Becomes Man in the Balkans." In Herdt, *Third Sex,* 241–81, 548–54.

Griggers, Cathy. "Lesbian Bodies in the Age of (Post)Mechanical Reproduction." In *The Lesbian Postmodern.* Ed. Laura Doan. New York: Columbia University Press, 1994. 118–33.

Grimm, Jacob, and Wilhelm Grimm. "The Fisherman and His Wife." In *The Complete Grimm's Fairy Tales.* Trans. Margaret Hunt and James Stern. New York: Pantheon, 1944. 103–12.

Hacking, Ian. *Representing and Intervening: Introductory Topics in the Philosophy of Science.* Cambridge, Eng.: Cambridge University Press, 1983.

Hall, Roberta M., and Bernice R. Sadler. *The Classroom Climate: A Chilly One for Women?* Washington, D.C.: Assn. of Amer. Colls. and Univs., 1982.

Hansot, Elisabeth. *Perfection and Progress: Two Modes of Utopian Thought.* Cambridge, Mass.: MIT Press, 1974.

Haraway, Donna J. "Situated Knowledges: The Science Question in Feminism and the Privilege of Partial Perspective." *Simians, Cyborgs, and Women: The Reinvention of Nature.* New York: Routledge, 1991. 183–201.

Hardin, Nancy Shields. "Doris Lessing and the Sufi Way." In Pratt and Dembo, 148–64.

———. "The Sufi Teaching Story and Doris Lessing." *Twentieth Century Literature* 23 (1977): 314–26.

Harris, Adrienne, and Ynestra King, eds. *Rocking the Ship of State: Toward a Feminist Peace Politics.* Boulder, Colo.: Westview, 1989.

Harrison, Barbara Grizzuti. *Unlearning the Lie: Sexism in School.* New York: Liveright, 1973.

Hawthorne, Nathaniel. "The Birthmark." 1843. In *Nathaniel Hawthorne,* 264–81.

———. *Nathaniel Hawthorne: Selected Tales and Sketches.* 3d ed. New York: Holt, Rinehart and Winston, 1970.

———. "Rappaccini's Daughter." 1844. In *Nathaniel Hawthorne,* 329–60.

Hayles, N. B. "Androgyny, Ambivalence, and Assimilation in *The Left Hand of Darkness.*" In *Ursula K. Le Guin.* Ed. Joseph D. Olander and Martin Henry Greenberg. New York: Taplinger, 1979. 97–115.

Heathcote, Owen. "Masochism, Sadism, and Women's Writing: The Examples of Marguerite Duras and Monique Wittig." *Nottingham French Studies* 32.2 (1993): 71–84.

Heilbrun, Carolyn. *Toward a Recognition of Androgyny.* New York: Harper Colophon-Harper & Row, 1973.

Hemingway, Ernest. "A Very Short Story." In *In Our Time.* New York: Scribner's, 1970 [1958]. 65–66.

Herdt, Gilbert. "Mistaken Sex: Culture, Biology and the Third Sex in New Guinea." In *Third Sex,* 419–45, 582–89.

———, ed. *Third Sex, Third Gender: Beyond Sexual Dimorphism in Culture and History.* New York: Zone Books, 1993.

Herman, David. "Introduction: Narratologies." In *Narratologies: New Perspectives on Narrative Analysis.* Ed. Herman. Columbus, Ohio: The Ohio State University Press, 1999. 1–30.

Holland, Norman N. "You, U. K. Le Guin." In Barr, *Future Females: A Critical Anthology,* 125–37.

Homans, Margaret. "'Her Very Own Howl': The Ambiguities of Representation in Recent Women's Fiction." *Signs* 9 (1983): 186–205.

hoogland, renée c. "Perverted Knowledge: Lesbian Sexuality and Theoretical Practice." *Journal of Gender Studies* 3 (1994): 15–29.

hooks, bell. *Ain't I a Woman: Black Women and Feminism.* Boston: South End Press, 1981.

Hospers, John. "Implied Truths in Literature." *Journal of Aesthetics and Art Criticism* 19 (1960): 37–46.

Howe, Florence. "A Conversation with Doris Lessing (1966)." In Pratt and Dembo, *Doris Lessing,* 1–19.

Hubbard, Ruth. "The Political Nature of 'Human Nature.'" In Rhode, *Theoretical Perspectives,* 63–73, 271–72.

Humm, Maggie. *The Dictionary of Feminist Theory.* 2d ed. Columbus, Ohio: The Ohio State University Press, 1995.

Hurston, Zora Neale. *Their Eyes Were Watching God.* 1937. Urbana, Ill.: University of Illinois Press, 1979.

Irigaray, Luce. *je, tu, nous: Toward a Culture of Difference.* 1990. Trans. Alison Martin. New York: Routledge, 1993.

———. "A Personal Note." In *je, tu, nous,* 9–14.

———. "The Power of Discourse and the Subordination of the Feminine." In *This Sex Which Is Not One,* 68–85.

———. "Questions." In *This Sex Which Is Not One,* 119–69.

———. *Speculum of the Other Woman.* 1974. Trans. Gillian C. Gill. Ithaca, N.Y.: Cornell University Press, 1985.

———. *This Sex Which Is Not One.* 1977. Trans. Catherine Porter with Carolyn Burke. Ithaca, N.Y.: Cornell University Press, 1985.

———. "When Our Lips Speak Together." 1976. Trans. Carolyn Burke. *Signs* 6 (1980): 69–79.

———. "Why Define Sexed Rights?" In *je, tu, nous,* 81–92.

Iser, Wolfgang. *The Act of Reading: A Theory of Aesthetic Response.* 1976. Baltimore, Md.: Johns Hopkins University Press, 1978.

———. *The Implied Reader: Patterns of Communication in Prose Fiction from Bunyan to Beckett.* 1972. Baltimore, Md.: Johns Hopkins University Press, 1974.

Iyer, Nalini. "Intergalactic Empires, Benevolent Imperialism and the Quest for Form." *Doris Lessing Newsletter* 20.1 (1999): 4–8.

Jacobs, Naomi. "Beyond Stasis and Symmetry: Lessing, Le Guin, and the Remodeling of Utopia." *Extrapolation* 29 (1988): 34–45.

Jaggar, Alison M. "Sexual Difference and Sexual Equality." In Rhode, *Theoretical Perspectives,* 239–54, 302–303.

James, Henry. *The Portrait of a Lady.* 1881. New York: Laurel-Dell, 1961.

Jameson, Fredric. "*History and Class Consciousness* as an 'Unfinished Project.'" *Rethinking Marxism* 1 (1988): 49–72.

———. *The Political Unconscious: Narrative as a Socially Symbolic Act.* Ithaca, N.Y.: Cornell University Press, 1981.

———. "World Reduction in Le Guin: The Emergence of Utopian Narrative." *Science-Fiction Studies* 2, pt. 3 (1975): 221–30.

Jardine, Alice. "Pre-Texts for the Transatlantic Feminist." *Yale French Studies* 62 (1981): 220–36.

Jones, Libby Falk. "Gilman, Bradley, Piercy, and the Evolving Rhetoric of Feminist Utopias." In Jones and Goodwin, *Feminism, Utopia, and Narrative,* 116–29.

Jones, Libby Falk, and Sarah Webster Goodwin, eds. *Feminism, Utopia, and Narrative.* Tennessee Studies in Literature 32. Knoxville, Tenn.: University of Tennessee Press, 1990.

Kaplan, Carey. "Britain's Imperialist Past in Doris Lessing's Futurist Fiction." In Kaplan and Rose, *Doris Lessing,* 149–68.

Kaplan, Carey, and Ellen Cronan Rose, eds. *Doris Lessing: The Alchemy of Survival.* Athens, Ohio: Ohio University Press, 1988.

———. "Lessing and Her Readers: Celebrating Difference." In Kaplan and Rose, *Doris Lessing,* 3–16.

Kessler, Suzanne J. "The Medical Construction of Gender: Case Management of Intersexed Infants." *Signs* 16 (1990): 3–26.

Khanna, Lee Cullen. "Frontiers of Imagination: Feminist Worlds." *Women's Studies International Forum* 7 (1984): 97–102.

———. "Truth and Art in Women's Worlds: Doris Lessing's *Marriages Between Zones Three, Four, and Five.*" In Barr and Smith, *Women and Utopia,* 121–33.

———. "Women's Worlds: New Directions in Utopian Fiction." *Alternative Futures: The Journal of Utopian Studies* 4.2–3 (1981): 47–60.

Kipen, David. "Le Guin Has a Lot to Say But Gets Lost in 'Telling.'" *San Francisco Chronicle,* 20 Sept. 2000: C1+.

Kristeva, Julia. "Un Nouveau type d'intellectuel: le dissident." *Tel Quel* 74 (1977): 3–8.

Krouse, Agate Nesaule. "The Feminism of Doris Lessing." Ph.D. diss. University of Wisconsin, 1972.

Laclos, Pierre-Ambroise-François Choderlos de. *Les Liaisons Dangereuses.* 1782. Trans. P. W. K. Stone. Harmondsworth, Eng.: Penguin, 1961.

Lafayette, Marie-Madeleine Pioche de La Vergne. *The Princess of Cleves.* 1678. Trans. Nancy Mitford. New York: New Directions, 1951.

Lake, David J. "Le Guin's Twofold Vision: Contrary Image-Sets in *The Left Hand of Darkness.*" *Science-Fiction Studies* 8, pt. 2 (1981): 156–64.

Lanser, Susan Sniader. *Fictions of Authority: Women Writers and Narrative Voice.* Ithaca, N.Y.: Cornell University Press, 1992.

———. *The Narrative Act: Point of View in Prose Fiction.* Princeton, N.J.: Princeton University Press, 1981.

Laqueur, Thomas. *Making Sex: Body and Gender from the Greeks to Freud.* Cambridge, Mass.: Harvard University Press, 1990.

Lefanu, Sarah. *Feminism and Science Fiction.* 1988. Bloomington, Ind.: Indiana University Press, 1989.

Le Guin, Ursula K. *Always Coming Home.* New York: Harper & Row, 1985.

———. "American SF and the Other." 1975. In *The Language of the Night,* 97–100.

———. "The Child and the Shadow." 1975. In *The Language of the Night,* 59–71.

———. *Dancing at the Edge of the World: Thoughts on Words, Women, Places.* New York: Grove, 1989.

———. *The Dispossessed.* 1974. New York: Avon, 1975.

———. "The Eye of the Heron." In *Millennial Women.* Ed. Virginia Kidd. New York:

Delacorte, 1978. 88–209.

———. "Is Gender Necessary? Redux." 1976, 1987. In *Dancing at the Edge of the World,* 7–16.

———. "It Was a Dark and Stormy Night; or, Why Are We Huddling about the Campfire?" In *On Narrative.* Ed. W. J. T. Mitchell. Chicago: University of Chicago Press, 1981. 187–95.

———. "Lagniappe: An Informal Dialogue with Conference Participants." In *Selected Proceedings of the 1978 Science Fiction Research Association National Conference.* Ed. Thomas J. Remington. Cedar Falls: University of Northern Iowa, 1979. 269–81.

———. *The Language of the Night.* Ed. Susan Wood. New York: Putnam, 1979.

———. Lecture at San Francisco State University. San Francisco. 7 May 1991.

———. *The Left Hand of Darkness.* 1969, Introduction 1976. New York: Ace-Grosset & Dunlap, 1976.

———. "The Marriages Between Zones Three, Four, and Five by Doris Lessing." *The New Republic,* 29 Mar. 1980: 34–35.

———. "National Book Award Acceptance Speech." In *The Language of the Night,* 57–58.

———, ed. *Nebula Award Stories 11.* London: Gollancz, 1976.

———. "A Non-Euclidean View of California as a Cold Place to Be." 1982. In *Dancing at the Edge of the World,* 80–100.

———. "The Ones Who Walk Away from Omelas." 1973. In *The Wind's Twelve Quarters,* 251–59.

———. "Re: Colonised Planet 5 Shikasta by Doris Lessing." *The New Republic,* 13 Oct. 1979: 32–34.

———. "Reply to Lem." *SF Commentary* 26 (1972): 90–93.

———. "Schrödinger's Cat." 1974. In *The Compass Rose: Short Stories.* New York: Harper & Row, 1982. 41–49.

Lessing, Doris. *Briefing for a Descent into Hell.* London: Cape, 1971.

———. *The Diaries of Jane Somers.* New York: Vintage-Random House, 1984.

———. *Documents Relating to the Sentimental Agents in the Volyen Empire.* New York: Knopf, 1983.

———. *The Four-Gated City.* 1969. New York: Bantam, 1970.

———. *The Golden Notebook.* 1962, Introduction 1971. New York: Bantam, 1973.

———. *The Good Terrorist.* 1985. New York: Vintage-Random House, 1986.

———. *The Making of the Representative for Planet 8.* London: Cape, 1982.

———. *The Marriages Between Zones Three, Four, and Five (As Narrated by the Chroniclers of Zone Three).* New York: Knopf, 1980.

———. *The Memoirs of a Survivor.* 1974. New York: Knopf, 1975.

———. *Re: Colonised Planet 5 Shikasta: Personal, Psychological, Historical Documents Relating to Visit by JOHOR (George Sherban), EMISSARY (Grade 9) 87th of the Period of the Last Days.* New York: Knopf, 1979.

———. *The Sirian Experiments: The Report by Ambien II, of the Five.* New York: Knopf, 1981.

———. "The Small Personal Voice." 1957. *In A Small Personal Voice: Essays, Reviews, Interviews.* Ed. Paul Schlueter. New York: Vintage-Random House, 1975. 3–21.

———. *The Telling.* New York: Harcourt, 2000.

———. "Winter's King." Rev. ed. *The Wind's Twelve Quarters,* 85–108.

Litt, Iris. *Taking Our Pulse: The Health of America's Women.* Stanford, Calif.: Stanford University Press, 1997.

Lorde, Audre. "The Master's Tools Will Never Dismantle the Master's House." *Sister Outsider: Essays and Speeches by Audre Lorde.* Trumansburg, N.Y.: The Crossing Press. 110–13.

Lukács, Georg. *Studies in European Realism: A Sociological Survey of the Writings of Balzac, Stendhal, Zola, Tolstoy, Gorki and Others.* 1948. Trans. Edith Bone. London: Hillway, 1950.

Lynn, Elizabeth A. *The Dancers of Arun.* 1979. New York: Berkley, 1980.

———. *The Northern Girl.* 1980. New York: Berkley, 1981.

———. *Watchtower.* 1979. New York: Berkley, 1980.

Lyons, John. *Introduction to Theoretical Linguistics.* Cambridge, Eng.: Cambridge University Press, 1968.

MacKinnon, Catherine A. "Legal Perspectives on Sexual Difference." In Rhode, *Theoretical Perspectives,* 213–25, 298–301.

Magie, Michael L. "Doris Lessing and Romanticism." *College English* 38 (1977): 531–52.

Mailloux, Steven, ed. *Rhetoric, Sophistry, Pragmatism.* Literature, Culture, Theory 15. Cambridge, Eng.: Cambridge University Press, 1995.

———. *Rhetorical Power.* Ithaca, N.Y.: Cornell University Press, 1989.

Manuel, Frank E., and Fritzie P. Manuel. *Utopian Thought in the Western World.* Cambridge, Mass.: Belknap-Harvard University Press, 1979.

Marks, Elaine, and Isabelle de Courtivron, eds. *New French Feminisms: An Anthology.* Amherst: University of Massachusetts Press, 1980.

Marlowe, Christopher. *Doctor Faustus.* 1604. Ed. Sylvan Barnet. New York: Signet-New American Library, 1969.

Martin, Wallace. *Recent Theories of Narrative.* Ithaca, N.Y.: Cornell University Press, 1986.

McCormack, Win, and Anne Mendel. "Creating Realistic Utopias: 'the obvious trouble with anarchism is neighbors': An Interview with Ursula Le Guin." *Seven Days,* 11 Apr. 1977: 38–40.

McIntyre, Vonda. *Dreamsnake.* Boston: Houghton Mifflin, 1978.

Meese, Elizabeth A. *Crossing the Double-Cross: The Practice of Feminist Criticism.* Chapel Hill, N.C.: University of North Carolina Press, 1986.

Mezei, Kathy, ed. *Ambiguous Discourse: Feminist Narratology and British Women Writers.* Chapel Hill, N.C.: University of North Carolina Press, 1996.

Millay, Edna St. Vincent. *A Few Figs from Thistles. Poems and Four Sonnets. Salvo One.* Enlarged ed. New York: Frank Shay, 1922.

Miller, J. Hillis. *The Ethics of Reading.* New York: Columbia University Press, 1987.

Miller, Nancy K. "Emphasis Added: Plots and Plausibilities in Women's Fiction." *PMLA* 96 (1981): 36–48.

Millett, Kate. *Sexual Politics.* 1969. Garden City, N.Y.: Doubleday, 1970.

More, Sir Thomas. *Utopia.* 1516. Trans. and ed. Robert M. Adams. 2d ed. New York: Norton, 1992.

Morris, Pam. *Literature and Feminism.* Oxford, Eng.: Blackwell, 1993.

Morrison, Toni. *Beloved.* 1987. New York: Plume-New American Library, 1988.

Moura, Jean-Marc. *L'image du tiers monde dans le roman français contemporain.* Paris: PUF, 1992.

Moylan, Tom. *Demand the Impossible: Science Fiction and the Utopian Imagination.* New York: Methuen, 1986.

———. *Scraps of the Untainted Sky: Science Fiction, Utopia, Dystopia.* Boulder, Colo.: Westview-Perseus, 2000.

Murphy, John P. *Pragmatism: From Peirce to Davidson.* Boulder, Colo.: Westview, 1990.

Newton, Adam Zachary. *Narrative Ethics.* Cambridge, Mass.: Harvard University Press, 1995.

Nussbaum, Martha. *Love's Knowledge: Essays on Philosophy and Literature.* New York: Oxford University Press, 1990.

———. *Poetic Justice: The Literary Imagination and Public Life.* Boston: Beacon, 1995.

O'Brien, Mary. "Feminist Theory and Dialectical Logic." *Signs* 7 (1981): 144–57.

Offen, Karen. "Defining Feminism: A Comparative Historical Approach." *Signs* 14 (1988): 119–57.

———. "Feminism and Sexual Difference in Historical Perspective." In Rhode, *Theoretical Perspectives,* 13–20, 265–66.

———. "Reflections on National Specificities in Continental European Feminism." *U.C.G. (University College, Galway [Ireland]) Review* 3 (1995): 53–58.

Okin, Susan Moller. "Feminist Interpretations of Political Thought." Jing Lyman Lecture. Stanford University, Stanford, Calif. 8 Feb. 1995.

———. "Thinking like a Woman." In Rhode, *Theoretical Perspectives,* 145–59, 288–91.

Oyĕwùmí, Oyèrónké. *The Invention of Women: Making an African Sense of Western Gender Discourses.* Minneapolis, Minn.: University of Minnesota Press, 1997.

Panshin, Alexei. "Books." Rev. of *The Left Hand of Darkness*, by Ursula K. Le Guin [and other works]. *The Magazine of Fantasy and Science Fiction* 37.5 (1969): 46–51.

Parrinder, Patrick, ed. *Learning from Other Worlds: Estrangement, Cognition, and the Politics of Science Fiction and Utopia*. Durham, N.C.: Duke University Press, 2001.

Patai, Daphne. "Beyond Defensiveness: Feminist Research Strategies." In Barr and Smith, *Women and Utopia*, 148–69.

Pearson, Carol. "Coming Home: Four Feminist Utopias and Patriarchal Experience." In Barr, *Future Females: A Critical Anthology*, 63–70.

Peel, Ellen. "Communicating Differently: Doris Lessing's *Marriages Between Zones Three, Four, and Five*." *Doris Lessing Newsletter* 6.2 (1982): 11–13.

———. "Contradictions of Form and Feminism in *Corinne ou l'Italie*." *Essays in Literature* 14 (1987): 281–98.

———. "Corinne's Shift to Patriarchal Mediation: Rebirth or Regression?" In *Germaine de Staël: Crossing the Borders*. Ed. Karyna Szmurlo, Madelyn Gutwirth, and Avriel Goldberger. New Brunswick, N.J.: Rutgers University Press, 1991. 101–12, 212–14.

———. "He Reads, She Speaks: How Narrative Form Conveys Conflicting Values in *Corinne, or Italy*." *Reader: Essays in Reader-Oriented Theory, Criticism, and Pedagogy* 40 (1998): 28–52.

———. "Leaving the Self Behind in *Marriages*." *Doris Lessing Newsletter* 11.2 (1987): 3, 10.

———. "Reading Piebald Patterns in Le Guin's *The Left Hand of Darkness*." *Women of Other Worlds: Excursions through Science Fiction and Feminism*. Ed. Helen Merrick and Tess Williams. Nedlands, Austral.: University of Western Australia Press, 1999. 29–40.

———. "The Riddle of Doris Lessing's Feminism." *Magazine* 11.1 (1992): 45–62.

———. "Utopian Feminism, Skeptical Feminism, and Narrative Energy." In Jones and Goodwin, *Feminism, Utopia, and Narrative*, 34–49.

Perelman, Ch., and L. Olbrechts-Tyteca. *The New Rhetoric: A Treatise on Argumentation*. 1958. Trans. John Wilkinson and Purcell Weaver. Notre Dame, Ind.: University of Notre Dame Press, 1969.

Pfaelzer, Jean. "Response: What Happened to History?" In Jones and Goodwin, *Feminism, Utopia, and Narrative*, 201–7.

Phelan, James. *Narrative as Rhetoric: Technique, Audiences, Ethics, Ideology*. Columbus, Ohio: The Ohio State University Press, 1996.

Piercy, Marge. *Woman on the Edge of Time*. New York: Fawcett-Crest, 1976.

Plato. *The Republic*. Trans. Paul Shorey. Vol. 2. Cambridge, Mass.: Harvard University Press, 1946.

Porter, David L. "The Politics of Le Guin's Opus." *Science-Fiction Studies* 2, pt. 3 (1975): 243–48.

Porter, Laurence M. "Writing Feminism: Myth, Epic and Utopia in Monique Wittig's *Les Guérillères*." *L'Esprit Créateur* 29.3 (1989): 92–100.

Pratt, Annis, and L. S. Dembo, eds. *Doris Lessing: Critical Studies.* Madison: University of Wisconsin Press, 1974.

Pratt, Mary Louise. "Interpretive Strategies/Strategic Interpretations: On Anglo-American Reader Response Criticism." *Boundary 2* 11.1–2 (1982–1983): 201–31.

Prince, Gerald. *A Dictionary of Narratology.* Lincoln: University of Nebraska Press, 1987.

Propp, Vladímir. *Morphology of the Folktale.* 1928. Trans. Laurence Scott. Ed. Louis A. Wagner. Rev. ed. Austin: University of Texas Press, 1968.

Rabinowitz, Peter J. "Assertion and Assumption: Fictional Patterns and the External World." *PMLA* 96 (1981): 408–19.

———. *Before Reading: Narrative Conventions and the Politics of Interpretation.* Ithaca, N.Y.: Cornell University Press, 1987.

———. "Truth in Fiction: A Reexamination of Audiences." *Critical Inquiry* 4 (1977): 121–41.

Rabkin, Eric S. "Determinism, Free Will, and Point of View in Le Guin's *The Left Hand of Darkness*." *Extrapolation* 20 (1979): 5–19.

———. "Metalinguistics and Science Fiction." *Critical Inquiry* 6 (1979): 79–97.

Rand, Ayn. *The Fountainhead.* 1943. New York: Signet-New American Library, 1971.

Rapping, Elayne Antler. "Unfree Women: Feminism in Doris Lessing's Novels." *Women's Studies* 3 (1975): 29–44.

Raymond, Janice. "The Illusion of Androgyny." *Quest* 2.1 (1975): 57–66.

Reid, Martha. "Outsiders, Aliens, and Exiles in the Fiction of Doris Lessing." *Doris Lessing Newsletter* 4.2 (1980): 3–4, 14.

Rhode, Deborah L. "Definitions of Difference." In *Theoretical Perspectives,* 197–212, 294–98.

———. "Theoretical Perspectives on Sexual Difference." In *Theoretical Perspectives,* 1–9, 263–65.

———, ed. *Theoretical Perspectives on Sexual Difference.* New Haven, Conn.: Yale University Press, 1990.

Rhodes, Jewell Parker. "Ursula Le Guin's *The Left Hand of Darkness:* Androgyny and the Feminist Utopia." In Barr and Smith, *Women and Utopia,* 108–20.

Rich, Adrienne. "Compulsory Heterosexuality and Lesbian Existence." 1980, 1982. In *Blood, Bread, and Poetry: Selected Prose, 1979–1985.* New York: Norton, 1986. 23–75.

Richards, I. A. *Practical Criticism: A Study of Literary Judgment.* New York: Harvest-Harcourt, Brace and World, 1929.

Richardson, Samuel. *Pamela; Or, Virtue Rewarded.* 1740. Ed. Peter Sabor. London: Penguin, 1985.

Richter, David H. *Fable's End: Completeness and Closure in Rhetorical Fiction.* Chicago: University of Chicago Press, 1974.

Roberts, Robin. *A New Species: Gender and Science in Science Fiction.* Urbana, Ill.: University of Illinois Press, 1993.

Rohrlich, Ruby, and Elaine Hoffman Baruch, eds. *Women in Search of Utopia: Mavericks and Mythmakers.* New York: Schocken, 1983.

Roof, Judith. *Come As You Are: Sexuality and Narrative.* Between Men-Between Women: Lesbian and Gay Studies. New York: Columbia University Press, 1996.

Rorty, Richard. *Consequences of Pragmatism (Essays: 1972–1980).* Minneapolis, Minn.: University of Minnesota Press, 1982.

———. "Introduction: Pragmatism and Philosophy." In *Consequences of Pragmatism,* xiii–xlvii.

———. "Pragmatism, Relativism, and Irrationalism." In *Consequences of Pragmatism,* 160–75.

Roscoe, Will. "How to Become a Berdache: Toward a Unified Analysis of Gender Diversity." In Herdt, *Third Sex,* 329–72, 566–79.

Rosenberg, Michael. "Virtual Reality: Reflections of Life, Dreams, and Technology, An Ethnography of a Computer Society." 16 Mar. 1992. msr@casbah.acns.nwu.edu.

Rosenblatt, Louise. *Literature as Exploration.* 1938. 4th ed. New York: Modern Language Association, 1983.

Rosinsky, Natalie M. *Feminist Futures: Contemporary Women's Speculative Fiction.* Studies in Speculative Fiction. Ann Arbor, Mich.: UMI Research Press, 1984.

Rothstein, Edward. "Paradise Lost: Can Mankind Live Without Its Utopias?" *New York Times,* 2 Feb. 2000: A13+.

Rowe, Marsha. "If you mate a swan and a gander, who will ride?" In *Notebooks/Memoirs/Archives: Reading and Rereading Doris Lessing.* Ed. Jenny Taylor. Boston: Routledge & Kegan Paul, 1982. 191–205.

Rubenstein, Roberta. "*The Marriages Between Zones Three, Four, and Five:* Doris Lessing's Alchemical Allegory." *Extrapolation* 24 (1983): 201–15.

———. *The Novelistic Vision of Doris Lessing: Breaking the Forms of Consciousness.* Urbana, Ill.: University of Illinois Press, 1979.

Ruppert, Peter. *Reader in a Strange Land: The Activity of Reading Literary Utopias.* Athens, Ga.: University of Georgia Press, 1986.

Russ, Joanna. *The Female Man.* 1975. Boston: Beacon, 1986.

———. "The Image of Women in Science Fiction." In Cornillon, *Images of Women in Fiction,* 79–94.

———. "Recent Feminist Utopias." In Barr, *Future Females: A Critical Anthology,* 71–85.

———. "What Can a Heroine Do? Or Why Women Can't Write." In Cornillon, *Images of Women in Fiction,* 3–20.

Sacks, Sheldon. *Fiction and the Shape of Belief: A Study of Henry Fielding, with Glances at Swift, Johnson and Richardson.* Berkeley, Calif.: University of California Press, 1964.

Sage, Lorna. *Doris Lessing.* London: Methuen, 1983.

Sammons, Jeffrey L. *Literary Sociology and Practical Criticism: An Inquiry.* Bloomington, Ind.: Indiana University Press, 1977.

Sand, George. *Lélia.* 1833, 1839. Trans. Maria Espinosa. Bloomington, Ind.: Indiana University Press, 1978.

Sargent, Lyman Tower. "An Ambiguous Legacy: The Role and Position of Women in the English Eutopia." In Barr, *Future Females: A Critical Anthology,* 88–99.

———. "Contemporary Scholarship on Utopianism." *L'Esprit Créateur* 34.4 (1994): 123–28.

———. "The Three Faces of Utopianism Revisited." *Utopian Studies* 5 (1994): 1–37.

Sargent, Pamela. "Introduction: Women and Science Fiction." In *Women of Wonder.* Ed. Sargent. New York: Vintage-Random House, 1975. xiii–lxiv.

Sargisson, Lucy. *Contemporary Feminist Utopianism.* London: Routledge, 1996.

Sarraute, Nathalie. *The Planetarium.* 1959. Trans. Maria Jolas. London: Jupiter-John Calder, 1965.

Saxton, Ruth. "The Bay Area." *Doris Lessing Newsletter* 8.2 (1984): 6–7.

Schaer, Roland, Gregory Claeys, and Lyman Tower Sargent, eds. *Utopia: The Search for the Ideal Society in the Western World.* New York: N.Y. Public Library; Oxford, Eng.: Oxford University Press, 2000.

Scholes, Robert. *Protocols of Reading.* New Haven, Conn.: Yale University Press, 1989.

———. *Semiotics and Interpretation.* New Haven, Conn.: Yale University Press, 1982.

———. *Structural Fabulation.* Notre Dame, Ind.: University of Notre Dame Press, 1975.

Scholes, Robert, and Eric S. Rabkin. *Science Fiction.* New York: Oxford University Press, 1977.

Schweickart, Patrocinio P. "Reading Ourselves: Toward a Feminist Theory of Reading." In Flynn and Schweickart, *Gender and Reading,* 31–62.

Scott, Melissa. *Trouble and Her Friends.* New York: Tom Doherty-Tor, 1994.

Seigfried, Charlene Haddock, ed. *Feminism and Pragmatism.* Spec. issue of *Hypatia* 8.2 (1993): 1–242.

———. *Pragmatism and Feminism: Reweaving the Social Fabric.* Chicago: University of Chicago Press, 1996.

Seligman, Dee, comp. *Doris Lessing: An Annotated Bibliography of Criticism.* Westport, Conn.: Greenwood, 1981.

Shakespeare, William. *Hamlet Prince of Denmark.* In *Complete Works,* 930–76.

———. *Romeo and Juliet.* In *Complete Works,* 855–93.

———. *The Tempest.* In *Complete Works,* 1369–95.

———. *William Shakespeare: The Complete Works.* Ed. Alfred Harbage. Rev. ed. Baltimore, Md.: Penguin, 1969.

Shelley, Mary. *Frankenstein: Or, The Modern Prometheus.* 1816. New York: Signet-New American Library, 1983.

Shikibu, Murasaki. *The Tale of Genji: A Novel in Six Parts.* [Ca. 1015]. Trans. Arthur Waley. New York: Modern Library, 1960.

Showalter, Elaine. "Feminist Criticism in the Wilderness." *Critical Inquiry* 8 (1981): 179–205.

———. "Introduction: The Rise of Gender." In *Speaking of Gender.* Ed. Showalter. New York: Routledge, Chapman and Hall, 1989. 1–13.

Sinclair, Upton. *The Jungle.* 1905. Cambridge, Mass.: Robert Bentley, 1946.

Slonczewski, Joan. *Daughter of Elysium.* New York: Avon, 1993.

Slusser, George Edgar. *The Farthest Shores of Ursula K. Le Guin.* San Bernardino, Calif.: Borgo, 1976.

Smith, Barbara. "Racism and Women's Studies." In *All the Women Are White, All the Blacks Are Men, But Some of Us Are Brave: Black Women's Studies.* Ed. Gloria T. Hull, Patricia Bell Scott, and Smith. Old Westbury, N.Y.: The Feminist Press, 1982. 48–51.

Snitow, Ann. "A Gender Diary." In Harris and King, *Rocking the Ship of State,* 35–73.

Solanas, Valerie. *SCUM Manifesto.* New York: Olympia, 1968.

Spelman, Elizabeth V. *Inessential Woman: Problems of Exclusion in Feminist Thought.* Boston: Beacon, 1988.

Spender, Dale. *Man Made Language.* London: Routledge & Kegan Paul, 1980.

Sprague, Claire. *Rereading Doris Lessing: Narrative Patterns of Doubling and Repetition.* Chapel Hill, N.C.: University of North Carolina Press, 1987.

———. "'Without Contraries Is No Progression': Lessing's *The Four-Gated City.*" *Modern Fiction Studies* 26 (1980): 96–116.

Staël, Germaine de. *Corinne, or Italy.* 1807. Trans. Avriel H. Goldberger. New Brunswick, N.J.: Rutgers University Press, 1987.

Stead, Christina. *The Man Who Loved Children.* 1940. New York: Holt, Rinehart and Winston, 1965.

Stimpson, Catharine R. Introduction. *Feminist Issues in Literary Scholarship.* Ed. Shari Benstock. Bloomington, Ind.: Indiana University Press, 1987. 1–6.

Stitzel, Judith. "Reading Doris Lessing." *College English* 40 (1979): 498–504.

Suleiman, Susan Rubin. *Authoritarian Fictions: The Ideological Novel As a Literary Genre.* New York: Columbia University Press, 1983.

———. "The Politics and Poetics of Female Eroticism." In *Subversive Intent: Gender, Politics, and the Avant-Garde.* Cambridge, Mass.: Harvard University Press, 1990. 118–40.

Suvin, Darko. *Metamorphoses of Science Fiction.* New Haven, Conn.: Yale University Press, 1979.

———. "Parables of De-Alienation: Le Guin's Widdershins Dance." *Science-Fiction Studies* 2 (1975): 265–74.

Swift, Jonathan. *Gulliver's Travels.* 1735. Ed. Robert A. Greenberg. 2d ed. New York: Norton, 1970.

Tan, Amy. *The Hundred Secret Senses.* New York: G. P. Putnam's, 1995.

Thürmer-Rohr, Christina. *Vagabonding: Feminist Thinking Cut Loose.* 1987. Trans. Lise Weil. Boston: Beacon, 1991.

Tiger, Virginia. "'The words had been right and necessary': Doris Lessing's Transformations of Utopian and Dystopian Modalities in *The Marriages Between Zones Three, Four, and Five.*" *Style* 27.1 (1993): 63–80.

Tiptree, James, Jr. "The Women Men Don't See." In *Warm Worlds and Otherwise.* New York: Ballantine, 1975. 131–64.

Tolstoy, Leo. *War and Peace.* 1869. Trans. Louise Maude and Aylmer Maude. Ed. Henry Gifford. Oxford, Eng.: Oxford University Press, 1998.

Tong, Rosemarie. *Feminist Thought: A Comprehensive Introduction.* Boulder, Colo.: Westview, 1989.

Tucker, Lindsey. *Textual Escap(e)ades: Mobility, Maternity, and Textuality in Contemporary Fiction by Women.* Westport, Conn.: Greenwood, 1994.

Varley, John. *Demon.* New York: Berkley, 1984.

———. *Titan.* 1979. New York: Berkley, 1980.

———. *Wizard.* 1980. New York: Berkley, 1981.

Vonarburg, Elisabeth. *The Silent City.* 1981. Trans. Jane Brierley. London: Women's Press, 1988.

Walby, Sylvia. "Post-Post-Modernism? Theorizing Social Complexity." In Barrett and Phillips, *Destabilizing Theory,* 31–52.

Walker, Alice. *The Color Purple.* 1982. New York: Washington Square-Pocket, 1983.

Walker, Jeanne Murray. "Myth, Exchange and History in *The Left Hand of Darkness.*" *Science-Fiction Studies* 6, pt. 2 (1979): 180–89.

Warhol, Robyn R. *Gendered Interventions: Narrative Discourse in the Victorian Novel.* New Brunswick, N.J.: Rutgers University Press, 1989.

Warren, Mary Anne. *The Nature of Woman: An Encyclopedia and Guide to the Literature.* Inverness, Calif.: Edgepress, 1980.

Watson, Ian. "Le Guin's *Lathe of Heaven* and the Role of Dick: The False Reality as Mediator." *Science-Fiction Studies* 2 (1975): 67–75.

Wenzel, Hélène Vivienne. "The Text As Body/Politics: An Appreciation of Monique Wittig's Writings in Context." *Feminist Studies* 7.2 (1981): 264–87.

West, Rebecca. "Mr. Chesterton in Hysterics: A Study in Prejudice." *The Clarion,* 14 Nov. 1913. Rpt. in *The Young Rebecca: Writings of Rebecca West 1911–1917.* Ed. Jane Marcus. Bloomington, Ind.: Indiana University Press, 1982. 218–22.

Whitbeck, Caroline. "Theories of Sex Difference." *Women and Philosophy: Toward a Theory of Liberation.* Ed. Carol C. Gould and Marx W. Wartofsky. New York: Capricorn-Putnam's, 1976. 54–80.

Willis, Gary. "Le Guin's *The Left Hand of Darkness:* The Weaving Together of Dualities." *Riverside Quarterly* 8 (1986): 36–43.

Wimsatt, W. K., and Monroe C. Beardsley. "The Intentional Fallacy." 1946. In *Critical Theory Since Plato.* Ed. Hazard Adams. New York: Harcourt Brace Jovanovich, 1971. 1014–22.

Wittgenstein, Ludwig. *Philosophische Untersuchungen/Philosophical Investigations.* Trans. G. E. M. Anscombe. 3d ed. Vol. 1. New York: Macmillan, 1968.

Wittig, Monique. *Les Guérillères.* Paris: Minuit, 1969.

———. *Les Guérillères.* 1971. Trans. David Le Vay. New York: Bard-Avon, 1973.

———. *Les Guérillères.* 1971. Trans. David Le Vay. Boston: Beacon, 1985.

———. "Homo Sum." *The Straight Mind,* 46–58.

———. *The Lesbian Body.* 1973. Trans. David Le Vay. New York: Morrow, 1975.

———. "The Mark of Gender." In *The Straight Mind,* 76–89.

———. "One Is Not Born a Woman." In *The Straight Mind,* 9–20.

———. *The Opoponax.* 1964. Trans. Helen Weaver. New York: Simon & Schuster, 1966.

———. "Quelques Remarques sur *Les Guérillères.*" *L'Esprit Créateur* 34.4 (1994): 116–22.

———. "The Straight Mind." In *The Straight Mind,* 21–32.

———. *The Straight Mind and Other Essays.* Boston: Beacon, 1992.

———. "The Trojan Horse." In *The Straight Mind,* 68–75.

Wittig, Monique, and Sande Zeig. *Lesbian Peoples: Material for a Dictionary.* 1976. Trans. Wittig and Zeig. New York: Avon, 1979.

Wolf, Christa. *The Quest for Christa T.* 1968. Trans. Christopher Middleton. New York: Farrar, Straus & Giroux, 1970.

Wolmark, Jenny. *Aliens and Others: Science Fiction, Feminism and Postmodernism.* Iowa City: University of Iowa Press, 1994.

Wood, Susan. "Discovering Worlds: The Fiction of Ursula K. Le Guin." *Voices for the Future: Essays on Major Science Fiction Writers.* Ed. Thomas D. Clareson. Vol. 2. Bowling Green, Ohio: Bowling Green University Popular Press, 1979. 154–79.

Woolf, Virginia. *Orlando: A Biography.* 1928. New York: Harvest-HBJ, 1956.

———. *To the Lighthouse.* 1927. New York: Harvest-Harcourt, Brace & World, 1955.

Wright, Austin M. *Recalcitrance, Faulkner, and the Professors: A Critical Fiction.* Iowa City, Iowa: University of Iowa Press, 1990.

Zerilli, Linda M. G. "Rememoration or War: French Feminist Narrative and the Politics of Self-Representation." *differences* 3.1 (1991): 1–19.

Index

The Theory and Interpretation of Narrative Series
James Phelan and Peter J. Rabinowitz, Editors

Because the series editors believe that the most significant work in narrative studies today contributes both to our knowledge of specific narratives and to our understanding of narrative in general, studies in the series typically offer interpretations of individual narratives and address significant theoretical issues underlying those interpretations. The series does not privilege any one critical perspective but is open to work from any strong theoretical position.